Additional Praise for *Brilliant Teaching*

For many years, Adeyemi Stembridge has been working with teachers throughout the country as a mentor and a coach. This book presents a compilation of reflections on what he has learned from these experiences. The keen insights he has obtained through observation and direct experience provides a treasure trove of valuable pointers that teachers can use to enhance their practice and increase their ability to reach every learner.

—Pedro Noguera, Dean, Rossier School of Education, Distinguished Professor of Education, University of Southern California

Dr. Stembridge's new book builds and expands on concepts from his decades of work in education. The mere fact that this new book is entitled *Brilliant Teaching* should whet the appetite of educators who have the desire to maximize the learning options for each and every student who sits in front of them!

—Dr. Connie Sims, Retired Educator of 58 years, and President, Sims and Sims, Inc.

Dr. Stembridge's framework for culturally responsive pedagogy is transforming how educators across the state of Washington see, understand, and work to engage each student. Read this book to restore the joy in teaching and learning where it has been lost, to ignite it where it has not existed, and to maintain it where it has always lived.

—Sue Anderson, Retired Director, Educator Effectiveness Office

T0284853

Brilliant Teaching

Brilliant Teaching

USING CULTURE AND ARTFUL
THINKING TO CLOSE EQUITY GAPS

Adeyemi Stembridge

JB JOSSEY-BASS™
A Wiley Brand

For general information on our other products and services or for technical support, please contact our Customer Care Department within the United States at (800) 762-2974, outside the United States at (317) 572-3993 or fax (317) 572-4002.

Wiley also publishes its books in a variety of electronic formats. Some content that appears in print may not be available in electronic formats. For more information about Wiley products, visit our web site at www.wiley.com.

Library of Congress Cataloging-in-Publication Data is available:

ISBN 9781119901129 (Paperback)
ISBN 9781119901136 (ePDF)
ISBN 9781119901143 (ePUB)

Cover Design: Wiley
Cover Image: © Dorothy Gaziano/Shutterstock;
Author Photo: © Gwen Phillips, Denver Headshot Co.
SKY1047755_051223

This book is a love letter to my friend, teacher, and mentor,
Charles A. Tesconi (1938–2020). A quarter-century since
we first met, and I'm still learning from you.
Thank you for everything.

TABLE OF CONTENTS

PREFACE

DO I, OR DO I NOT, TAKE THIS PICTURE?

In every direction, as far as I could see, nothing was left untouched by the destruction.

It was June 9, 2007. I was a freshly minted PhD embarking on the first research project of my academic career in which I was the lead investigator. Along with two exceptionally bright and committed graduate students, Thanh Ly and Ebony Duncan, our task was to spend time with a reconstituting Upward Bound program in New Orleans. We were interested in learning more about how an education program with a successful track record for preparing students for college would rebuild nearly two years after Hurricanes Katrina and Rita had effectively wiped out the Lower Ninth Ward, the district that was home to most of its student participants.

In order to understand the story of this program's rebuilding, we wanted to first know what it was that made it successful *before* the storms. In other words, what was the essence and ethos of this Upward Bound program that was worth reviving—even as the students, most returning to New Orleans for the first time in more than 18 months, had endured trauma beyond the comprehension of most Americans.

Upon arrival, I had thought of myself as disconnected to New Orleans. Like most, I watched closely on the national news networks as the hurricanes narrowly avoided a direct hit of the city, but leaving behind instead failed levees, a more insidious anguish. My disconnectedness served me well, I thought. I could conduct my research with the distanced objectivity of a well-trained social scientist. I was unburdened by the personal need to redeem anything lost to me.

My colleagues and I decided to see the Lower Ninth Ward for ourselves in advance of our first visit to our research site in order to gain some perspective and context for the conditions in which this rebuild was being attempted. How do you restore something that is extraordinary when the staff and students have, in many cases, quite literally lost every physical possession that couldn't be tucked into a backpack upon evacuation?

I wouldn't have been able to comprehend the devastation in the Lower Ninth Ward until I was there to see it for myself. The water had lifted homes from their foundations, moving some of them hundreds of feet out of place. There, in the thick, stifling Louisiana heat, we soon came across a house that had been floated on top of a car, a surreal image that forces the observer into recognition of the havoc wrought by the flooding. I saw the car first, and my mind flooded with calculations for how this could have happened. *Exactly how much water was flowing through these neighborhood streets?* I wondered aloud. . . . *This was someone's home.* I could only imagine the stories and memories, the lived experiences that had accumulated inside of this structure.

I think it's important to take pictures in research. Photographs can record details and insights that language struggles to convey. As I positioned myself to capture a clear and compelling image of this home mangled by the disaster, I noticed writing across the front of the house. I was confronted by a message left for curious onlookers.

1600 People Died 4 U 2 take this picture

It felt like I was being called out. Challenged. And though there were only three of us out there on that sweltering swamp-hot afternoon, it felt like I was spotlighted on a stage in front of millions.

Do I, or Do I Not, Take This Picture?

I decided to document the image—but not without some soul-searching. The question at hand in that moment for me was more philosophical than technical, more existential than methodological. *Why am I doing this? What are my intentions? Who am I in this moment? Why am I here?*

Many years later, I continue to interrogate myself and my intentions as I deepen and extend my understanding of why some classrooms work better for our most vulnerable learners than others. I still have more questions than answers. In fact, I now understand that the brilliance that I most admire is that which values the questions . . . because the capacity for generating thoughtful and well-constructed questions is unlikely to become stale, or worse, *certain*. It is the uncertainty of the inquiring mind that is the source of its brilliance because uncertainty is necessary for understanding.

Research, like teaching and also much like making art, is a kind of philosophizing. The philosopher seeks answers to the questions of personhood.... As in: *Who am I?* and *How have I come to be?* We were there to study an educational program's effort to rebuild its former efficacy. We were asking of the program and the people of it: *Who are you? And how have you come to be?* But to pose those questions, I was reminded that I must first engage in the deliberation of those questions of myself . . . or the entire episode would be a farce based on the false pretense of certainty—and a farce is not what I would consciously choose to be.

In the end, I took the picture because it was part of the story I was hoping to tell, and I wanted to honor the participants of my study by telling their story in the most honest and informed way possible. I interpreted the author's intent of the writing across the front of the house, whoever they were, as a personal exhortation to me in that moment to be clear about my intentions because there were consequences for ambiguity. I felt then, as I do now, that I am accountable to any who would pay attention to my words and ideas to present the full story, ugly parts included, because only the full story is truly worth telling. All else is ultimately folly.

WHAT IS THIS BOOK ABOUT?

In this book, I am making the case that Equity is the historical heir in the legacy tracing all the way back to the origin story of American public education. Hence, Equity is to be centered as the essential purpose of teaching, and teaching for Equity is a function of creating opportunities that match the social, political, and economic context in which teaching occurs. And further, the craft of creating these opportunities is what we call *pedagogy*, and pedagogy in the interest of Equity is a lot like making art. Most importantly, I am making the case that Equity in education that isn't responsive to or doesn't empower learners to reach their own goals is neither responsive nor empowering but more likely manipulating. Worse yet, teaching that isn't responsive underserves vulnerable student populations by compromising their preparedness for the forthcoming tasks and challenges of life. Until the artmaking sensibilities for teaching are normalized and supported by education systems, the Equity gaps we see currently will persist because our prevailing models do not empower learners, and neither the policy nor practice environments are designed to be responsive.

This book is divided into two parts. In Part 1, I define *Equity* as the quintessential purpose of education. The goal of Equity in education is to remove educational disparities as a hindrance to the ethos of individual freedoms, "life, liberty, and the pursuit of happiness." Equity is not the same as equality, though they are conceptually related. A primary difference between the two is a matter of measurement. Equality is measured by sameness of inputs whereas Equity is measured by outputs. We will know that we have achieved Equity when neither race, nor class, nor income, nor gender, nor language background, nor physical (dis)ability—when no social disparity or measure of identity—is a barrier to or predictor of educational achievement. In the sense of Equity, fairness is a differentiating process through which opportunity is mediated. I am further building on the argument I make in *Culturally Responsive Education in the Classroom: An Equity Framework for Pedagogy* (2019) that culturally responsive teaching is useful for closing Equity gaps.

In Chapter 1, I offer guidelines for how to think about teaching as an artmaking endeavor—particularly in such a way that prioritizes student empowerment as both a process and outcome goal for instruction. In Chapter 2, I revisit the definition of *Equity*—which is to say that Equity in Education is broadly concerned with the extent to which students are effectively prepared through quality learning opportunities for the social and economic world beyond school. But there is a terrible flaw in our logic in terms of how districts and schools have largely attempted to solve the problems of Equity through top-down driven approaches to reform and innovation. As a former classroom teacher, this has always struck me as agonizingly inadequate in addressing the inequities that persist in American education.

There is a troublesome disconnect among the analytical perspectives taken to understand the Equity problems that yield fragmented solutions that rarely ever solve much of anything. These disjunctured perspectives prevent the collective systems of American education to move schools, teaching, and learning forward beyond the woefully outdated factory models of the past.

The fracture in perspectives I refer to can be summarized in terms of *people groups and people*. Administrators in school systems are responsible for tracking the data of students' performance and achievement across classrooms and even school buildings, and sometimes much larger territories than school districts. From this analytical perspective, the questions asked about the data seek to find answers to the problem of uneven outcomes among the different people groups, which can be disaggregated in numerous ways. From this analytical perch, Equity problems are understood and addressed in terms of how some people groups fare better-or-worse in outcomes relative to others.

Teachers, on the other hand, have a different perspective by dint of their role in the education system. Teachers know kids, and when you know kids, you come to comprehend something . . . which is, there's a kind of irreducibility about individual kiddos. They are all, in effect, one-of-a-kind . . . and though they belong to people groups, they can only be understood as people.

The teachers who are paying attention realize that culture and identity can be understood and leveraged in the interest of student engagement, but to truly know any one student invariably means you are able to recognize them as a unique individual and not as a cardboard cutout of any people group. In fact, even well-intentioned efforts to use our knowledge of people groups for predictive purposes in teaching risks great harm to the very students who most need to be seen, understood, and validated for them to see, understand, and validate school as a place where they belong. And we know full well that our most vulnerable students don't often engage unless and until they are confident in their belonging.

A consequential aspect of the problems we face in American education is the poor understanding of the meaning of Equity, which has experienced substantial concept creep in the past few years. In Chapter 3, I delve more deeply into the discussion of how Equity properly understood is now and has always been the guiding purpose for the work of schools and teaching. In Chapter 4, I contend that all learning is cultural; and further, intelligence can't be understood separate from culture.

In Part 2, I take the approach of the essayist in exploring further the connections between artmaking—production and performance, that is—and culturally responsive pedagogy. Chapter 5 is entirely dedicated to telling the story of a unit-long learning experience in a high school science class. The teacher, whom I will refer to as Mr. Andre Derain, and I plan together drawing on the Culturally Responsive Education (CRE) mental model (Stembridge, 2019). My goal is to provide a text that can be used to highlight how our CRE planning shapes and directs our pedagogy over several weeks of instruction. I'm not so much trying to describe what's *happening* in the classroom; I'm trying to describe the way it feels to be alive and engaged in the work of the classroom, right there and then. Chapter 5 is intended to bring the reader inside of the design process for culturally responsive learning experiences. The hope is that you, the reader, can see through Mr. Derain's eyes the ways in which he attempted to empower his students by exposing them to rigorous learning opportunities and centering their inquiry and experiences in the instruction.

I focus on several key concepts, including improvisation (Chapter 6), story (Chapter 7), audience (Chapter 8), and assessment (Chapter 9) as essential ingredients of the culturally responsive teacher's philosophizing toolkit. In Chapter 7, I consider how we teachers can best design learning experiences that center students' identities. In Chapter 8, I make a defense of incentives by drawing on, among others, the fields of cognitive science, anthropology, and cultural psychology. The topic of Chapter 9 is assessments; more specifically, I put forth the argument that culturally responsive assessments are those that allow students to effectively draw on their assets and cultural fluencies in order to perform their learning and developing competencies.

My desire in writing this book is not so much to refute existing premises regarding Equity or Culturally Responsive Education but rather to build out an argument based in multiple disciplines that seeks to explain what teachers can do in their classrooms to close the stubbornly persistent gaps in educational outcomes that frustrate educators and stifle our societal collective capacity to maximize the talent of the youth. As Albert Bandura, Peter Richerson, Robert Boyd, Richard Wrangham, Joseph Henrich, Robert Sapolsky, and many others have argued, the secret of the human species' success lies not in our raw intellect or reasoning powers, but in our capacity to learn from those around us and then diffuse what we've learned outward, through our social networks, and down to future generations.

My teachers are the many teachers who've thought-partnered with me in professional development and classroom spaces where we share our collective brain power and experience to solve for problems of Equity not at some far-off level of abstract theory, but at the granular level of the classroom. Teaching is perhaps the most human profession of all because we can learn from others (most especially our students) and integrate insights from diverse populations. Each of us teachers is invited to tap into a rich, dynamic, ever-growing, and improving repertoire of tools, skills, techniques, goals, motivations, beliefs, rules, and norms. As teachers, we are either growing in our practice or we risk a kind of inertia that is harmful to the learners who most depend on our own engagement to serve as a model and inspiration for theirs. In this way, innovation is less the invention of something altogether "new," but more commonly a recombination of inspired insights that have the potential to show up in our practice in the most profoundly specific, relevant, and personal ways.

TO WHOM AM I SPEAKING?

Human beings are a tribal species. We create tribes on all sorts of levels. That's why culture—the formal and informal rules that govern human interactions—is such a dynamic and critical feature of humanity. As humans, we understand each other through the identities and cultural inheritances we share within our social groups. Our tribes are those with whom we have common goals, fashion, and ways of being. Here, I welcome all readers, *but I know my tribe*—and I write for *you. You* are the teachers who see teaching as your *craft*. To you, teaching is a kind of cause, and you aspire to be brilliant for *all* your students. You seek ideas to add to the quality of your craft. You like ideas, but because you're a teacher, you especially like ideas that you can use in your practice.

The publication of this book comes on the heels of what may be the hardest few years to be a teacher in the history of the world. The moment is pressing. I'd rather not waste time grandstanding. My message is twofold. First, schools today are more important than ever, and Equity-focused teaching is the essential task of schools. In my view, the most important work of schools is to provide meaningful opportunities to learn—opportunities that are rigorous and engaging—for *all* students. *All* means we must give specific attention to the groups of students that have historically been underserved because they're the ones most likely to be overlooked. We cannot be satisfied with schools that predictably serve some groups better than others. That violates our most fundamental ethic. Our goal is to teach in ways that every student will have a fair opportunity to learn and the support to take advantage of the opportunity. That's Equity, and I believe that culturally responsive teaching is an effective pedagogical pathway for closing Equity gaps. In the American multiracial, multiethnic, multilingual, multicultural, pluralistic democracy, free and public schools serve a purpose, and that purpose is Equity. *That's what schools are for.*

My second message is that culturally responsive teaching that creates equitable opportunities does not follow some narrow, prescriptive form. It isn't an algorithmic, paint-by-numbers type of endeavor. Yes, there are important themes and ideas with which teachers should be familiar, but culturally responsive teaching is a function of mindset. My goal in writing this book is to provide source material for your pedagogical philosophizing that will help you to make good ideas functional in your practice.

It is true that artists are creative—but what they do is make art. Making art with our pedagogy is Equity work. I embrace the pragmatic value of CRE, but culturally responsive teaching is at least as much a function of mindset as it is of any technical skill. The great challenge in making art is that it invariably reveals that our flaws and weaknesses are at once both obstacles to our getting work done and inspiration as well. Teaching is inherently frustrating not because the process is halting and often disjointed, but because we imagine it to be fluid, seamless, and immediate. Similarly, "most artists don't daydream about making great art—they daydream about having made great art" (Bayles & Orland, 1993). Only the teacher with artmaking sensibilities can discern how important small maneuvers and micro-choices are in engaging students. These details of artmaking are mostly uninteresting to lay audiences (and frequently to disengaged teachers) perhaps because they're almost never visible—or even knowable—by merely examining the finished work.

I hope that the readers of this book will feel both challenged and inspired to evolve their practice. Though my primary intended audience is teachers, I know that others, policymakers and educators in administrator roles, may also be interested in what I have to say. I want administrators who read the book to also feel challenged, but I want them to feel it differently. I want administrators to know that Equity work requires that they thoughtfully revise the very systems and structures in which teaching and learning occur. I want administrators to read this book and know that they must make an effort to create the circumstances in which this artmaking teaching is possible . . . which means that administrators and policymakers have to do something beyond the issuing of proclamations. Too many are seeking answers to "chequity" questions—the questions you ask when you want to mark items off an Equity checklist. I am asking you to engage more deeply than that. The circumstances necessary for culturally responsive, artmaking teaching that closes Equity gaps require a re-centering of students and a re-imagination of the prevailing organizational models for schooling. In fact, until administrators and policymakers take on the challenge of re-imagining the systems and structures for school, brilliant teaching will be a subversive act carried out in spite of the policy environment and not because of it. For those who work in executive and policymaking roles, the question I hope you will consider is: What systems and structures will directly support the types of artmaking and culturally responsive teaching discussed in this book?

This book may offer the reader an opportunity for some existential, philosophizing reflection, as in: *Why am I doing this? What are my intentions? Who am I in this moment? And why am I here?*

To teach without clear insight into these questions is an exercise that is, at best, ripe with frustration and the attendant feelings of inadequacy, and at worst, a pedagogical catastrophe in waiting. To teach with clarity, however, renders a great deal possible to ourselves and our students. In fact, it is the only way for us to truly achieve Equity in the work that we do.

PART ONE

CULTURALLY RESPONSIVE ARTMAKING TEACHING

"Education is the acquisition of the art of the utilisation of knowledge. This is an art very difficult to impart."

—A. N. Whitehead (1929)

CHAPTER 1

What Does It Mean to Think Like an Artist?

"The precise role of the artist, then, is to illuminate that darkness, blaze roads through that vast forest, so that we will not, in all our doing, lose sight of its purpose, which is, after all, to make the world a more human dwelling place."

—James Baldwin

WHAT IS ARTMAKING?

Technically, I am a consultant for Equity in education—but I'm not fond of the term *consultant*. I much prefer to think of myself as a *freelance teacher*. As such, I provide site-based, professional development with particular attention to pedagogy in schools and classrooms where there are Equity gaps. But I'm not fond of the term *professional development* either. It's compromised with the fiction that some outside *expert* can provide answers to teachers' problems of practice. In supporting teachers, I try very hard to thought-partner with them in developing a deeper understanding of our students and the contexts in which they are learning. It's a heuristic approach. Also, I enjoy thinking; and I find that the best answers to teachers' questions about Equity are usually those that empower them to be thoughtful as well.

So, in that vein, you should think of this book as one long thought experiment. Here's the scenario:

Imagine that you are a teacher. You are a teacher in any grade you like, but you are teaching in the current year of your reading of this book. If you're a secondary school teacher, choose any subject area or discipline you want. You can be a teacher in any type of school you like. It might be an urban school, but it could also be suburban, or even rural. Doesn't matter. It can be a large school with several thousand students or a tiny school where you literally know every kiddo's name in the building. Any school, anywhere.

Mind you, you are not just any teacher. You are a teacher who cares deeply and wants to teach brilliantly. Let's say that brilliant teaching closes Equity gaps in which case, it's really important to you that you are both brilliant and equitable in your teaching. . . .

Having established this as our premise, the central thought-experiment question is: What does Equity mean *in* your teaching? Or put another way, how do you *do* Equity?

Let's Begin at IKEA . . . Yes, You Read That Correctly—IKEA

My unrecognized and underappreciated talent is that I can always find a reason for a trip to IKEA. One should have a system for these types of things. Because I know what I'm doing, my IKEA routine *obviously* begins at the cafeteria, and my order is always the same—the Swedish meatballs. They're delicious . . . and it puts me in just the right mood to buy the three things I intended to purchase and the additional dozen or so items that mysteriously find their way into my shopping cart before I make it to the cashier.

Did you know you can buy those very same delicious IKEA Swedish meatballs to prepare at home? In fact, you don't even have to take a trip to IKEA. The recipe for making Swedish meatballs is freely provided on the internet by IKEA itself. Here's the thing though: you must follow the directions closely, or your meatballs are going to taste weird, which is the opposite of the goal of your project. You want your meatballs to taste just as if you were savoring them in an IKEA cafeteria. Your goal is to replicate. The good news is that if you acquire the exact ingredients and follow the instructions precisely, the Swedish meatballs you make at home will be basically just as tasty as they are at IKEA—better actually, if you factor in that you don't have to second guess all those impulse purchases from the kitchen section.

Let's consider that teaching is like making Swedish meatballs, and we want to make the most scrumptious meatballs possible. If every teacher was tasked with preparing the perfect dish of meatballs—that is, if every teacher were to teach brilliantly—it would also be true that every teacher would be responsible for something more than following the cooking directions precisely. An excellent *kitchen cook* pays careful attention to accurately repeating the steps for preparing a dish. To follow directions is an algorithmic approach to cooking and teaching; but in this analogy, the teacher would require a skillset much more like that of a *chef* because the dining audience of every classroom is uniquely different than any other.

Chefs also know how and when to follow directions, but chefs think artfully. They exercise a kind of innovative autonomy and carry forward decisions with myriad variables, all of which—when arranged well—contribute to the serving-up of memorable and satisfying experiences for patrons in the culinary context (Haykir & Çalışkan, 2021).

If the teacher's task is to (metaphorically) make delicious meatballs—but each classroom is a distinct mosaic of students' backgrounds, interests, personalities, and ambitions—the teacher can't merely be expected to follow even the most detailed of instructions because each classroom is a qualitatively singular commixture of humanity. Rather, these teachers with the responsibility for managing many variables would have to be able to think like chefs, which is different than how kitchen cooks think. The teacher with a chef mindset is required to be innovative, to analyze and synthesize, to combine the available parts in the interest of a unique creation that is responsive to the dining audience. The goal is to create an *experience* of meatballs—but the steps taken in doing so are informed and influenced by the context in which the dish is being served.

There are, however, limits to this analogy. The work of teaching is not the same as preparing meatballs. Teaching is the work of developing students to have the capacities for intelligence; and to be clear, intelligence should be understood as something different than intellect.[1] I will return in greater depth to the discussion of intelligence in Chapter 4, but for now intelligence should be thought of as competencies that cultivate understandings. Intelligence is that which integrates reason and affect, that which speaks to the relationship of the parts to the whole, and that which expands students' awareness for accurate self-assessment and self-regulation. Intellect, on the other hand, is something related to intelligence but qualitatively different. Intellect, as I'm referring to it, references the accumulation of topic- and context-specific knowledge (facts, dates, phraseologies, and algorithms) that demonstrates a specialistic recognition of patterns and phenomena in particular fields. *Intelligence* and *intellect* are, of course, not mutually exclusive and can be complementary. Further, an intelligent person may lack knowledge that an intellectual person cites readily, but it can also be said that an intellectual person is not necessarily intelligent.

In this book, I want to make the argument that teaching that closes Equity gaps is much more artful than algorithmic. Teaching is the art of empowering students with understandings. And further, the art of teaching is performed through learning experiences that position students in proximity to concepts such that their cultural fluencies are useful to them in integrating understandings into a schema of meaningful knowing.

There is an artistic sensibility in the work of teaching that is indispensable for Equity broadly and Culturally Responsive Education specifically. Artists—all artists—struggle with their art.[2] That's part of what it means to be an artist. The stories of struggle are epic and taken as evidence of the artist's commitment to their craft. The problems of Equity in education are complex and cannot be answered by an out-of-context algorithm or global program. Complex problems require adaptive and not technical solutions. It's important that we are willing to think deeply about teaching. The search for simple fixes to complex problems is more dangerous than the problems we seek to address; therefore, the approaches to solve must be more artful than algorithmic.

Making art is purposeful and integral to one's identity. In fact, those who make art can be said to be driven by a kind of philosophical directive more than a simple task-oriented impulse to produce something. And though artmaking is channeled through tools including the familiarity with certain algorithmic methods—artmaking draws from one's very sense of being in a way that following directions does not.

Artmaking and Philosophizing . . .

Teachers, like artists (and most people for that matter), are drawn to philosophy, by which I don't necessarily mean the philosophy of the Socrates, Diogenes, or Plato variety. The word *philosophy* is derived from the Greek word *philos* ("loving") and *sophia* ("wisdom") and etymologically means "the love of wisdom."[3] The balance of one's fundamental convictions about truth, right, wrong, good, bad, beauty, ugliness, work, family, concepts of god and spirituality, and the like can be said to constitute a personal philosophy. Teachers and any persons who are moved to find meaning in life, those who question where they are going, why, whether it's all worthwhile, and so forth, can be said to be *doing* philosophy. And if we are thinking and feeling people, that kind of activity recurs throughout our lives. To be a thinking and feeling person is not without consequence. To think and feel condemns us to question, to take ruminative strides toward understandings, to unsnarl the complex forces which play upon us—in short, to *philosophize* (Tesconi, 1975).

To philosophize forms the basis of what human beings are inclined to do—to make sense out of our life situations, to find or create meaning in or out of them. To philosophize for teachers means to bring to one's own awareness the beliefs and assumptions that underscore how we approach our craft. It's not an anchor but rather a rudder that steers our thinking toward understandings that are useful and consistent with the highest goals of teaching. To philosophize is to engage cognitively, to compose a view of one's philosophy of life, and by extension for us teachers, a philosophy for our craft.

This implies that the responsibility of teaching bears with it the commitment to investigate our own relationship with the ideas and techniques of our craft. To carry this responsibility there must be the love of *understanding* and not mere learning for the acquisition of knowledge. In this way, philosophizing is an exercise in self-knowledge, and self-knowledge is more than superficial adjustment; rather, it is the capacity to understand one's own patterns of thought, including one's biases and blind spots, and it is the perception of how intelligence can be applied to the influence of one's existence. Of what value is knowledge to the individual if one continues in their confusion? The craft of teaching is too complex to take on uncritically. It demands careful and reflective thinking—an inclination for the philosophical as a companion to practice.

As I will discuss in Chapter 2, our understanding of Equity and what it requires of teaching is the result of a multigenerational, societal inquiry through which the central and essential purpose of schools has been clarified relative to the principles of American democracy. Put another way, Equity in education is a product of public philosophizing. The goal of

Culturally Responsive Education is to operationalize Equity in the classroom. Culturally responsive pedagogy that is effective in creating equitable opportunities for kiddos is more than knowledge. There is a difference between being knowledgeable (which strikes me as something more like a *technical* attribute) and artful (which though may rely in some way on technical knowledge is critically *adaptive* in nature).

Art, in general, is about the sharing of aesthetics, communicating meaning, and promoting the aspirations of a society. Teaching, especially in a culturally diverse context, is an artful endeavor intended to draw out a reaction (i.e., engagement) from the audience (i.e., students) while developing products for posterity (i.e., intelligence and understandings). Artful teaching entails the skillful presentation of concepts and the intentional design of conditions in which students can learn most effectively—and this art demands much of us.

Craft

Brilliant teaching, while encouraging the learning of knowledge and technique, should accomplish something of far greater importance; it should impart upon students the means of *how* to think rather than *what* to think. *How* to think is also a kind of artistic endeavor. If we accept that intelligence is the capacity for *how* to think, then we can also say that the intelligence we hope to develop through artful teaching yields students' understandings of their own relationships with and responsibilities within their intersecting and overlapping communities—not in isolated terms but as a total process. Taken together, these communities comprise society, and society is the relationship between each one of us and every other.

The craft of teaching should empower students to solve the many problems of existence at their respective levels. The interactional tools necessary for the solving of personal, community, and societal problems necessitate an intelligence that integrates specialistic knowledge (separated as it is into various categories) into a cohesive whole (Zimmerman, 1995). To approach problem solving otherwise indicates an utter lack of comprehension. By extension, brilliant teaching should empower students with the intrapersonal capacities to understand themselves as whole beings constituted by the intellectual, emotional, psychological, and cultural parts in order to summon the agency to influence the circumstances of their existence. If school is to be perceived as relevant, then it should at the very least provide students with the tools to understand themselves as a total process of the various parts. This integrated understanding is required if there is to be any possibility for inward transformation through learning, and this manner of learning (i.e., intelligence) is essential because without it, life and all that can be studied become a series of themeless, threadless chaotic events—and meaning is difficult if not impossible to ascertain.

I think of culturally responsive teaching as a type of artistic expression that exists in concert with a kind of philosophical outlook. More specifically, culturally responsive teaching creates opportunities that close Equity gaps by engaging learners in rigorous thinking through the leveraging of culture in the interest of amassing understandings. I describe in greater detail what I mean by culturally responsive teaching in *Culturally Responsive Education in the Classroom: An Equity Framework for Pedagogy* (2019). Of course, there are technical and scientific principles, but be assured, this type of teaching doesn't make lessons, it makes art; and teachers who make art approach the craft from a fundamentally different philosophical outlook than teachers who make lessons.

Where brilliant art is created with paint or cameras or through storytelling or performance, brilliant teaching is created on the canvas of experience. Whether it be physical, emotional, or cerebral, it is through the compelling medium of experience that understandings are forged. In my vocabulary of effective teaching, I prefer the term *brilliance* over *mastery* because *brilliance*, in my view, is indicative of a more artful, dynamic, and ongoing process to build one's capacity to engage learners in rigorous and meaningful thinking.[4] There is no single expression of brilliance, and brilliance evolves. This could be said to be the critical difference between the proverbial one-hit wonder and an artist of generational significance. The generational artist is more likely to have evolved their craft and expression of their artmaking self so that they continue to create when the one-hit wonder has exhausted their capacity to be brilliant in one, or very few, productions.

When I talk about brilliance, I don't mean to suggest that artmaking teachers bring some supernatural, inaccessible, genius-level insight to the craft. Brilliance, as I am describing it, is earned, not granted by the heavens. When the artist learns to incorporate their technical skill inside of a larger vision, their work takes on expanded dimensions. Similarly, when the teacher finds their voice and purpose, they can create from a higher level of perspective and with an intention tailored to match the specific context in which their pedagogy is performed. And once artists understand themselves as creatives, they must never stop evolving—or the most dangerous of fates awaits them . . . inertia . . . which is to no longer produce from a heartfelt purpose but rather to copy one's previous successes.

Artmaking involves skills and habits that can be learned, but scripts and simple directives just won't suffice. Our philosophizing habits can take us in a more (or less) fruitful direction, so it's important to pay attention to what those philosophical conventions are—to inquire if they're serving our purpose well or not. This is, of course, not such a mystery or a provocative thing to say. It mostly requires a certain discipline, an awareness, a reverence if you will, of the gravity inherent in what teachers do.

Like many who may be reading this, I am a person who seeks to understand myself in relation to the world in which I live. I see this as a kind of philosophizing; or said another way, I consciously try to live such that my view of the world—my beliefs and core values—is something more than abstractions but rather an operationalized expression of my being. I am not an ant driven only by instinct and group membership. I can and do think for myself, though often in error, but (nearly) always in pursuit of that which I can reliably claim to be justified beliefs based on some measure of epistemic demand. This requires that I have tools for vetting the quality and usefulness of ideas. I am too engaged to consume concepts without philosophical critique. That would betray the very awareness and sense of purpose I bring to my craft.

The central question of this book—*How do you do Equity?*—is only partially about the classroom methods and activities we choose; it's a philosophical question we ask of ourselves relative to teaching. *What are my convictions about the craft? And how are these convictions operationalized in my pedagogy?*

SOCIAL LEARNING

Defining *Culture*

I am making the case that where brilliant art is created on easel-mounted canvases or on stages with the tools of paint, cameras, and/or performance, brilliant teaching creates through the medium of experience. This raises many questions beginning with: If experience is the canvas for the artmaking of teachers, then what are the tools? The tools for the artmaking craft of Culturally Responsive Education are revealed in the name itself. Education, of course, refers to the central pedagogical task, the effort to create fair and meaningful opportunities to learn. Responsiveness is a function of understanding, validation, and care (Reis & Clark, 2013; Reis, 2014). Culture, however, is the wildcard. Brilliant teaching leverages culture in order to engage students. Culture is what the artmaking teacher must take great effort to understand.

Culture resists a simple definition—*which is sort of the point of this book.* We must be willing to think rigorously in order to see the opportunities for employing our understanding of culture in the design of learning experiences. There are many definitions for culture.[5] For now, we can define culture as "information (i.e., ideas, beliefs, attitudes, and values) stored in human brains and social artifacts including its manifestations (i.e., norms, practices, techniques, motivations, heuristics, and institutions) that are commonly shared by a social group and acquired by new generations through what anthropologists and cognitive scientists call social learning" (Barrett, 2020; Gendron et al., 2020). I also appreciate an even more intuitive definition of *culture*: *culture* is how we do and think about things, transmitted by nongenetic means (Sapolsky, 2017).

The task of pinning down *culture* to a simple, static definition is so difficult precisely because of the immense role it plays in the human experience.

(It's the proverbial equivalent of explaining the concept of water to a fish.) *Culture* is human knowledge, skills, and any kind of mental state—conscious or not—that can affect individuals' behavior. It is acquired or modified through observation, imitation, inferencing, direct teaching, and other forms of social transmission (Boyd & Richerson, 1985). In the social and cognitive sciences, the collective of cultural information inherited through social transmission is referred to as the *cultural repertoire*. *Cultural variants* are specific elements (i.e., ideas, skills, symbols, beliefs, attitudes, and values) of the cultural repertoire, and the application of one's cultural repertoire employed within any particular social group is referred to as *cultural fluency* (Boyd & Richerson, 1985).

Our artmaking, philosophizing task of designing culturally responsive learning experiences requires a sophisticated understanding of culture in order to support pedagogy that is robust enough to close Equity gaps in the performance and achievement of our students. Our task is to facilitate our students' learning by providing opportunities for them to draw from their cultural repertoires in order to build understandings and show competence in academic spaces. This starts with both a nuanced understanding of culture and a healthy appreciation for the scope of its influence in the human experience. As we will discuss further in Chapter 4, every human culture contains an enormous amount of information. Humans leverage their cultural fluencies in all sorts of manners in their everyday lives (Boyd & Richerson, 1985; Morgan et al., 2012). No single story of any individual human can be told without reference to the fact of culture.

Culture and Learning

We humans are a cultural species. *But that statement only scratches the surface of the truth.* Humans are characterized by a profound dependence on the complex integration of culturally transmitted information gathered over time, information encompassing nearly every aspect of the human experience ranging from food preferences to beliefs about germs to rituals and traditions for mating (Brown, 2004; Henrich, 2016; Morgan, et al., 2012; Rendell, et al., 2011).

Culture is transmitted through social learning. The term *social learning* has a specific meaning and is a principal pillar in the arguments I make in this book. We can begin to define social learning as "learning that is facilitated by observation of or interaction with another individual or the products of other individuals' learning" (Hoppitt & Laland, 2013). When social learning occurs, naive (i.e., unlearned) individuals observe others in their environment, make inferences, and then develop their own beliefs, attitudes, ideas, and values that influence theirs and others' behavior. Social learning is a less costly process for acquiring valuable information than *individual learning.* Individual learning refers to self-directed, trial-and-error learning, and innovations stemming from first-hand experimentation (Rendell et al., 2011).[6] Innovation (in the sense of process) is the introduction of novel procedural variants into a population's repertoire and results in new or modified learned behavior. An innovation (in the sense of product) is a new or modified learned behavior yielding a particular outcome not previously found in the population.

Social learning, in the way I am using the term in this book, is unique to the human species. It isn't that other nonhuman animals, including our primate relatives, lack capacities for social learning, but rather that social learning in nonhuman species leads to the spread of behaviors that individuals could, and routinely do, learn on their own if they aren't already stored in the genes. And further, in many cases, the byproducts of nonhuman social learning are short-lived. Social learning limits the risks of individual learning by allowing individuals to interpret and respond to environmental and social cues selectively. This suggests that human social learning is not merely a downstream outcome of sociality and cumulative individual learning capabilities, but rather requires special-purpose mental mechanisms unique to the human species. In other words, our brains are built for learning culture (Hoppitt & Laland, 2013).

Humans can adapt to live in a wider range of environments than other primates because human culture allows for the rapid accumulation of effective strategies for successfully navigating many types of ecological spaces. Other nonhuman organisms speciate in order to occupy novel environments, whereas humans predominantly rely upon complex, highly evolved cultural information. In this way, humans are distinct from all other known life forms. In fact, human cultures are so imbued with meaning, so permeated with symbolism, and so reliant on uniquely human qualities of cognition, that to liken them to the social habits of animals is nonsensically remedial and flatly misses the point.

Humans acquire rules of behavior in specific social settings through social learning. This means that the essence of culture isn't any observable behavior but rather the encoded information that consciously and non-consciously prompts the behavior. As such, culture is fluid, meaning that any particular cultural rule may lead to different behaviors given different environmental contingencies.

Language also encodes and transmits tremendous amounts of cultural information about social roles and moral norms. Even before the emergence of written language, myths and stories were devices that conveyed vast quantities of ideas woven together into coherent cultural narratives. Language is both a function and reflection of culture. In all sorts of ways, language provides a kind of psychic structure for human sociality. Just as the syntax of a language is made up of a system of interdependent rules, so are the cultural meanings embedded in systems of kinship, traditions, and law to name just a few facets of humanity. These systems connect and facilitate social groups, and they require a variety of often complex, social institutions that together produce the *essential ingredients* of human societies—cooperation, coordination, and division of labor (Boyd & Richerson, 2008).

Social Transmission

The question of how culture is transmitted is, of course, a focus of great concern to us teachers. The classroom environment is a social space, and culture is shared through *social transmission* wherever humans interact.[7] In other words, social transmission is the process for the accumulation, refinement, and increased homogeneity of behaviors, norms, and traditions within social groups that no single individual could invent on their own. Further, the effects of social transmission extend beyond the period of the individuals' interactions exerting a lasting causal influence on the rate at which other individuals acquire and/or perform said behaviors, norms, and traditions.

Our goal here is to understand the general principles of social transmission for two reasons. First, we should be knowledgeable of the influence of culture on society so that our classroom spaces (which are microcosms of our larger society) can be designed with greater intentionality for the distribution and norming of values and behaviors conducive to students' academic success—and second, so that our teaching can support the processes that best facilitate opportunities for every student's cultural repertoire to be useful to them in showing their competence.

Social transmission, in the way I am using the term, refers to any time an individual's learning is influenced by others, and it includes many kinds of psychological processes. Social traits and cultural variants can be transmitted in three primary means: observation, exposure to products, and through verbal or written instruction. In terms of observation, the process begins with the acquisition of a trait, as in learner A is able to perform the trait which is observed and acquired by learners B and C through their inferences about the meanings, motivations, and usefulness of these traits in the context of the social environment. When successfully incorporated into their own cultural repertoire, these newly acquired traits and cultural variants may prove to be an efficient shortcut to trial-and-error learning. Social transmission also happens when learners B and C acquire traits through exposure to the products left behind by learner A. Finally, the acquisition of traits and variants by learners B and C is also a function of instructions of learner A's performance of the trait (Bandura, 1985; Henrich, 2016; Hoppitt & Laland, 2013).

Social learning occurs when information in one person's brain generates some behavior that prompts information in other persons' brains to infer meaning and thus generate some similar behavior. (Though if we could look inside people's heads, we would find that individuals have different mental representations of the observable behavior even when they may seem to behave in the same way.) Most importantly for our purposes in designing quality and effective learning opportunities, social transmission allows individuals to avoid at least some of the costs of learning for themselves while acquiring the locally preferred adaptations (Boyd & Richerson, 1985).

Environmental Niches and Cultural Inheritance

Here's a rather random question: Have you ever watched a newborn giraffe learn to walk? I can't precisely trace the YouTube rabbit hole that brought me to it, but I have! It's not very graceful, but it's super interesting because the baby giraffe isn't given lessons from the other giraffes as much as it's just given space to figure it out. This happens in the first hour of its life, and it's critical because in the giraffe's natural habitat, a baby giraffe is a tasty snack to a lion or hyena. Giraffes often don't have long stretches of time where a vulnerable infant is likely to survive if it can't move itself. But what's most interesting to me is that giraffes are born with this knowledge embedded in their DNA. It's just part of being a giraffe.

Humans, however, are not like giraffes. Humans learn how to *human (v)* from other humans.

Human infants are born with highly sophisticated brain hardware that requires the upload of the organizing software that enables its functionality. Though admittedly not as impressive as the feats of a newborn giraffe, it's pretty awesome to see how babies take in the environment as they begin to make sense of what it means to be human. Have you noticed that when an infant or young child encounters something with which they are unfamiliar in the environment, they will often look to some caregiver or other adult to check for the guidance of a reaction? If the attending adult shows an encouraging affect, they often proceed to investigate the novel object. If the adult seems to discourage the child, they back off (Henrich, 2016). Through a combination of speech, touch, pointing, expressions of emotion, and the back-and-forth switching of gaze—which cognitive scientists call sharing attention—more experienced humans alert the baby to which parts of the environment matter and which parts don't. Sharing attention teaches a developing mind to read, manage, and reliably reference its own environment based on what is relevant to its well-being and what can be ignored in the environmental niche (Barrett, 2020).

Cognitive scientists refer to an *environmental niche* or *cognitive niche* as the social space in which an individual accumulates the know-how, capacities for communication, familiarity with norms, shared values, and culturally encouraged motivations in order to navigate the networks of interactions necessary to sustain oneself and contribute to the well-being of one's social-groups (Barrett, 2020). Your cognitive niche is where you learn how to *human (v)*. One of the main unique characteristics of our species is the ability to use the environment in a way that is epistemically relevant. "In other words, human success primarily relies on the ability to gather and exchange information and knowledge from the environment" and on the ability to make use of what is learned in the interest of attending to various orders of human need (Bandura, 1985; Bertolotti & Magnani, 2016; Pinker, 2010).

We humans learn both through individual and social learning. The environments in which we share references and learn to make inferences from our observations offer a kind of template for *humaning*. Your character and personality, the ways in which you view and understand the world, the very essence of your humanity are derivatives of your cultural inheritance—the data downloads that fill your cultural repertoire. Despite how intuitive some of your inclinations may seem to you, and regardless of how deeply you may feel aspects of your identity, each of us learned how to *human (v)* through our cultural inheritance and in a cognitive niche.

The process of cultural inheritance is efficient and frugal because evolution doesn't have to genetically encode all our wiring instructions. We humans are able to out-source much of the encoding of our neurocognitive instructions to the social world around us (Boyd & Richerson, 2008; Barrett, 2020). I often ask teachers to imagine or remember a time when you were in a foreign country where you do not speak the language. You enter a coffee shop or some dining establishment: How do you know what to do to receive service? Should you rely on individual learning? The more prudent world traveler could greatly improve their prospects by observing the locals. Their behaviors are likely to reveal clues as to the social norms in the space.

It's important to make it abundantly clear that humans are immeasurably benefited by the cultural knowledge bequeathed throughout human history. It isn't even just that we are served by what we inherit by being better able to reason and solve problems. It's much deeper than that. While every human has their own individual dispositions and agency, we are all profoundly shaped by the cultures in which we learned to engage with other humans. Our cultural inheritance involves every aspect of our lives and informs how we think, what we like, and what we can make. Culturally acquired standards or values guide our efforts at individual learning, and as I will make note of in Chapter 4, social norms effectively supply training regimens that shape our minds and our literal brains in various ways—ranging from expanding our hippocampus to thickening our corpus callosum, the information highway that connects the two halves of our brains (Henrich, 2016).

Recall that *culture* is (mostly) information stored in human brains which gets transmitted from brain to brain by way of a variety of social learning processes (i.e., social transmission). We develop our schema for the causal structure of the world around us through social learning. As we humans engage in using our intelligence to communicate, reason, and problem solve, we draw on funds of accumulated knowledge that contribute to tasks as mundane as the preparation of a favorite meal to the complicated choices we make in parenting and just about everything in between.[8]

It's astonishing to stop and consider just how much cultural inheritance goes into the most trivial of human activities. Think about it this way: What have you done so far today? Have you had a cup of coffee or tea? Is a meal available to you at some point? Are you indoors? Will you move about in a motor vehicle of some kind? Each of these mundane circumstances is made infinitely easier by what you have inherited from the human brains that have preceded you. Every major technological advance in human history resulted in psychological shifts in the approach to the associated task.[9] Most of the readers of this book benefit from our cultural inheritance in ways beyond what might be routinely appreciated. Much of what I will do on the day of my writing this sentence is less a reflection of personal accomplishment than it is an amalgamation of many integrated techniques, innovations, and motivations learned in my cognitive niches.

The "success" of our species—*success* here is defined by the capacity to survive in a range of ecological environments—is not due to any superior, raw, problem-solving, mental abilities in individual humans. Over time, useful skills and practices began to accumulate and improve, which favored the cultural learners who could more effectively tap into the ever-expanding body of adaptive information available. These cultural adaptations relate to every aspect of human existence: from sophisticated projectile technologies, to food taboos, to gender roles, language conventions and various packages of social norms. Cognitive scientists refer to these cultural variants and adaptations that are passed down through social groups as *cultural inheritance*. This is a central theme in the story of humanity (Barrett, 2020; Henrich, 2016; Odling-Smee & Laland, 2011; Whiten, 2017).

Thus, *learning is cultural.* Our capacities for learning from others are themselves finely honed products of an evolutionary process that far predates the origin story of any modern-day people group. We are adaptive learners who, even as infants, carefully select when, what, and from whom to learn (Bandura & Walters, 1977; Henrich, 2016). Caregivers curate a baby's abilities for navigating their environment by, as just one example, sharing attention to guide the baby's developing brain in learning their niche. The cognitive niches in which we learn to *human (v)* shape our sociality by influencing what we attend to, perceive, process, and value. Individual human brains are essentially optimized for the particular social and physical environment in which they are developed (Gendron et al., 2020). Our very sense of selves is filtered through our cultural inheritances.[10]

As I hope to make super clear in this book, for us teachers, it is culture that is the critical variable in our efforts to *do Equity* in the classroom. That doesn't mean that we ignore other aspects of the human experience like race, ethnicity, gender expression, and socio-economic status, but we must be able to think deeply about culture and use our knowledge of it in the artful design of learning experiences. Further, my claim is that our greatest hope in the closing of Equity gaps is in the craft of teachers and not in policy mandates.

There is much to learn from the work of cognitive scientists, biologists, and also anthropologists, particularly in the field of cultural psychology. I find the research methodologies compelling and the data informative. I like to borrow from these fields to support our understanding of the role that culture plays in shaping humanity. We teachers, however, are most benefited by deepening our own sense of how culture influences the thinking and behaviors of our students in the here and now. In Chapter 4, I will offer a brief statement on what is interchangeably referred to as Gene-Culture Coevolution or the Theory of Dual Inheritance. These, I've concluded, are sufficiently beyond the scope of our work in the classroom, and therefore, while plenty interesting, not directly relevant to the central claims of this book. Our sociality is the driver of our humanity. We are human because we are social; and it is our sociality that is both fed and produced by culture.

Through social learning, we inculcate the essential ideas shared within our social groups including those moral and visceral notions regarding truth, right, wrong, good, bad, beauty, ugliness, work, family, concepts of God and spirituality—ideas so elemental to one's being that they can evade conscious recognition. In a species with cumulative cultural knowledge that raises the prospects for success, but only in such a species, faith in one's cultural inheritance often favors greater survival and reproduction (Henrich, 2016). Because of social learning, we have developed an array of mental dispositions that mold the individual's psychology in ways that allow them to engage with their culturally constructed, social worlds (Bandura & Walters, 1977). When we have an understanding for how these cultural processes influence our students' thinking, we are in a position to deliver much more brilliant teaching to our kiddos.

Culture Matters

I return to my claim regarding the centrality of culture in brilliant teaching: if experience is the canvas on which teachers create, then culture is a primary tool with which the artmaking teacher executes their craft. We will discuss cultural identity further in Chapters 3 and 4, but for now, let's synthesize the discussion of culture by considering the following:

1. The key to understanding how humans evolved and why we are so different from other animals is to recognize that we are a social species with a profound dependency on culture. By *culture* I mean the information and large body of practices, techniques, heuristics, tools, motivations, values, and beliefs that we all acquire through social learning.

   It's almost impossible to overstate the massive influence culture has on human behavior. The perception of all experience is a function of culture. Through a process of cultural evolution, culture generates social norms that, if violated, can result in a bad reputation, denial of status, or other punishment (Boyd & Richerson, 2008; Henrich, 2016). These are powerful arbiters of human beliefs and behavior. No human is so independent as to not be a product of cultural indoctrination. This means that all human experience is performed and understood through a cultural lens. Culture influences the meaning one derives from any life event, big or small. It is the omnipresent dark matter of our social world. No brain operates in a culture vacuum. Culture filters the constant stream of information into the brain and influences not only our perceptions but also the frequency of behaviors (Sapolsky, 2017).

   Cultural processes are at the crux of the most interesting (and important) questions about our pedagogy. To be able to leverage an understanding of culture in our teaching starts with a nuanced understanding of the significance of culture in the story of human kind. We humans share a "collective brain" through which we learn from others in the social transmission of culture. This allows us to live in large and widely interconnected social communities. You, for example, received a massive cultural inheritance that included a convenient base-10 counting system, Arabic numerals for easy quantifying, a vocabulary of at least 60,000 words (if you are a native English speaker), and working examples of all sorts of concepts that you would have been unlikely to invent on your own, including pulleys, springs, screws, bows, wheels, levers, and adhesives. Culture also provides problem-solving heuristics and sophisticated cognitive skills (like reading) that have evolved to both fit and, to some degree, modify our brains and biology. We don't have these tools, concepts, skills, and heuristics because of our individual capacities for intelligence; rather, we are intelligent because we have culturally evolved a vast repertoire of tools, concepts, skills, and heuristics. It is culture that makes us intelligent (Henrich, 2016).

2. Learning abilities are cultural adaptations. We learn how to learn in the same social spaces in which we inherit our cultural repertoires. In other words, we are socialized to be particular types of learners with uniquely arranged interests, motivations, and expressions of competence.

Socialization is the process of forming fundamental dispositions—intellectual and emotional—toward nature, humankind, society, and the individual (among other things). Therefore, we teachers must be aware that the expressions of culture have the potential to confuse our interpretations of students' competencies. Cultural differences inform the conscious and nonconscious inferences we make about the abilities of our students. Rather than succumbing to the tribal urge of *deficitizing* difference, we should be mindful of seeing culture as a tool for our craft.

This brings a particular caution to mind. We should treat the topic of culture with great care and reverence because our cultural lens biases us all in our interpretation of other social groups' cultures. This is no small observation. It should humble us. It calls for a constant awareness of how culture influences your own views and interpretations of the world. I've heard it described this way: Imagine that your cultural lens is an actual pair of blue-colored sunglasses. If in your most sincere intention, you seek to see the world through the eyes of a student with a different cultural background, you cannot merely look through their eyes because their cultural sunglasses may be, let's say, yellow-shaded. This means that when you make even your best effort to see the world from their vantage point, your view of their yellow-shaded perspective won't be yellow, and it won't actually be blue, but rather green. To look through the cultural lens of another is still filtered through one's own cultural lens resulting in a view that is different from both but not identical to either. The differences in shaded perspectives do not necessarily reflect any specific deficits, but without the awareness of how our views are biased by our cultural indoctrinations, we may inaccurately perceive our students and thus thoughtlessly limit their opportunities to learn.

3. *This one is super important.* Culture is much more useful to teachers as a descriptive rather than a predictive tool. To use culture to make predictions for how students will behave is inherently risky because it opens the door for stereotypes and generalizations when our most vulnerable learners are the very ones who need to be seen in the highest, individualized definition possible. Overgeneralizations are rarely useful in understanding specific difficulties. The limitations of analysis at the macro-, social-group level are prone to stifle our best efforts in understanding the local and immediate context in which our pedagogical philosophizing occurs.

The culturally responsive, artmaking teacher is especially attuned to both the symbols and functions of culture. Cultural differences are of degree, not of kind. To understand the cultural differences among social groups, try not to think of culture as a panel of on/off switches with some features turned on for some cultures and off in others. Think about it in terms of sliding scales—with each group having some measure of expression of every feature. What I find to be most profound about the history of the human species is that many groups, through their own independent devices, invented variations of agriculture, writing, pottery, embalming, astronomy, and coinage. The anthropologist Donald Brown is but one of many on a long roster of scholars who have proposed categories of cultural universals including:[11]

the existence of and concern with aesthetics, magic, males and females seen as having different natures, baby talk, gods, induction of altered states, marriage, body adornment, murder, prohibition of some type of murder, kinship terms, numbers, cooking, private sex, names, dance, play, distinctions between right and wrong, nepotism, prohibitions on certain types of sex, empathy, reciprocity, rituals, concepts of fairness, myths about afterlife, music, color terms, prohibitions, gossip, in-group favoritism, language, humor, lying, symbolism, the linguistic concept of "and," tools, trade, and toilet training.

And that's only a partial list. (Sapolsky, 2017)

My point is that it is far more important for teachers to have a *descriptive* understanding of what culture is and how it functions in our species than to try to accrue some *predictive* inventory of the specific cultural symbols and practices of any social group. Instead of thinking about the specific group features of culture, it is more useful to ask: *What does culture do?* The understanding of, in the descriptive sense, how cultural fluency serves the individual learner provides great insight into the ways in which culture can be leveraged in responsive learning environments. And, in fact, our students are our best teachers of their social-group cultural references precisely when they are invited to draw from their full repertoires for knowing while they are engaged in meaningful learning.

A goal of this book is to avoid simple categorical thinking particularly as it relates to culture. Putting facts into neatly demarcated buckets of predefined explanations has its advantages but it's a remedial form of knowing. Rigorous understandings are nuanced and disciplined. The boundaries between categories in our understandings are often arbitrary, but once we give credence to some arbitrary boundary, we soon forget that it is arbitrary and are inclined to ascribe to it all manners of unfounded (or unexamined) significance. Categorical thinking about culture and identity can obfuscate inter-group similarities and intra-group differences. We want to see the students we teach as whole beings in order to design learning experiences that they can perceive as culturally responsive, but this is made more difficult by broadly categorizing and labeling them.

NOTES ON ARTMAKING: INFLUENCE AND INSPIRATION

Me: "This isn't nearly as impressive as I was expecting it to be."

Who isn't familiar with the *Mona Lisa*, one of the world's most famous paintings? I was in Paris at the Louvre, and as an art admirer, this was a bucket-list moment; but once in the gallery and upon first seeing the *Mona Lisa*, I was more than a little disappointed. The hype didn't match the actual painting.

To start, it was much smaller than I anticipated, and because of the arrangement of the room and the constant crowd in the gallery, I couldn't get within 30 feet of it—which meant it was basically not possible for me to make out any of the detail that might have confirmed the great skill of the brilliant artist, Leonardo da Vinci.

Leonardo da Vinci is known as one of the more important artists and thinkers in world history, and he was highly acclaimed during his lifetime, which meant he was a sought-after mentor and teacher to young and aspiring artists. As was the custom in the early 16th century, famous and successful artists had workshops where a select few would be able to spend time as apprentices. A common practice was for the mentor artist's paintings to be prominently displayed throughout the workshop so that students could copy them, a type of qualifying exam to test their skill for managing the tools of the craft.

The *Mona Lisa* is thought to have been a fixture of da Vinci's workshop for many years, and dozens of unknown apprentices would have seen it and taken on the challenge of copying its subtleties. There is one such copy on display at the Prado in Madrid, nearly identical to the masterpiece, displayed without fanfare or large crowds. It's become one of my favorite destinations. At the Prado, one can stand within inches of this version of the Mona Lisa, which makes it much more possible to appreciate its brilliance; and now I tell everyone: If you want to see the *Mona Lisa*—don't go to Paris, go to Madrid!

The artist to whom I feel closest and whose backstory I probably know best is Jean-Michel Basquiat (1960—1988), a Brooklyn-born neo-expressionist style painter of Haitian and Puerto Rican descent. Basquiat and I shared mentors, both of us having attended the same high school in

New York City. Through his enormous investment of time and attention, Basquiat, like all artists of note, developed an unmistakable aesthetic that took the art world by storm. His paintings are uniquely a product of his hand, his story, his vision of the world, and his role in it.

Every artist learns from and is influenced by others, but I think the notion of influence is too often misunderstood. Robert Farris Thompson, professor emeritus of Art History at Yale University and an authority of African diasporic art philosophy, gave a quote in a fantastic documentary on the life of Jean-Michel Basquiat (*The Radiant Child*, 2010) articulating what the brilliant artist himself understood about influence. Basquiat, Thompson said, never mindlessly copied the work of other artists but rather he "improvised revisions." Basquiat understood that "influence is not influence. It's simply someone's idea going through my new mind."

Take a moment and google Jean-Michel Basquiat's version of the *Mona Lisa*. It isn't anything like the copy at the Prado, though it is easy to see what work is influencing Basquiat's hand. Basquiat famously drew from a range of source material. His catalog of work embodies the sentiment that the artist is eternally responsible for their own inspiration. The inspired artist is a philosophizing artist. Inspiration is a function of expansion; it is the illustration of one's commitment to staying engaged. The moment one loses their sense of awe and curiosity for the craft is the moment one shifts from artist to copyist.

One way to think of the role of culture in the human story is as an agent of influence and inspiration, and much of what I want to explore in this book resides at the intersections. By influence, I am referring to that which causes direct, indirect, or intangible effects in the thinking, actions, and motivations of groups and individuals. The etymology of the word *inspiration* can be traced to the Latin *inspiratus*, which means "to breathe into," and since the mid-16th century, the literal meaning of inspiration in English is "the drawing of air into the lungs." So *inspiration* can be defined as both that which sustains life and also that which has "the action or power of arousing the intellect or emotions."

As a teacher, I am reminded that my work is to be a source of both inspiration and influence for my students. I want to inspire my students to engage, and I want to influence an empowered trajectory in their lives. What they do with the inspiration is ultimately up to them, and though the long-term yield of my influence is but one factor in a much larger multivariable equation, I would hope to be seen as having an effect that empowers my students. Further, and just as relevant, as one (much like you, I suspect) who is committed to making art with my teaching that serves the learning interests of my students, I have a responsibility to cultivate channels of influence that affect and sustain my own inspiration for my craft.

CHAPTER NOTES

1. In the estimated 45,000-year history of anatomically modern humans, the purest definition of intelligence is the ability to learn that which allows one to survive. The extent to which early humans were able to retain and make use of the knowledge shared within their social group was directly aligned with the likelihood of individual survival and passing on their DNA into the species' gene pool.

2. I have tried very hard to limit the word *creativity* in this book because it is, in my view, mostly tainted by its overuse and misuse. *Artmaking* includes what might be colloquially referred to as creativity, but I mean it to be considered as something much more specific and intentional in relation to the craft of teaching.

3. For Diogenes, the logic and motivation of philosophy was clear: to actively engage in an inquiry of truth and falseness affords the individual a greater responsibility for their own life output. When asked what it did for him, the Greek philosopher is reputed to have replied that it enabled him to do willingly and responsibly what others did out of fear of the law, ignorance, and established custom (Tesconi, 1975).

4. Rigor is neither about a particular type of text, nor the volume of work assigned, nor even how "hard" some task is. . . . Rather, I deploy the definition of rigor used by Karin Hess in her design of the Cognitive Rigor Matrix (Hess, Jones, et al., 2009), which is a function of the cognitive processes related to how students think—as in, "rigor refers to the type(s)

of cognitive processes (i.e., Bloom's taxonomy) in addition to the depth of content understanding and scope of learning activities (i.e., Webb's Depth of Knowledge)." "Both the thinking processes and the depth of content knowledge have direct implications in curricular design, lesson delivery, and assessment development and use" (Hess, Carlock, et al., 2009).

5. The definition I am using could be classified as "psychological with an explicit emphasis on learning."

6. In the chapters that follow, the discussion of cognition is intended to highlight the processes that matter most to teachers in the context of classroom-based instruction. I don't aim to speak about the brain, intelligence, or thinking, for that matter, at a biological level. Rather, I am discussing cognition as a psychological phenomenon heavily influenced by human sociality generally and culture more specifically. I do not intend to speculate about the cerebral or neural processes that underlie the psychological processes of engaged learning beyond that which can be useful to teachers in the design of culturally responsive learning experiences.

7. There is debate about whether direct teaching falls into the category of social learning. For our philosophizing purposes, I am following the lead of Bennett Galef (2009) and others who have defined social learning as the transmission of durable cultural variants by direct teaching, observation, imitation, verbal instruction, and inferencing of all sorts—basically anything that isn't unfacilitated individual learning. Some disagree, contending that guided learning (i.e., learning from direct teaching) is not cultural transmission because the naive individual must acquire their own information from teaching by a process of reinforcement that is almost as costly as ordinary individual learning. Since the focus of our craft is pedagogy, however, I find it most useful to include direct teaching in the category of social learning mechanisms. Research in the field of developmental psychology suggests that it is the exposure to others problem solving, using artifacts, and trying to "do things" that most effectively sparks the causal inference machinery in our minds (Meltzoff et al., 2012; Henrich, 2016).

When I refer to teaching and learning in this book, I am primarily referencing classrooms in schools where students and teachers share a physical space. Ultimately, we are most concerned with designing learning environments in which students will be able to maximize all the tools available to them—socially and individually—in the interest of building understandings and demonstrating what they've learned. The very fact of the shared space makes it, in my view, a social learning experience.

8. Do you like your food spicy? Well, consider that many spices are antimicrobials that kill pathogens in foods, and in many societies—particularly those near the equator—the customary use of spices is a product of cultural inheritance. Globally, the most common spices are onions, pepper, garlic, cilantro, chili peppers (capsicum), and bay leaves. So the very manner in which we season our foods suggests a cultural adaptation to the problem of food pathogens and particularly meat. Your taste for and tolerance of spicy food, not to mention some of your favorite family recipes, are a function of your cultural inheritance (Henrich, 2016).

9. This speaks to an aspect of the role of culture in the human experience, which is beyond the scope of my arguments in this book. I say more about this in Chapter 4, but Gene-Culture Coevolutionary Theory (or Dual Inheritance Theory) proposes that culture interfaces with our genes and biology through the social transmission of things like fire, cooking, cutting tools, projectile weapons, water containers, artifacts, tracking know-how, and communicative patterns (Wrangham, 2009). These processes, the theory goes, create selective pressures that yield genetically evolved responses to the environment. Among our numerous features, this theory would help explain our small teeth, short colons, shrunken stomachs, poor plant-detoxification abilities, accurate throwing capabilities, nuchal ligaments (head stabilizer for running), numerous eccrine sweat glands, long post-reproductive lives, lowered larynxes, dexterous tongues, whitened sclera, and enlarged brain (Henrich, 2016). The arguments I make in this book do not

depend on this theory of Dual Inheritance, but it makes a fascinating case that the genetic and anatomical evolution of our species is attributed to, at least in part, culture and social learning. Suffice it to say that your life would be quite different depending on which cultural software functions as your neurophysiological operating system.

10. "This isn't to ignore the consequential effects of conditions like poverty on capacities for learning. Research shows that early and long exposure to poverty is bad for the developing brain. The circumstances of poverty may alter the development of the prefrontal cortex, the brain area involved in a range of critical cognitive functions, including attention, language, and emotional self-regulation. The full effects of poverty on brain development are not yet fully understood, but we do know that it's linked to poorer performance in school and fewer years of education. These ramifications ultimately increase a child's risk of raising their own children in poverty and living in communities where the intergenerational effects of poverty are compounded by the intense concentration of impoverished conditions" (Barrett, 2020).

11. I will ask for forgiveness in advance because, in some instances, I'm going to quote long original-source passages. When I do so, it's because I don't think I can paraphrase the original sentiment any clearer than the author, and I want you to hear the observation directly from them rather than filtered through my interpretations.

CHAPTER 2

Defining Equity . . . and the Problem of Fairness

"But what of public education? What rational prescriptions can be made for it during these times? How can the school fulfill its traditional socialization functions when the norms, values, attitudes, and convictions that have traditionally shaped these functions are often in conflict with, or at least out-of-joint with emerging beliefs and values, or are merely lacking in support owing to the fragmentation of social experience? In short, where does the school find its values and locate authority for transmitting them and for constructing curricula in a time when just about everything appears to be relative and so transient?"

—Charles A. Tesconi

A PROBLEM OF FAIRNESS

I like to make the argument at get-togethers and festive occassions that free and public education is one of the coolest social inventions of all time! (Yes, you guessed it. I am lots of fun at parties.) Many Americans, if not most, take the existence of public schools as a given, a right of citizenship so basic it hardly needs to be justified; but the creation of public education in America is a remarkable feat of human cooperation and an integral social apparatus of Western society. Though we may have been desensitized over time to the miracle of public schools, the very notion was indeed a radical departure from the ways in which nearly all of human societies had been organized in the training of youth.[1] From the onset, however, the promise of public education in the United States has been hampered by a recurring dilemma—a *problem* of fairness.

The source of both the promise and the problem of public schools is *opportunity*. It is precisely because of the opportunities for social and occupational mobility between generations that the fairness dilemma arises to begin with (Coleman, 1968), and "since its inception, the public school has been thought to be the major instrument through which social equality and, more specifically, equality of opportunity would be ensured" (Tesconi, 1975).

The expectations placed on public schools are inextricably interwoven with the institution's purpose; and so, in order to define *Equity*, we are required to wrestle with (at least) two essential questions of concern: *What is the role of schools in a pluralistic, multiracial, multiethnic, multicultural, democratic society?* And: *How can we know if schooling—the systems, structures, policies, practices, and the opportunities therein—is fair?*

But if public education were to be the vehicle for equality of opportunity in society at large, there must be fairness in the accessing of *educational opportunity*. This has long been recognized and affirmed in principle if not practice, and yet, from the very beginning, the attempts to live out the concept of equality of educational opportunity have been like walking through quicksand. *But why the difficulty?* To answer this, a latent conceptual relationship is necessarily made explicit: fair access to educational opportunity is imperative to the American opportunity ethic itself; the former, at least in part, is also a function of the latter. There is an interdependent, mutually supportive and benefiting, reinforcing relationship between these two ideals (Feinberg & Soltis, 1998; Tesconi, 1975).

The question of fairness is clearly a matter of first-order, national interest, and weakening the correlation between social status and school achievement is the principal measure of fairness in American public education. Whether or not schooling functions in this way is an empirical question, but the fact remains that most people have long thought it does and/or should (Ballantine et al., 2018; Tesconi & Hurwitz, 1974).

Equity in Education Is . . .

The origin story of Equity in education is as old as the "common school" movement itself, and to define *Equity* requires that we associate the purpose of free and public schooling with the very goals of the American project because the arguments I make throughout this book are largely *not* dependent on the political divisions of the current or any particular historical period. Rather, I seek to convey the point that Equity in education is not a partisan argument at all, but rather the existential *sine qua non* of American public education. Without it, the institution would never have come to be nor will its expense and effort be reasonably justified.

Equity in education is the policy and practice directive to provide quality and effective learning opportunities so that background and identity are neither correlative nor predictive of student performance and/or achievement outcomes. This definition of Equity is based in the half-century-plus-long legal, policy, and scholarly discussion of the concept. *Equity*, as I am defining it, consists of three interdependent pillars:

1. *It's about outputs.* Given the purpose of American public education, Equity is *measured by outputs* in contrast to equality, which is measured by inputs.

2. *Opportunity brings achievement.* Equity requires *quality* learning opportunities that are *effective* in bringing about achievement.

3. *Differences aren't deficits.* Though there are *differences* in cultural, linguistic, racial, ethnic, and language backgrounds, as well as differential access to resources among students, socio-ethnolinguistic groups do not differ from each other in the capacity for intelligence in any important way; and thus, *differences do not equate to deficits in ability.*

Each of these interdependent pillars is integral to our understanding for the policy and practice directives inherent in the Equity concept. The rest of this chapter is a further explanation of these three definitional pillars.

MEASURED BY OUTPUTS

1. *It's about outputs.* Given the purpose of American public education, Equity is *measured by outputs* in contrast to equality, which is measured by inputs.

Defined by Purpose . . .

Horace Mann famously claimed in his 1848 annual report on education that free public schooling is "beyond all other devices of human origins the greatest equalizer of the conditions of man—the balance wheel of the social machinery." Among the most persuasive arguments in favor of the common school was that such schooling would open wide the gateway to opportunity that would otherwise be closed to many young people, and that an educated populace would reliably avert the social inequalities that plagued other nations (Hurwitz & Tesconi, 1972).

From its earliest iterations, American public education has always had a sorting function, the sorting itself intended to fairly identify the talent and develop the intelligence from among the youth of the various communities. This is vital because in the context of the young American democracy, intelligence was both a private and public commodity affecting both the private and public good alike. Establishing common schools, it was said, would improve the position of the poor by providing them the same access to society's inheritance of funded knowledge from which the rich profited (Tesconi & Hurwitz, 1974). Fairness in schooling was philosophically intended to provide an equally accessible and quality education for all of America's youth irrespective of social status, race, gender, language background, religious belief, or any other characteristic of identity or lineage—at least in mission if not in its actual performance.

Long before *Brown v. Board of Education* (1954) and other landmark cases, discrimination on the basis of background and identity was argued to be antithetical to the very institution of public education itself. In a widely read and referenced teacher training text, Myers and Harshman (1929) noted the imperative of fairness as synonymous with the purpose of schooling in a democratic society:

The principle of equality of educational opportunity excludes any discrimination based on sex, race, social status, confession, or political opinion. No class or minority shall enjoy any special privileges or suffer under any disadvantages in this matter of opportunity for education. Every mother, every father shall know that their children by their own effort will make a new start in life, and will attain, inside a friendly and cooperative society, exactly the goal that their talents and efforts bring within their reach. Only if every young generation makes, in this sense, society new again, can democracy live and avoid senility and sterility. Only by this application of equality of opportunity can the natural aristocracy of talents replace what Jefferson called the Tinsel Aristocracy based on privileges only.

Schools have also functioned as a social transmission device. They streamlined habits, customs, concepts, premises, and ways of knowing that became central threads in the larger societal narratives, scripts, and affects. This is an especially significant role to play in Western society where the social and transactional connections that bind the larger population are assisted by the individual's abilities to interact among a variety of persons hailing from multiple socio-ethnolinguistic groups. To make a living in this society, one must have the tools and knowledge to successfully engage across social group lines.

So I return to the questions I raised at the start of this chapter: *What is the role of schools in a pluralistic, multiracial, multiethnic, multicultural democratic society?* And: *How can we know if schooling—the systems, structures, policies, practices, and the opportunities therein—is fair?* I re-center these questions because it is my contention that the teaching and the policy environment of schooling should be organized relative to its highest aim. To define *Equity*, we must consider public education in the light of its *purpose* in American life. Notably, in the *Brown* decision, the Supreme Court establishes as a baseline for its unanimous opinion that:

> Today, education is perhaps the most important function of state and local governments. Compulsory school attendance laws and the great expenditures for education both demonstrate our recognition of the importance of education to our democratic society. It is required in the performance of our most basic public responsibilities, even service in the armed forces. It is the very foundation of good citizenship.

Brown v. Board

By the 1950s, there was a well-organized campaign in place to strike down the segregation of students by race in American public schools. Segregation was permissible under the Supreme Court's 1896 decision in the *Plessy v. Ferguson* case that "separate but equal" schools were not in violation of fundamental constitutional rights. This view prevailed until 1954 when the Supreme Court ruled unanimously that another input variable, racial mix, was a crucial ingredient in the interpretation of Equal Educational Opportunity (Tesconi and Hurwitz, 1974).

On May 17, 1954, Chief Justice Earl Warren read the following words from the bench of the Supreme Court: "We conclude that in the field of public education the doctrine of *separate but equal* has no place. Separate educational facilities are inherently unequal." *And the world changed.*

At issue was the legality of the "separate but equal" doctrine, the custom of the American South (and much of the North) in segregating not only schools but also most of society's public spaces. The school districts took the position of defending their practices by arguing that the input factors, tangible and otherwise, were comparable between the White and "Negro" schools. The Court's unanimous opinion reads:

> We come then to the question presented: Does segregation of children in public schools solely on the basis of race, even though the physical facilities and other "tangible" factors may be equal, deprive the children of the minority group of equal educational opportunities? We believe that it does.[2]

This was a watershed cultural moment for the United States. In *Brown*, the Court ruled that the segregation of students by race constituted a violation of fundamental freedoms not because of an input deprivation, but rather because of the implications for outputs:

> Here, unlike [previous cases in which the equivalence of resources is in question], there are findings below that the Negro and white schools involved have been equalized, or are being equalized, with respect to buildings, curricula, qualifications and salaries of teachers, and other "tangible" factors. Our decision, therefore, cannot turn on merely a comparison of these tangible factors in the Negro and white

schools involved in each of the cases. We must look instead to the effect of segregation itself on public education.

Brown v. Board of Education is widely viewed as a quintessential victory for *equality*. If, however, we interrogate the logic structure of the Court's opinion, we can see that it opened the conceptual door for Equity in that the essence of the Court's judgment was that the *effects* of separation were the actual basis for its illegality. The Court determined that the *effects* of the separation *were* the injury and thus a violation of rights of citizenship, and therefore the effects of schooling were the measure by which "separate but equal" was deemed unconstitutional and therefore unfair.[3] Before 1954, Equal Educational Opportunity (EEO) was conceptualized in relation to the input view whereas after the *Brown* decision, Equity was to be seen as a function of the output view. Thus, the opposite of equality is inequality; and the opposite of EEO is inequity.

The Beginning of an Era

Therefore, Equity is not equality—in terms of the sameness of inputs. Equality assumes that *fair* means sameness. Equity, however, posits that equality isn't necessarily *fair* because the social, economic, historical, and political contexts in which students learn impact how they perceive and are able to take advantage of their educational opportunities. The concept of equality is more-or-less a matter of resource distribution, but Equity is defined by its purpose in our society.

The traditional input notion of equality of educational opportunity consisted of two major elements. First, anyone who wishes to do so must have access to schooling. Second, and most significant, the schools available must have approximately equal resource inputs in terms of materials, teachers, curricula, and the like (Tesconi & Hurwitz, 1974). The traditional input view says that the fact that certain social groups may not benefit equally from the system has nothing to do with the system so long as the inputs are distributed equally. After *Brown*, however, the input view is insufficient, and thus yields to the output view which holds public education accountable differently (Tesconi, 1975).

The *Brown* decision turned the attention from what seemed a simple definition of inputs to the consequences of schooling. This conceptual pivot introduces a new interpretation of the notion of fairness as measured by results of schooling and signifies the beginning of the Equity era (Havighurst, 1973; Tesconi, 1975; Yudof, 1972). The work of Equity, however, poses numerous difficulties in a society in which systems beyond schools contribute to the social and economic inequalities that render some students less ready to take advantage of traditional educational opportunities. What's more, this work of Equity requires the specifying, justifying, and ordering of criteria for fair treatment. Resistance to this premise was soon mounted, most often in the cordoning of resources and the proliferation of suburban and affluent school districts because those who benefit from arbitrary privileging distinctions are often quite loathe to see them dissolve.

QUALITY AND EFFECTIVE

2. *Opportunity brings achievement.* Equity requires *quality* learning opportunities that are *effective* in bringing about achievement.

The Coleman Study (1966)

As we have seen, Equity, as a construct and organizing principle, is related to equality, but more specifically, it is born from the notion of Equal Educational Opportunity (EEO), which has been implicit in some form in the mission of public education from its inception into the 21st century (Reese, 2011; Tesconi, 1975). While the concept of EEO is generally uncontroversial in theory, to fairly operationalize it in practice is another challenge altogether. What do we imply when we assert that the opportunity of student X to get an education is fair relative to that of student Y? It can be argued that since the amount and kind of education a person acquires are functions of their inherent abilities to learn, and since these abilities vary among persons, fairness in educational opportunity ought to be a function of and determined by the capacity to profit from education (Tesconi, 1975).

This requires something in addition to the desegregation of schools. Following *Brown*, an inventory of the overall educational opportunity structure was in order to determine the conditions and appropriate actions necessary to advance schools toward fairness.

A little noticed provision of the 1964 Civil Rights Act called for "a survey and report to the President and the Congress, within two years of its enactment, concerning the lack of availability of equal educational opportunities for individuals by reason of race, color, religion, or national origin in public educational institutions at all levels in the United States, its territories and possessions, and the District of Columbia." James Coleman, a Johns Hopkins University sociologist, would be named the principal investigator in what was one of the more ambitious, important, and controversial social science research projects of the 20th century—which is commonly referred to as *The Coleman Study* (1966). The Coleman Study found that access, opportunity, and the capacity to profit from education are related to pivotal factors including socio-economic background and the kinds of social and cultural fluencies young people bring with them in addition to the input resources available to students in school (Kahlenberg, 2001; Tesconi, 1975). More specifically, the Coleman Study contended that the capacity to benefit from equality of educational opportunity does not start in the school (Borman & Dowling, 2010; Tesconi, 1975). The Coleman Study showed that academic achievement was likely in causal relationship with students' cultural inheritance and middle-class social fluencies. At the time, the study was controversial because it suggested that schools made little difference in achievement outcomes, but there is debate regarding this interpretation.[4]

In a 1968 paper presented at a conference on the campus of Harvard University, Coleman himself took center stage to review the controversial study.[5] The disciplined social scientist that he was, the first action of surveying the accessibility of Equal Educational Opportunity was to clarify a definition for the term. He used a thought experiment to frame the original intent of the concept of EEO and to expose a hidden assumption for public schooling that was revealed in the *Brown* decision:

Suppose the early schools had operated for only one hour a week and had been attended by children of all social classes. This would have met the explicit assumptions of the early concept of equality of opportunity since the school is free, with a common curriculum, and attended by all children in the locality.

Coleman posited that while a one-hour-a-week model may be said to be equal and impartial, it obviously would not have been accepted as fair in terms of providing equality of opportunity because its effects would have been so minimal. Though in the scenario, every child would have the *same* opportunity to be educated, it would not be fair because the more affluent families would have supplemented the one-hour-per-week school inputs with private resources, which would have created gross inequalities in results. Coleman thus confirmed that since the inception of public schools, EEO was never expected to be purely input driven, but rather to be measured by the effectiveness of those inputs for bringing about learning outcomes.

Inequality

The glaring contradiction in the American opportunity narrative broadly and the purpose of public education specifically are the anti-democratic and unmeritocratic systems that privilege the social elite. These systems, networked and intersecting, functionally limit the discovery, recruitment, and training of the talent from among the various subgroups in the general population. Furthermore, the unequal distribution of rewards in one generation tends to result in the unequal distribution of hope and motivation in succeeding generations (Tesconi, 1975). Central to the principles of Equity is the claim that social inequalities are not mirror images of inequalities in the distribution of human ability across populations but rather the result of social stratification that cause the conditions that perpetuate disparate outcomes (Howe, 1999).

Isabelle Wilkerson, Michelle Alexander, Gibran Muhammad, Richard Rothstein and others have written about the systems of social stratification in America in terms of a hierarchy, a ranking system that formalizes unequal access to resources and opportunities. Hierarchies establish and maintain a status quo by ritualizing inequalities. It's important to note that social inequalities based on race do not require racial animus as much as they are maintained through tradition and indifference. Michelle Alexander (2010) argues that mass incarceration in America, as an example, is a system that locks economically poor people—and disproportionately economically poor people of color—into something functionally approaching a permanent, second-class status tantamount to a kind of American caste system. It is, in her view, the moral equivalent of Jim Crow:

> The notion that all racial caste systems are necessarily predicated on a desire to harm other racial groups, and that racial hostility is the essence of racism, is fundamentally misguided. All racial caste systems, not just mass incarceration, have been supported by racial indifference. Many whites during the Jim Crow era sincerely believed that African Americans were inferior, and that segregation was a sensible system for managing a society composed of fundamentally different and unequal people. The sincerity of many people's bigoted racial beliefs is what led Martin Luther King Jr. to declare, "Nothing in all the world is more dangerous than sincere ignorance and conscientious stupidity."

I want to be deliberate in my explanation here. I do not intend to make the claim that patterns of inequality and disparate access to resources in 21st-century America serve the same codified function as slavery or Jim Crow. My argument is that as we define Equity relative to the American ethos of *life, liberty, and the pursuit of happiness*, we are responsible for acknowledging that these systems "have operated as a tight network of laws, policies, customs, and institutions that collectively enact the subordinate status of a group defined largely by race" (Alexander, 2010). Public education has failed in many ways to meet its highest calling, but it is also true that schools inherit the impacts of social inequalities that complicate the essential task of teaching and learning. It strikes me as naive and disingenuous to argue otherwise; the concerns of Equity speak to the effects of systems on the experiences and opportunities of society's most vulnerable and historically marginalized social groups.

James Coleman suggested that if equality of educational opportunity is to be measured not by equal inputs, but by the effectiveness of those inputs for bringing about learning outcomes, the focus of efforts to improve educational outputs should not be limited to school facilities and educational practices, but rather to include fair access to supportive human resources— that is, what children take to school. Given that schools function in alignment and cooperation with other societal systems, the work of Equity in education must entail more than improvements in school-based pedagogy alone. Equity requires the consideration of the larger societal context or it may otherwise result in the competing among underserved populations for improved outcomes and status in the hierarchy without challenging the systems that perpetuate the inequitable status quo. This is a critical observation because without it, underserved populations may be blamed for the injustices they endure, or they may be inclined to fight among themselves for improved opportunities by vying for the claim of most aggrieved. This kind of competition would require a jockeying for position that risks denying the humanity of other groups, which is short-sighted, and ultimately, counterproductive. More importantly, it lets systems escape accountability and criticism for failures to provide the types of quality educational opportunities that are most likely to yield rigorous and engaging learning experiences for the most vulnerable student populations.

The Clarification of Equity

The goal of Equity in education is to remove educational disparities as a hindrance to opportunity in broader society. The inequities of the public school system affect more than those left behind in the lower rungs of the social hierarchy. The systematic educational deprivation that has been inflicted on generations deprives everyone of the tangible social and economic benefits that can be realized when all are afforded equitable opportunities (Green, 1971; Tesconi, 1975).

In the early definitions of Equal Educational Opportunity, the role of the school was relatively passive; it was primarily expected to provide a set of free public resources. The responsibility for profitable use of those resources lay with the child and their family. But the evolution of the concept into what we now call Equity has revised these roles. With this shift, the school's responsibility changed from increasing and distributing equally its *quality* to increasing the quality of its students' achievements (Coleman, 1968). Thus, it is more accurate to say that Equity in education is not so much a re-defining of EEO as it is the clarification of it. Equity means the *effective* equality of opportunity—that is, equality in those elements that are *effective* for learning (Coleman, 1968).

The work of Equity in education bears a special responsibility. In the Equity paradigm, the responsibility of schools is to re-engineer the opportunity pipeline so that as students enter racially integrated and equitably resourced schools, they are also provided with quality and effective opportunities to learn and benefit from education—which is something different than manipulating outcomes. Equity says that fairness is the differentiating process through which opportunities are designed. In terms of Equity, the work of classroom instruction requires that we consider the social and environmental factors to tailor the opportunities for students without compromising the integrity of the learning targets.

As I will discuss further in the second part of this book, the instructional task in closing Equity gaps is accomplished through increasing rigor and situating meaningful learning targets in terms that are relevant and accessible to students through the leveraging of their cultural fluencies. By increasing rigor, I am not referring to definitions that are synonymous with teaching with particular types of texts, or even the volume of work assigned, or for that matter, a specific level of "difficulty." Rather, when I refer to *rigor*, I am thinking about the ways in which students are able to extend concepts beyond specialistic knowledge into more integrated understandings that are equitable precisely because they are inclusive of expressions of knowing in a range of cultural fluencies.

The work of Equity in education is removing the effects of social disparities that induce gaps in performance and achievement; or more accurately, the work is developing instructional practices that create and sustain fair and meaningful learning opportunities for all students. From the perspective of Equity, it is necessary to determine the effect of the various pedagogical factors upon students' learning outcomes—conceiving of outcomes inclusively, referring not only to traditional metrics of achievement (i.e., standardized testing), but also the performative expressions of integrated understandings. This provides various measures of schools' quality in terms of its effects upon students.

DIFFERENCE ≠ DEFICITS

3. *Differences aren't deficits.* Though there are *differences* in cultural, linguistic, racial, ethnic, and language backgrounds, as well as differential access to resources among students, socio-ethnolinguistic groups do not differ from each other in the capacity for intelligence in any important way; and thus, *differences do not equate to deficits* in ability.

Achievement

All of what has been discussed to this point in this chapter raises an important question: What could we say Equity would look like if it is attained? In other words: How would we know when we have reached some plateau that we can think of as Equity?

A massive tension in Equity work is the trepidation surrounding the discussion of the root causes of the gaps in achievement across social groups. I understand the hesitation, but the discussion is necessary because the ways in which we make sense of the differences in school performance inform how we address our Equity problems. Plus, it's not good to make as if achievement differences do not exist. To do so requires one to pretend to not see what is apparent to all—and this may lead to reckless and irresponsible interpretations of the differences. In my experience, most teachers reject concepts that require them to suspend disbelief or muffle their own questions. As there are differences among social groups in achievement that have persisted over time, it is important for us to give honest, transparent consideration to their possible explanations.

Generally, we do not worry if different individuals come out of the schools with different abilities, talents, honors, rewards, and the like.

We have thought of this as a natural consequence of effort and aptitude among the students. On the other hand, if certain social groups generally achieve far less or more than other social groups, then we have an Equity problem (Tesconi, 1975).

Having established that *Equity in education* is to be defined, at least in part, in terms of achievement outcomes implies that fairness will be realized when the variance of individual achievement is as wide or narrow within one social group as it is in another, but this begs many questions such as: What do we mean by *achievement* exactly? Can we assume that achievement is a reliable correlate of intelligence? What kind of knowledge is most representative of achievement? What kind of intelligence is measured in schools? What learning is of most worth in our current society? And how do we measure achievement? These are questions that are working in the background of our philosophizing. The ways in which we answer them have huge significance both in terms of pedagogy and our approaches to measuring the efficacy of our Equity work.

It's helpful to have a conceptual understanding of the distribution of achievement to support our understandings of Equity in theory and practice. Think about the bell curve, a graphic representation of the distribution and range of individual instances inside of a total data set which has a shape reminiscent of a bell (Figure 2.1). A line drawn straight down the

Figure 2.1 A (Normal Distribution) Bell Curve

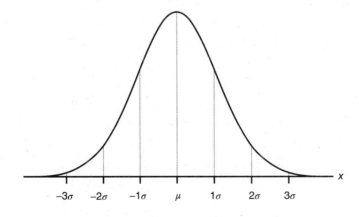

middle from the tip-top point of the curve shows the mean, mode, and median of the total data set. Its standard deviation depicts the bell curve's relative width around the mean. So the bell curve can help to illustrate the gaps in achievement *between* social groups. The difference, for example, in achievement at grade 12 between the mean achievement of any socio-ethnolinguistic group and the mean of any other is, in effect, the degree of inequity; and the reduction of that inequity is a responsibility of the school. The bell curve can also be used to represent the range in achievement *within* social groups.

Equity in education would mean that we should see a more-or-less comparable distribution of achievement (i.e., similar bell curves) when calculating the standard deviation within the various subgroups. Importantly, when we see disparities in achievement, the bell curve doesn't tell us *why* we have inequity; rather, disparities in the variance of achievement between the bell curves of different social groups merely tell us *that* we have inequity. In order to solve for the problems of Equity, we should consider the possible explanations for dissimilar patterns in performance and achievement. To avoid these considerations threatens the credibility of any claims we may make in the interest of Equity. Here, I will offer comment on the three buckets of potential explanations for persistent gaps in achievement:

1. a group is inherently inferior/superior relative to another due to the genetic makeup of social groups (i.e., the eugenics' claim);
2. a group is culturally handicapped relative to another (i.e., the cultural deficit claim);
3. a group is disadvantaged by the practices and policy environment of the school (i.e., school itself is precipitating achievement gaps).

Explanation #1: Gaps in achievement are attributed to inherent traits of social groups that render some more or less able to achieve than others in school (i.e., the eugenics' claim).

Usually when this explanation is posed (subtly or not), it's framed around race, but my response can be applied to any human social group or subsocial group. I want to be clear, however, regarding Equity as it pertains to race so I'll fashion my comments accordingly.

My first observation is that scholars in the social and natural sciences have long agreed that the notion of race as a fixed, biologically based classification system is spectacularly rubbish. Aside from capturing something of the migration patterns of ancient people groups, the racial categories developed historically by Europeans—such as Caucasian, Negroid, and Mongoloid—convey very little, if any, useful genetic information. The Human Genome Project and other well-supported and methodologically sophisticated studies have only served to further underline this point. Skin-color genes, as an example, are heavily influenced by a combination of UV radiation and diet.[6] This means that people in New Guinea and the Sub-Saharan African continent are both very dark skinned despite being from opposite ends of our species' family tree (Henrich, 2016).

We have been so consumed with the matter of race that our interest evoked the pseudo-scientific field of eugenics that gained great popularity in the 20th century and which inspired the paradigms for intelligence testing and standardized achievement testing that continue to occupy mainstream and enormous revenue-generating status in public education today (Stoskopf, 1999; 2002). The theory that any "racial" group is inherently inferior or superior in any biological way ignores the truth of overwhelming scientific evidence that human beings are all members of the same species of primate, Homo sapiens. Race is not synonymous with species. There are no subgroupings of human beings that reflect any genetic or biological difference. If race (and the phenotype characteristics associated with racial groups) were a reliable proxy for some group-specific biological or genetic traits, we humans would be speciated like many of the nonhuman genus groups on Earth. But we are not that. In fact, depending on the gametes involved, a human being of any "race" can produce a healthy zygote with a human being of any other racial group. Therefore, no biological construct of race can be an explanation of performance and achievement gaps in schools because there is no essential, inherent, irreducible, immutable quality of race shared by the members of any racial group. Race, as a biological explanation for gaps in achievement, is an invalid response because there is no single trait to which an individual's race can be reduced.

Race categories in the United States have much more to do with custom than anything significant about the character, ability, and interests of an individual. I like to point to the fluidity of race to disprove its legitimacy. In the United States, for example, at the start of the 20th century, Italians, Irish, and European persons of Jewish heritage were all considered non-White (Golash-Boza, 2002; Kolbert, 2018; Yang & Koshy, 2016); but today, all of those groups are classified as White.[7] The fact that a group can move from non-White to White in less than a century is confirmation in and of itself to the lack of any rigorous, scientific merit underscoring the concept. Race is something we made up in America to filter and distribute freedom and opportunity. Though racism is a very real by-product, race itself is junk science. And we are wise to remember this as we discuss so that we do not fall prey to thinking it has any real analytical merit in the understanding of the contexts and learning needs of our students.

Explanation #2: A group is culturally handicapped relative to another (i.e., the cultural deficit claim).

Is it possible that gaps in educational achievement are attributed to some flaw or flaws in the cultural ways of being and social preparedness that disproportionately affect some groups relative to others? My answer to this question may surprise you (or not): Quite obviously, yes. Please note that this observation does not argue for what should be; rather, it calls attention to what is. If cultural background disadvantages some groups, then that would reveal a problem with the systems of schooling more so than it does with any social group—unless, of course, we are willing to admit that our schools aren't intended to develop the intelligence of students, but rather a particular brand of cultural fluency.

But for the sake of argument, let's go with the cultural deficit claim for a moment. We can define the *cultural deficit claim* as resting on the assumption that communities under conditions of poverty and cultural dysfunction are disorganized and morally insufficient, resulting in various forms of behavioral and intellectual deficit. Since a disproportionate number of the economically poor are members of non-White racial and ethnic groups, racial identity has been taken by many as a stand-alone indicator of cultural deficit that lessens the intellectual capabilities of individual members of these affected groups (Cole & Bruner, 1971).

To consider this from a researcher's standpoint, one would need to articulate a normed cultural standard in order to assess the degree of cultural difference and thus relative inferiority/superiority between groups. Theoretically, then, we could argue that some students are culturally deficient, but unless we believe that they are genetically inferior, that still wouldn't release teachers of the responsibility of leveraging our awareness of students' culture in order to bring them to the skills and conceptual understandings that are useful to them in the 21st-century, information-age economy.

As discussed in Chapter 1, culture is mostly information residing in the mind that influences behavior which is largely gained through social learning. In schools, we teachers want to develop the intelligence of students, and we espouse to engage students from an array of cultural backgrounds in doing so. Since human beings rely so profoundly on culture to support our sociality, and since learning is so social in nature, teaching that builds on a rich understanding of culture and the ways in which it influences thinking is more likely to contribute to equitable outcomes than otherwise. Further, the leveraging of students' culture begins with the attention to your own cultural indoctrinations because you are only assessing the culture of others through the filters of your own. The cultural references that you bring to bear—What is right? What is wrong? What is good? What is bad? What is appropriate? What is inappropriate?—are all wrapped up into how you learned to *human (v)* . . . which is by definition *biased*, because your learning occurred in a cognitive niche with mediating cultural norms and values.

The cultural deficit claim, however, fails in any rigorous interrogation as an explanation of gaps in academic achievement because: (1) there is no such thing as a culturally neutral space to measure or substantiate the claim of cultural deficit; and (2) considering the work of John Hattie and others confirming that the collective sense of efficacy of teachers has among the greatest effects on learning outcomes, it follows that the belief in the cultural deficit of students is itself a limiting factor in students' achievement.[8] In short, the investigation of the claim of cultural deficit as an explanation for underperformance is methodologically doomed by human bias, impossible to measure empirically, and ultimately, underscored by attitudes we know to be harmful to vulnerable student populations as a prerequisite for consideration.

So, whether or not you believe that your students are culturally deficient, what your school needs are teachers who absolutely, relentlessly view your students as capable. Put another way, teachers who view their students as having cultural deficiencies also don't believe their teaching is efficacious, which is a barrier to learning. If you're wondering if you are one of these obstacles for your students' learning, you should ask yourself: What beliefs of mine advance the achievement of my students, and what beliefs are impediments?

Explanation #3: A group is disadvantaged by the practices and policy environment of the school (i.e., the school itself is precipitating achievement gaps).

One of the more significant findings of the Coleman Study was that students from lower socio-economic classes, regardless of race, achieved at a rate significantly below their age and grade peers from higher classes. The disparities in achievement increased, found the study, the longer children stayed in school.

If my arguments in this chapter are held valid, it is infeasible to view socio-ethnolinguistic identity (and race specifically) as a determinant of intelligence and ability (explanation #1). Further, it's fatally unproductive and intellectually shortsighted to the task of teaching to view some students as culturally deficient, and thus, in effect, unteachable (explanation #2). That then would indicate that there is something likely happening in the schools that is contributing to the underperformance of some social groups which requires our attention. In which case, I can argue that schools are complicit in a kind of criminal conspiracy against students of the lower-performing social groups because compulsory education laws in this country require that they attend schools in which their underachievement relative to other groups is predictable and exacerbated the longer they attend.

This is not to say that those properties and expressions of intelligence which are *presently* most valued for success in our schools are randomly distributed. To the contrary, a reasonable conclusion of the Coleman Study is that the skills and abilities fostered by some social and cultural environments are not relevant to success in the schools as they are presently constituted (Borman & Dowling, 2010; Cole & Bruner, 1971; Tesconi, 1975). This is an Equity problem—defining what counts as the properties and demonstrations of intelligence, or in this case, determining which abilities are to be singled out for reward by the school. Who is to define such attributes and abilities? How are they to be measured? A student raised and nurtured in an environmental niche in which the intellectual abilities, talents, and skills fostered were not those which the school used to develop and measure intelligence would not have an equitable opportunity to benefit from the school's rewards compared to those whose indoctrinations more closely matched the culture of the school.

Difference Interpretations and Deficit Ideologies

The controversy in the discussion of achievement exists because of the implications it has for how we think about intelligence as in: *What groups may be said to be more or less intelligent than others?* We'll investigate further an operational definition of intelligence for the classroom in Chapter 4, but for now, a broad definition will do: *intelligence*, in the anthropological sense, is the ability to learn that which is necessary for one's survival. In hunter-gatherer times, that meant intelligence was a function of being able to take in and make use of the knowings and skillsets of others in one's clan that served the interests of physical survival. In our modern times, survival is a function of decision making and problem solving—so we can say that intelligence is the ability to learn that which is useful and necessary for decision making and problem solving in the interest of one's own well-being and also by extension one's community.

Intelligence quotient (IQ) is not synonymous with *intelligence*, and intelligence is not a guarantee of high academic achievement. Neither is IQ synonymous with any meaningful character descriptions like morality, wisdom, compassion, and so on. One can convincingly argue that cognitive ability is too complex to be represented by a single number (Kovacs & Conway, 2019; Murray, 2021), but it is accurate to say that IQ tests measure a specific (i.e., narrow) aspect of the mental agilities associated with collating disparate bits of information and then inferring and deducing conclusions from that information. Going back many decades now, studies have indicated that there is no genetic component to inter-racial, interethnic variation in intelligence as measured by IQ (Labov, 1970; Cole & Bruner, 1971; Boyd & Richerson, 1985; Sternberg et al., 2005; Nisbett, 2009; Greenspan, 2022; Giangrande & Turkheimer, 2022). This is consistent with the hypothesis that the differences between the mean IQ scores of various social groups primarily result from cultural and environmental differences.

The Equity view is compatible with widely studied linguistic anthropological and psychological theorizing, which concentrates on describing the way in which different socio-ethnolinguistic groups categorize and make sense of familiar areas of human experience (Brown, 2004; Tyler, 1970). These arguments say that different conclusions about the world are the result of variant but equally logical ways of analyzing and interpreting evidence. From this perspective, descriptions of the "deficit" of some ethnolinguistic groups would be inadequate. The *deficit hypothesis'* assessment of the source of social group differences in intellectual performance relies on an assumption that the intelligence and learning capacities of lowerachieving social groups are a function of flaws and failures in some social group communities, and these shortcomings are revealed in various forms of achievement deficit. But the question needs to be asked: Deficit from what point of view?

I do not intend to argue over the existence or nature of such things as "a culture of poverty," although such an idea seems implicit in the view of most deficit theorists. These kinds of debates detract from the Equity work of designing culturally responsive learning experiences for students. I am, however, making the assertion that the cultural variants which differently affect the learning skills, habits, and motivations that facilitate decision making, problem solving, and perceiving essential meanings are not equal to cognitive deficits. I argue that we cannot reliably discern the underlying intelligence of those who have had limited versus greater exposure to a particular culture when cultural fluencies are part and parcel to our conceptions and measures of school achievement. The crux of the Equity argument is that those social groups ordinarily viewed as culturally deprived have the same underlying capacities for competence and intelligence as those in the mainstream of the dominant culture. The differences in achievement can be accounted for by the social situations and cultural contexts in which the competence is expressed. "One can find a corresponding situation in which the member of the low-performing cultural group can perform on the basis of a given competence in a fashion equal or superior to the standard achieved by a member of the dominant culture" (Cole & Bruner, 1971).[9]

To be clear, individual students vary in their capacity to benefit from formal education, but this uncritical observation is misleading because it fails to consider what properties and expressions of intelligence are most educationally relevant for school achievement and how students come by these properties and capacities. In some significant measure, individual capabilities are functions of cultural inheritance and the fluencies obtained from the cognitive niche through social learning. Therefore, if it could be established that as a matter of empirical fact, educationally relevant intelligence is not randomly distributed, then it seems possible to conclude that the educational system would be justified in distributing benefits disproportionately (Tesconi, 1975).

Are All "Men" Created Equal?

Equity does not denote equality of intelligence and physical capacities of all students in all places. Equity does not strive to eliminate the distinctions among people; it is not a drive for "sameness" or homogeneity. Equity does not mean that every individual must reach the same level of achievement. It means that the range of achievement and the distribution within that range should be comparable for each social group. We will know that we have achieved Equity when neither race, nor class, nor income, nor gender, nor language background, nor physical (dis)ability—when no social disparity or measure of identity—is a barrier to or predictor of educational achievement. Debates over the meaning of *all men are created equal* and fairness, then, are not about whether people possess in equal measure the same talents, potentials, and so on. They are about the criteria that are signaled out as the bases for achievement (Tesconi & Hurwitz, 1974).

Raising the achievement of students from underperforming social groups can very well be the test of the school's effectiveness (Tesconi, 1975). Equity is determined by the intensity of the school's influence relative to the external divergent influences. That is, Equity is not determined by equality of the resource inputs, but by the power of these resources in bringing about achievement (Coleman, 1968).

WHAT SCHOOLS CAN DO

There is a final and yet critical point to be added to the definition of *Equity*. Equity in education is an idea which is intended to be operationalized rather than merely pontificated. Though I may be called naive to retain belief in the promises of public schooling, my faith is buttressed by concern for the alternatives. If there is no public education option, I am dubious about the notion that the privileged in our society will downgrade the quality of the educational opportunities available to their own children; rather, the greatest harm will be incurred in the communities that are most reliant on schools as an avenue to access opportunities in society. To dismantle public schools will profoundly exacerbate vulnerabilities. I don't think it's hyperbole to say that the lack of access to public education will likely concretize a functionally permanent underclass of economically and politically marginalized communities, which will, in turn, have a catastrophic effect on American society. Without schools, to be born into the lower classes of American society will require lottery-like circumstances to escape.

The concept of Equity rests in part on assumptions relating to the origins of inequalities. It assumes that social inequalities stand in the way of educational opportunity and thus constitute barriers to Equity. The goal of Equity in the context of public education is to provide learning experiences that offset the impact of larger social and economic disparities as limiting factors in the accessing of opportunity, and thus, Equity in education requires that schools will have to broaden both their offerings and their notions about educationally relevant abilities. An essential point of the Equity view is the assumption that intelligence is randomly distributed among the various socio-ethnolinguistic groups and subgroups throughout society. My argument in this chapter as I attempt to define *Equity* relative to its origin story is that it should be centered as the unifying impetus to direct the classroom's pedagogical craft.

Some argue that schools do not contribute significantly to social, economic, and political fairness in society at large. The central premise of their claim is that the systems that maintain the various and persistent stratifications of American society stifle any meaningful impact that schools could have in assisting the prospects of greater group social and economic mobility. In order to attain fairness in the broader society, the argument goes, changes in our economic and political institutions are of much greater consequence than changes in our schools.

These arguments might be correct, but the problem is that they have jumped from an uncertain premise to a conjectured conclusion. That is to say, schools as they are presently designed, *may* very well fail to contribute to the goal of an equitable society. But it's also possible the school could be an agent of change if schools and society changed in certain ways (Tesconi, 1975). To further address systemic gaps in health care, mass incarceration, and the effects of long-standing housing discriminatory practices could all have great potential for improving the conditions for teaching and learning. Schools on the other hand should strive to expand the views of what constitutes educationally relevant intelligence and develop the institutional capacities so that all students will have access to learning experiences that are responsive to their cultural repertoires for knowing.

NOTES ON ARTMAKING: THE HEART OF EQUITY

One of my favorite places to watch live music is Small's Live Jazz Club in the West Village, New York City. It's a tiny, little place. There are fancier and more famous venues for live jazz in the city, but Small's is where one can go to get a pure musical experience. Some very well known performers regularly do shows at Small's, but there are also late-night jam sessions during which "unknowns" are welcomed to share the stage with musicians of great acclaim. It's a laboratory for collaborative thinking. I learn a lot there.

Jazz is a lot like Equity, and Equity is a lot like jazz. Jazz and Equity are both output-focused constructs. In the case of jazz, its quality is measured differently than, say, classical music. For example, I appreciate Beethoven. I often write and view art with my favorite symphonies playing in the background of my thinking. I've seen Beethoven performed, and the expectation is that it will match the details of my memory for the composition. If the pacing is too fast or slow, or the melody is off pitch, or the rhythms seem frayed, I am disappointed because the point of a good show of classical music is that it matches closely the original product, which is not the case for jazz. Jazz isn't expected to be uniform; in fact, the point of a jazz performance is to see how the combo will uniquely deliver the musical goods. Even a mistake is an altogether different entity between the genres. A mistake in classical music is deeply embarrassing, almost certainly revealing some gap or deficiency in understanding, whereas a mistake in jazz might be the coolest thing that happens in a performance! A good mistake in a jazz set potentially on-ramps a once-in-a-lifetime riff that stirs up unknown and untapped inspiration for the experience. Good jazz is measured by the quality of the product, its effectiveness in bringing about for the audience the feeling of being engaged with and connected to the tune. Jazz, like Equity, is measured by the experiential output.

Jazz makes room for the expression of brilliance without the limiting restrictions of static, situationally indifferent expectations for performance. An orchestra concert of classical music is quite different from a jazz set because the goals are not the same. In classical music, there are far fewer liberties that can be taken in crafting an extraordinary act. Classical music is considered most brilliant when it sounds exactly like other performances of the same pieces, when it most closely follows the sheet music, and when it draws with the greatest fidelity from the cultural expressions of the original composition.

Every jazz tune has a personality, as does every class we teach. In a jazz set, the particular tune contributes to the shape and color of the performance. The tune itself is a kind of puzzle, something for the musicians to figure out and put together. A jazz tune is a kind of problem for musicians to solve using the tools of the craft. In a performance of classical music, the artist is required to employ their technical skillset to relay the composer's vision for the piece. In jazz, however, even as the notes may be printed on a sheet, the artist must take that melody and present it to the audience so that they can perceive it as worth following and relatable to their interests and lived experiences.

The art of jazz is based in the science of acoustics and the principles of pitch, volume, tempo, and rhythm and conducted with instruments that represent the height of advancements in musical technology. The essence of jazz is improvisation—the musician's unique response to, partnering with, and interpretation of the tune. The purpose of improvisation is to create a unique experience for those listening. The problem of figuring out and performing the tune so that it resonates with the audience is at the heart of the music-making.

I also think of the craft of teaching as an art based in scientific principles. The science is heavily informed by the cognitive sciences and the social sciences particularly in the areas of culture, sociology, and human psychology. Though we teachers don't have to memorize scales and have a knowledge of chord structures, we perform our craft with pedagogical tools. We use what we know and can learn about culture and pedagogy to convey expansive and integrated understandings through the medium of experience.

Just like no two jazz sets at Small's Live are ever identical, no two classrooms are the same. Each is its own ecosystem of personalities, needs, assets, and interests, and each requires a perspective that is unique and specific to the context in order to facilitate engaging experiences. The teacher must set the tempo and tone of the class, but the real learning occurs when students have a chance to share in the discovery of new understandings. I especially enjoy getting to know the personality of a class, which is also like solving a puzzle. We teachers seek to create the best fit in our classes between what it is we want for students to experience in a learning community and who they are as cultural and asset-filled beings. The compatibility of a class temperament with the environment created by the teacher often determines the outcome of the class (Luquet, 2015).

The problem at the heart of any jazz performance is improvising a tune to fully engage an audience. The goal of figuring out the tune, putting it together for the benefit of those listening, is the driving force for all decisions made in the execution of the craft. If the jazz musicians refuse to improvise, they will have failed because they didn't understand the assignment. No one goes to Small's to hear an exact replica of a previous performance. It isn't jazz if it doesn't improvise.

At the start of this chapter, I defined the essence of Equity work in education as the policy and practice directive to provide quality and effective learning opportunities so that background and identity are neither correlative nor predictive of student performance and/or achievement outcomes. The work of Equity is focused on solving the problems of fairness—all those factors that interfere with students' access to culturally responsive learning opportunities.

It is fair to ask how an individual teacher may solve for the problems of Equity when they seem to be so massive relative to the limited scope of influence in the classroom. Just as the problems of jazz are at the heart of its making, we should be reminded that the problems of Equity—the problems of fairness—are at the heart of our pedagogy and the learning experiences we design for students. That is, we design with Equity in mind. Equity is at the heart of our artmaking.

CHAPTER NOTES

1. There are many texts that I am fond of that present thorough and compelling reviews of the relationship between schools and the larger society given the various epochs of formal education in the United States. Among the readings that document the ideas I'm reporting in this chapter, I would especially recommend: Arum et al., 2021; Ballantine et al., 2018; Coleman, 1968; Feinberg & Soltis, 1998; Gutmann, 1999; Hurwitz & Tesconi, 1972; Reese, 2011; Spring, 2021; Tesconi, 1975; Tesconi & Hurwitz, 1974; Urban & Wagoner, 2004.

2. *"We believe that it does."* Literally, every single time I read these words. . . . I get all the chills. I am immensely inspired by the background story leading up to this moment, which includes cases going back as far as *Roberts v. Boston* (1850) and precedent-setting decisions in *Missouri ex rel. Gaines v. Canada* (1938), *Mendez et al v. Westminster School District of Orange County* (1947), *Sweatt v. Painter* (1950), and *McLaurin v. Oklahoma State Regents* (1950).

   Chief Justice Warren was not known for any track record or particular accomplishments in the interest of civil rights. He was a constitutionalist, and as such, his decisions were made (at least in his own mind) not according to a social justice metric, but rather according to his best interpretations of the intentions of the signers of the Constitution of the United States of America.

3. Even "separate but equal" indicates the philosophical commitment to equally accessible and quality education for all including non-White children. The moral justification for the *Plessy* doctrine attempts to reconcile the separation of students by race with the ostensible obligation to equalize the resources. Though we know this never happened, anywhere, anytime, the point is that even for the staunchest advocates of racism, the philosophical premise that fairness in educational opportunity was a critical contributor to fairness in the larger society remained intact.

4. The economist Samuel Bowels, among others, argued, for example, that the evidence in the Coleman Study actually suggests that student achievement *can be* positively and significantly affected by the level of input resources to a school with a reconsideration of the arrangement of the variables in the study. For example, the amount of variance in achievement scores of 12th-grade "Negro" students explained by the variable "teacher's verbal ability" more than doubles if this variable is brought into the analysis first, rather than after the social background variables (Bowles, 1968).

5. "Coleman and his colleagues expected to discover massive differences in the quality of schools based on their racial make-up. While Coleman did find the inequalities he predicted, much to his surprise,

he found that differences in school quality, when measured by traditional input criteria, were not strongly correlated to differences in student achievement. On the contrary, the massive survey showed that no children from a given socio-economic class—regardless of racial/ethnic background—did significantly better in schools with high resource inputs. Coleman did find that the achievement scores of Black children were higher in racially mixed classes than in all Black or predominantly Black schools. This was not a new finding, but Coleman added that improvements in educational achievement among Black students from economically poor backgrounds was owing to the fact that they picked up, somehow, conventional middle class academic skills and associated cultural fluencies, important to school success by mixing with middle-class White students. The crucial point, according to the Coleman Report, is that schools' inputs, as constituted at the time, had little influence on student achievement that is independent of students' social, economic, and cultural background" (Tesconi, 1975).

6. https://www.genome.gov/human-genome-project.

7. Yang and Koshy (2016) point out that it's probably less accurate to say that these groups became "White" than it is to say that these groups advanced in the social-group hierarchy from ethnic "minority" groups to being able to access the privileges of the majority White group though it required the shedding of pesky ethnic identifiers as part of the exchange. This further confirms that what we term *race* is not a scientific designation, but rather a proxy identifier that is meant to signal status in society.

8. See the Visible Learning website that publishes annual reports on the meta-analysis of effect sizes related to student achievement: www.visible-learning.org.

9. Even in controlled experiments, the only thing that is controlled is the external stimulus. *Tell me everything you can about this* is the prompt, "but the interpretation of the request, and the action believed to be appropriate in response is completely uncontrolled. One can view these test stimuli as requests for information, commands for action, or

meaningless sequences of words. . . . With human subjects it is absurd to believe that identical stimuli are obtained by asking everyone the same question. Since the crucial intervening variables of interpretation and motivation are uncontrolled, most of the literature on verbal deprivation tells us nothing of the capacities of children" (Labov, 1970).

"We can abstract several assertions from this key passage: (a) Formal experimental equivalence of operations does not insure de facto equivalence of experimental treatments; (b) different subcultural groups are predisposed to interpret the experimental stimuli (situations) differently; (c) different subcultural groups are motivated by different concerns relevant to the experimental task; and (d) in view of the inadequacies of experimentation, inferences about lack of competence among black children are unwarranted" (Cole & Bruner, 1971).

CHAPTER 3

Shifting Paradigms

"I'm just playing with this idea of expanding the way people think about things."

—Senga Nengudi

EQUITY PROBLEMS OF PRACTICE

Let's pause here to re-frame things with this book's central thought-experiment question: You're a teacher, and you want to be equitable. What does Equity mean *in* your teaching? How do you *do* Equity?

Let's construct a scenario: *You have an Equity problem.* You have some students whom you can't ever seem to get fully involved in your lessons, and they tend to be from the same social group. When they do engage, it isn't with any real enthusiasm, but just to turn something in. Maybe it's your Black students? Or your Latino students? Or your Pacific Islanders? Or Hmong? Or your boys? Or your girls? Or your language learners? Or the kids from that *other* side of town? Choose your own criteria for dis-aggregating your data. Your Equity problem is that there is a particular background- or identity-group that predictably underachieves. Not every single kiddo in the category is a low performer, but based on your data and observations, there are students at greater risk of negative outcomes based on their social group. *That's an Equity problem,* so let's philosophize.

Whatever Equity problem you face in the classroom is made doubly difficult by pandemics, social division, political partisanship, threats of nuclear war, and any other number of local and/or world events. Nothing about teaching in the United States will ever again be the same as it was before March 2020 (the initial closing of schools and pandemic-driven quarantining of society) and the murder of George Floyd a few months later. The pandemic caused a fundamental adjustment in how instruction is delivered, and the summer of 2020 saw the largest sustained, social justice, protest movement in American history. We are now operating within a new paradigm—and the practice of teaching must evolve in order to keep the institution of public education relevant.

In many respects, this paradigmatic shift is welcomed indeed—but it is also fraught with challenges. Given the persistent gaps in school achievement between various socio-economic demographic groups, it should be clear that the factory model of American public education has run its course; it neither serves students nor the larger economy any longer, and it must be retired. A radical departure from the status quo of traditional models of public-school instruction is in order. And yet, we know enough about pedagogy now to understand that in updating our methods and models, there is time-tested wisdom to which we are prudent to abide, such as:

- Instruction should be centered on the needs, interests, and learning styles of the students.
- Students learn better when they know, trust, and respect the persons teaching them and find the content of their learning to be meaningful (i.e., relevant to their lives and ambitions).
- When students are behaviorally, affectively, and cognitively engaged, they are better learners and more willing to think rigorously.
- Big ideas and essential understandings are more engaging learning targets than out-of-context, content-specific facts, dates, skills, and procedures.

So, if we philosophize about our Equity problem of practice—a disproportionately high percentage of a particular student social group are disengaged in learning—one way of understanding this is as an issue of community. Why community? Because students who aren't invested in the core activities of any social space (like a classroom) are generally not perceiving themselves as members of the community. When we humans don't perceive ourselves as belonging to a community, the norms, expectations, and behaviors valued within the group fail to resonate with us. But what exactly is community? Before we begin the discussion of community, let's start with something of a metaphysical observation:

Mentalizing

We all live in a world of social reality that exists only inside our human brains (Barrett, 2020).

In truth, this isn't such a metaphysical observation after all. Consider that the Earth itself with all of its biomes and geographic features is physical reality. If, for example, you were to stub your toe while walking barefoot in a bed of rocks, there would be little doubt as to the explanation for the sharp painful sensation that you are feeling in your lower extremities. You have had an encounter with physical reality. Humans, however, create social reality with other people (Barrett, 2020; Frith & Frith, 2006; Koster-Hale & Saxe, 2013; Schaafsma et al., 2015). Our brains have a kind of mirror system allowing us to share the emotions of others, which is arguably one of the defining characteristics of the human experience. I can remember elaborate games my childhood friends and I created with nothing but space and our imaginations. We were able to construct a social reality in which a different set of rules governed our interactions than those which shaped the societal norms outside of our group. I can now look back and see this as an experience in social learning. We co-constructed meaning, directly and indirectly abstracting the physical reality for the purposes of our shared play experience.

Recall from Chapter 1 that culture is transmitted through social learning, and social learning is defined as the inferences drawn from observation of or interaction with other individuals or the products of other individuals' learning (Bandura, 2001; Hoppitt & Laland, 2013). The theory of social learning provides a conceptual framework for how students pick up on shared norms and behaviors through interacting in the social spaces where they learn how to *human (v)*. A central aspect of the human capacity for social learning is the ability to anticipate and understand the thoughts and feelings of other people. Through social learning, we humans make inferences about the goals, preferences, motivations, intentions, beliefs, and strategies of other humans. These cognitive abilities relate to what is variously termed mentalizing or Theory of Mind (ToM). Mentalizing is part of the core architecture of the human brain and is specialized for learning about mental states.[1]

Our artmaking craft is aided by the ability to assess what our students know and feel. In effect, we are trying to decipher their thinking so that we can influence their thought processes in the direction of an understanding.

Our teaching is more effective when we can interpret the desires, beliefs, and goals of our students because we are better able to present the opportunities to learn in a clearer context of what is meaningful to the minds we are seeking to influence.

The intersections of culture and learning are so important for us teachers to think about because they give us insight into how students make perceptions and take in information about social spaces and interactions. Social learning occurs when information in person A's brain generates some behavior that rouses information in a person B's brain to infer meaning. Our minds are inference-making, mentalizing machines, and culture is the software that operates these applications. A cornerstone of the human capacity for social learning is the ability to reason about invisible causes. You make decisions through conscious and non-conscious reasoning, and these decisions rely on both observable and abstract entities to predict outcomes. Mentalizing happens against the backdrop of our cultural repertoires. The signposts for mentalizing are derived from and highly influenced by our cultural inheritance.

We mentalize all the time. Have you ever taken a seat in some public place to people-watch? People-watching is an exercise in mentalizing. Whenever we try to imagine a person's story with no evidence other than what we see and infer from their actions in the here and now, we are essentially mentalizing by ascribing a causal relationship to the observed behavior. We naturally explain people's behavior on the basis of our mentalized perceptions of their knowledge, desires, and beliefs.

These mentalizing, inference-making mechanisms fuel social learning and also comprise a key ingredient in community. We most accurately mentalize in the social spaces in which we are most familiar. Our capacities for mentalizing are core to our identities and the ways we perceive (and are perceived) in relation to specific social groups and particular communities. This is, in effect, what it means to be in community. We can be confident in our belonging to any given community based on, in large part, our own cultural fluencies, which facilitate the capacity for mentalizing and abstracting within the group's shared cultural repertoire.

We humans have a unique propensity for abstraction. The psychological definition of *abstraction* concerns our ability to perceive meaning in symbols and situations. *Abstraction* is the process that allows us to form and store information gleaned across our experiences. Through abstraction, we are able to discern what various objects and events have in common, and group them together into conceptual understandings. *To abstract* refers to a dynamic process—continually updated via experience and operating across individual and group references—from which concepts arise that seek meaning beyond the literal interpretation of people, places, and events.

Community

The human cognitive capacity for abstraction is what makes community possible. The term *community* has rather specific referents and is immediately related to culture and social learning. In community, culture is an organizing force for the configuration of values and belief structures "comprising the patterns, norms, and goals as revealed in the mores, the folkways, the traditions, the faiths, the fine arts, the philosophies, the play-activities, and generally the modes of living of social groups" (Tesconi, 1975). The intellectual and emotional development of individual identity is a function of acting on values, norms, and so forth within the social framework of community. Both culture and community then, are a process and product of social learning.

A classroom community problem is a social learning problem. It means that your students have not established an identity within the value-structure of the learning community, or at least not well enough to justify their investment in the activities of the classroom. The solution to these kinds of problems of practice require that students see themselves as belonging alongside other learners, sharing in the connections to a group identity, doing the things that members of this community do, showing their competence in doing so, advancing toward their own individual goals, and contributing to the greater good of the group. Ultimately, students who are willfully not engaged do not feel connected. As such, disengaged students are neither likely to subscribe to the cultural norms nor pick up the relevant cultural fluencies that signal group membership to others because identity is an attribute of community. We, like our students, feel most at ease, empowered, and invested in the spaces where we feel connected to community.

In Chapter 1, we referred generally to social learning to understand how culture is shared within social groups. It's important to clarify that ideas are not transmitted unedited and fully intact from one brain to another. Instead, the cultural variant in one brain generates some behavior which is observed by a cultural learner who then creates a cultural variant that generates a similar behavior. If we could look inside people's heads, we would find that individuals have different mental representations of the observable behavior even when they may seem to behave in the same way. The point is that social transmission isn't a simple, linear equation. It's much more subtle than that. And any number of factors in the environment or the minds of the cultural learners may lead to a range of different inferences from the same observation (Boyd & Richerson, 1985; Hoppitt & Laland, 2013).

Identity, community, and culture are concepts that travel hand-in-hand; and these are all critically important in our thinking about Equity broadly and Culturally Responsive Education more specifically. As we consider this Equity problem of practice, we are intentional about how we invite the identities of our students into the learning community of the classroom.

RACE

Identity is a core concept in the work of culturally responsive teaching, and race is uniquely relevant in the discussion of identity. A bit of redundancy is in order in support of the larger arguments I make in this book, and so I shall repeat the sentiment once more from the previous chapter: race is a socially constructed, pseudo-scientific myth that we humans use to classify categories of *Us* and *Them's* (Berreby, 2008). The appeal of race is largely due to the highly tribal nature of the human species. *Race* is a social group designation that refers to a conspicuous set of biological attributes including skin color, facial features, hair texture, and region of national origin as an identity marker. Science, however, fails to confirm the intuitions we may have about the genetic basis for race. What we call race is actually a biological continuum rather than discrete categories, meaning that genetic variation is generally as great or greater between as it is within *racial* groups.[2]

America has an especially colorful history of complex taxonomies and symbolic demarcations of group boundaries about different types of racial *Us/Them's* (from seemingly arbitrary traits to much more complex rationalized ideologies). The racial *Us/Them* dichotomy in the United States is rooted in the American origin story in which the social group categories of race were manufactured in order to justify the enslavement of Africans, which became a central feature of the earliest iterations of the American economy. But there is no internal coherence to the concept of race other than its consistent use as a divisive and oppressive *Us/Them* identity metric; further, the rules which supposedly determine racial classifications are fluid and influenced by any number of social, political, and economic trends in various time periods. Consider that "at various times in the history of the U.S. census, *Mexican* and *Armenian* were classified as distinctive races, and southern Italians were identified as a different race from northern Europeans; and just as arbitrary, a person with one black great-grandparent and seven white ones was classified as white in Oregon but not Florida" (Lee, 1993; Strmic-Pawl et al., 2018; Sapolsky, 2017). This is race operating as a social *Us/Them* dichotomy rather than a biological construct.

But while race is a social fabrication, racism, the product and output of the contrived fiction of race, is, in fact, quite real. Racism has profound and material ramifications for our society—many of which show up in racially disparate social and economic stratified inequalities.[3] Most important, none of us is beyond the influence of these multiple racialized *Us/Them* dichotomies that operate stealthily in our subconscious (and thus, beyond our conscious intentions) to shape our perceptions of people and events.

In terms of our work as teachers regarding issues of racial Equity and racial identity, we need to be aware that though we might resolve to eliminate these fictional racial classifications and all its accompanying baggage from our perceptions, it is also empirically true that our brains are actively attuned to recognize physical attributes including skin color, facial features, and hair texture. Flash a face for less than a tenth of a second, so short a time that people aren't even sure they've seen something, and multiple studies using brain-imaging technology have shown that the amygdala activates, signaling the frontal cortex in categorizing the race of the face as either in- or out-group (Harris & Fiske, 2006; 2007; Morrison et al., 2012).[4] Have them guess the race of the pictured face with that one-tenth of a second worth of observational data and there's a better-than-even chance of accuracy. Though we may aspire to judge someone by the "content of their character" rather than by the color of their skin, our brains have evolved to promptly and effectively note skin color nonetheless. Our brains are constantly processing stimuli that influence frontal cortical activation during cross-racial interactions (Kubota et al., 2012). That your frontal cortex is activated says nothing about your individual character; it merely implies that the cross-racial nature of the interaction is informing your cognitive processing and prompting executive control.[5] It's important to talk about race precisely so that we can bring the invisible processes of the brain into our conscious awareness so that our best intentions aren't thwarted by our subconscious tribal cognitive inclinations.

It can be difficult to hold on to multiple, seemingly contradictory truths when we think about race, but it is imperative that we do; otherwise, we can easily be consumed in false and unfounded narratives about racial identity. Equity in education is not limited to the consideration of race. Schools occupy a unique space in society, one in which every social group and cultural community is invested in some way. Race is relevant in the design of systems and structures that contribute to the distribution of resources throughout society. I am one who agrees with author Isabel Wilkerson's assessment of the American opportunity structure as something functioning as a caste system, an artificial hierarchy placing people in a graded ranking of human value that determines one's standing and access to opportunities based on race and class status. "Caste is the bones," says Wilkerson, "race is the skin, and class is the clothing. Race is the cue, the physical manifestation used to signal where individuals fit in the hierarchy" (2020).

But What Can I Do?

Much of what is daunting about racial Equity work is the immensity of it all. It can feel intractable at times given the scope and reach of racism as an historical arbiter of (in)opportunity in American society. Michelle Alexander makes a compelling argument regarding mass incarceration in her now classic treatise *The New Jim Crow* (2010) that I think is also applicable to American education. It is the indifference, writes Alexander, and lack of understanding, that is necessary for the perpetuation of racist policies and practices:

> Claims that mass incarceration is analogous to Jim Crow will fall on deaf ears and alienate potential allies if advocates fail to make clear that the claim is not meant to suggest or imply that supporters of the current system are racist in the way Americans have come to understand that term. Race plays a major role—indeed, a defining role—in the current system, but not because of what is commonly understood as old-fashioned, hostile bigotry. This system of control depends far more on racial indifference (defined as a lack of compassion and caring about race and people belonging to certain racial groups) than racial hostility—a feature it shares with its predecessors.

For we teachers who want to *do* Equity in our classrooms, indifference is not an option. We must be willing and able to thoughtfully consider racial Equity precisely because of the significance of race as a measure of identity for so many of our students—and identity is an essential resource of brilliant teaching. The effort and any discomfort are justified by our deep-seated commitment to providing the most meaningful opportunities for our learners.

The racial Equity problems that you face in your classroom with your students are never textbook because they are deeply personal and specific to the unique environment in which you are teaching. I encourage teachers to think of race and racial identity as one of the socio-ethnolinguistic identity variables interacting with other identity markers that can help us to tap into our students' rich cultural inventories of knowing. We teachers aren't necessarily interested in racial Equity in the way that politicians, statesmen, cognitive scientists, anthropologists, sociologists, or other social scientists might be. *Our* questions gravitate toward the pedagogical. We have pressing concerns; as in, given racially disparate outcomes in student performance and achievement: *What can I do to build community and racial equity in my classroom?*

"*But what can I do?*" is not merely one question but multiple inquiries bundled together, each engaging a different tension in our craft. In their article, "*But What Can I Do?*": *Three Necessary Tensions in Teaching Teachers about Race* (2009), Pollock et al. describe the tensions in the form of three questions:[6]

1. What can I *do*? Teachers routinely search for *concrete, practical steps* they can take in their classrooms and schools, questioning how abstract ideas or theories about racial inequality and difference can help them.

2. What *can* I do? Teachers routinely question the power of the individual educator to counteract *structural or societal problems* of racial and race-class inequality via the classroom.

3. What can *I* do? Teachers routinely question their own *personal readiness* to become the type of professional who can successfully engage issues of race and racism in his or her life and classroom practice.

These three tensions require explicit attention in teacher professional development, and further, the efforts necessary to ready teachers to effectively close racial Equity gaps are greatly enhanced when teachers are encouraged and given tools to keep all three tensions in play as a career-long habit. The tensions speak to the practical, structural, and personal challenges teachers face in coming to useful terms with how we bring together our theory and craft. To engage these tensions is to pursue philosophical positions that can usefully frame how we understand and interpret Equity problems of practice. *"What can I do?"* resists simple answers, and instead requires of those who pose it, the imminent risk of revealing their own vulnerabilities and the limitations of what they may currently know.

Pollock et al. share a journal entry from a teacher who participated in a semester-long, race-oriented teacher education course, a White man named Henry, which summarizes a key takeaway. In Henry's words:

> What does it mean to be an antiracist educator? Can my unconscious racial beliefs hurt my students? How can teachers be effectively taught to undo racism in their classes and in their schools? I cannot claim to have answers to these questions. Rather, I would claim that the pursuit of answers may be more important than the answers themselves.

I agree with Henry. Though I've heard many variations of the *"What can I do?"* question, I've come to realize that the question by itself is not only insufficient but also potentially misleading. So much of what makes us uncomfortable in the matters of race is the inherent uncertainty of it all, but certainty is an antagonist of Equity in the sense that it more likely stifles our artfulness rather than inspires it. The spirit of artmaking insists that we wrestle with the practical, structural, and personal tensions (among others) in our craft; and it insists—to be done with integrity—that we consider *whom* is being centered in the inquiry.

"What can I do?" is exactly the question many White educators ask in the discussion of racial Equity, but the articulation of the question also centers the White person asking. A more salient question is *"What can I understand?"* As in: *"What do you (or this situation) need me to understand?"* But the question must be asked with humility (if it is to be considered an honest inquiry) and a careful interrogation of one's own cultural biases. Humility in this regard is a reflective lens; it is a kind of antonym to certainty. Too often, we think of certainty as virtue when it can just as well be a major obstacle to the growth in understanding that is available to us. If one approaches a problem with the confidence that they know all about it, then there is little to be learned from the problem itself. To learn from any

problem requires that we are humble in order to recognize the limitations of our knowing.

Humility is also the corrective device that helps us to overcome the limitations of ego. Humility isn't so much a low regard for oneself (as per the dictionary definition). Humility is to be in possession of the mature self-awareness to rigorously examine one's judgments and the curiosity to discover new information that might lead to updates in perspective. Humility is the willingness to define oneself not by belief of one's own rightness, but rather by the willingness to evolve and expand one's proactive rather than reactive awareness. *"What can I do?"* asked by someone lacking humility can allow them to feel absolved from any pertinent responsibility when the response is "just be a good person." This conversation happens frequently and is inadequate for progress toward racial Equity.

Some readers may think, *But I still don't know what to do!* To which I would reply: In many cases, the understanding *is* the doing. The understandings and attitudes of educators have massive ramifications for any efforts to reform both our systemic infrastructure and our models for equitable teaching in the classroom. It is through our understanding that we can stretch beyond the invisible boundaries of our cultural purview. Understandings require cognitive empathy and shifts in points of view. Through perspective-taking, we can clarify our own beliefs and understandings and also infer what others believe and understand given their experiences in the world.

The responsibility to pursue the philosophical interrogation of our conscious and nonconscious beliefs is integral to the ways in which we show up as teachers. A philosophical outlook is formed over time and through deliberate reflection. It is often some tension in philosophizing that raises one's core beliefs to the level of critical consciousness. Central to the capacity for *doing* is the willingness to question one's own judgments and to remain committed to the curiosity to uncover new insights and understandings by rethinking that which has been assumed. Hence, the understanding is essential to the doing if the doing is going to address the problems of Equity.

NONSTARTERS

I am often disheartened by our species' slow progress toward a less racist, fairer, and more just society. (The human urge toward tribalism is powerful indeed.) While I agree that teachers should be exercising their capacity for thoughtful discourse on race, I also cringe when I see the topic manipulated in ways that alienate rather than empower. It has led me to three nonstarters for how I talk about race. I use these nonstarters as part of my philosophizing to vet ideas. They are useful in identifying and avoiding dogmatic appeals, and they serve the important role of limiting principles that more likely steer my thinking in alignment with my core values. I strive for an overall ethical and unified cohesion in my thinking, and I hold myself accountable to remain aware of my epistemic standard for investing in ideas—because ideas have consequences.

By *nonstarter*, I don't mean to issue any edict or even imply judgment. I am defining *nonstarter* as a plan, initiative, or idea that has no reasonable chance of succeeding or being effective on its own merit because of some fatal flaw in its logic. I do not intend to offer these as tools for policing the thinking of others. We all have the responsibility of investigating the meaning of race in ways that are consistent with our own personal philosophical outlook. The way we talk about race influences our beliefs, and it's important to believe responsibly because beliefs are potential action (or action at the level of potential). So, a word of caution: Choose your philosophies wisely because we are profoundly impacted by the ideas we invite to take up residence in our minds.

Essentializing

Personal nonstarter #1: There is no essential characteristic that defines what it means to be a member of any particular "racial" group (Golash-Boza, 2022; Kolbert, 2018). This isn't some naive *Why-can't-we-all-get-along?* take on race. Biologists' and geneticists' understanding of human genetic variation, derived from studying the sequencing and distribution of human genetic material (i.e., the entire genome), completely invalidates any remaining shreds of the old notions of racial groupings. When teachers talk about racial identity and racial groups, what we are really talking about are socio-ethnolinguistic groups—or groups bound together by cultural variants, references, and fluencies (i.e., ideas, customs, norms, language, often religion, and region of historic origin) that inform and influence beliefs, traditions, and ways of being.

I am not suggesting that we are living in any kind of postracial society where race no longer factors into the trajectories and opportunities of groups and individuals, but when we humans give into our tribalizing nature, we are actually *more* susceptible to indulge stereotypes and prejudicial thinking, which in turn affect our perceptions, automatic intuitions, and rapid judgments. My argument is that essentialized thinking about race reinforces the *Us/Them* dichotomies that undermine quality and effective pedagogy. Essentialism is all about viewing *Them* as homogeneous and interchangeable. It's the tempting idea that while we *Us's* are individuals, they *Them's* have a monolithic, immutable, predictable essence. *Us/Them* paradigms fuel essentialist thinking, namely, the cognitive cartwheels of those occupying the privileged positions to justify the existing system's unequal status quo (Berreby, 2008; Jost & Hunyady, 2005; Leyens et al., 2000; Sapolsky, 2017).[7]

Studies have shown that *Us/Them* thinking makes us more accepting of racial hierarchies and social inequalities. When our racial-essentialist group thinking is left unchallenged, we tend to think of *Us* as noble, loyal, and composed of distinctive individuals whose failings are due to circumstance while *Them's*, in contrast, seem disgusting, ridiculous, simple, homogeneous, undifferentiated, and interchangeable (Avenanti et al., 2010; Berreby, 2008; Sapolsky, 2017). These beliefs are often tacitly (and sometimes explicitly) rationalized in the school policy environment, increasing the likelihood and frequency of antagonistic, competitive, aggressive, and zero-sum conceptualized interactions between "racial" groups.

Essentializing is an especially pernicious and prejudicial way of viewing our students, opening the door for all kinds of biases—specifically, attribution and confirmation biases that can be used to justify automatic *Them*-ing (Weiner, 2012; 2014). These essentializing biases rationalize automatic *Them*-ing by remembering supportive rather than opposing evidence and probing bias-disconfirming outcomes with greater skepticism than bias-confirming outcomes.

We are much less effective with our pedagogy when we think in terms of *Us/Them* paradigms and allow ourselves to believe that race reveals anything real or true about an individual or group. The resistance to essentialized thinking elevates the humanity of our students such that we are more likely to be able to view them as whole persons with multifaceted cultural identities, which is much more likely to support our pedagogy in providing access points and on-ramps to rigorous and engaging learning experiences.

Using the Knowledge of Race to Empower Students

My second nonstarter is that in any space where the larger conversation is focused on schools and teaching, race should be employed exclusively for the purposes of focusing our attention on that which is likely to empower students in learning experiences. I find that when anything other than student-empowerment is centered in the dialogue on race, ego and agenda can corrupt the real and potential opportunities to better serve our most vulnerable learners. Let's talk about race, yes. And let's make sure that in doing so we center students' educational needs and assets and the Equity goals for our pedagogy.

In the interest of precision, *empowerment* is a term which we should define. Empowerment should be understood as something more like a psychological construct than a technical skill. According to Marc Zimmerman (1995), empowerment is a context-dependent process by which people, organizations, and communities gain mastery over issues of concern to them. *Empowerment* should be defined by its purpose—specifically as it relates to the psychological output of the individual in terms of perceptions of personal control, a proactive approach to learning, and a critical understanding of the sociopolitical environment.

In an empowerment model, the teacher's role is to be a resource and to serve in the capacity of collaborator and facilitator rather than expert deliverer of information. We share rather than give. The nature of the teacher's role is understood in terms of the purpose of empowerment. It both frames and informs the task of teaching—which by dint of mission must depend primarily on a particular place with specific students rather than any general goal, particular resource, or scripted, pre-packaged inputs. By definition, the quality of our empowering efforts is dependent on our capabilities to learn about the local social and cultural context in which teaching and learning occur. Further, the quality and effectiveness of our work to empower requires that we accept and acknowledge the values of that social context as pedagogically meaningful and culturally relevant to our students and their communities.

Empowering teaching places students in control of their learning, with effective supports, so that our kiddos have opportunities to become intelligent and independent problem solvers and decision makers (Zimmerman, 1995). The evidence of empowered learning is performative in nature; it looks like students' perceived sense of efficacy, control, motivation, and critical awareness of environment. Empowering learning experiences are those opportunities in which students learn to see a closer correspondence between their goals and a sense of how to achieve them.

Authentic empowerment in the classroom is an opportunity for students to express, explore, and expand both their sense of agency and their views of the world. If empowerment is not prioritized in the learning environment, then it may be that I am not necessarily teaching my students as much as I am requiring them to follow my directions (well-meaning though those directions may be). And while it is important for students to be able to follow directions, it is not as important as my desire for them to experience empowered thinking. Students therefore aren't empowered when they are taught *what* to think; students are empowered when they are taught *how* to think.

Equity is empowering for students, communities, and teachers. Students are empowered to pursue the full development of their abilities and dreams in the interest of their own well-being and that of the communities to which they belong. Communities are empowered through the development of their most valuable asset, the talent from within. Teachers are empowered to meet the needs of their students without compromising the integrity of rigor and high expectations.[8]

The Limitations of Violence

Last, I personally do not subscribe to arguments or tactics that compel, encourage, or celebrate violence. The philosopher Howard Thurman (1951) wrote:

> Violence is very deceptive as a technique because of the way in which it comes to the rescue of those who are in a hurry. . . . The fact that it inspires resistance is underestimated, while the fact that it inspires fear is overestimated. This is the secret of its deception. . . . Violence rarely, if ever, gets the consent of the spirit of those upon whom it is used. It drives them underground, it makes them seek cover, if they cannot overcome it in other ways. It merely postpones the day of revenge and retaliation.

It is objectively true that the principles of nonviolent civil disobedience led to material and legislative progress in American society that dramatically changed the world. Yes, there is still much work to do, but it is an utterly unserious argument that violence is a justified tool for the social justice movement of the 21st century because of any lack of efficacy in the nonviolent strategies and tactics of the 1950s and 1960s Civil Rights Movement. This isn't to assert a sovereign rectitude of the leaders of the Civil Rights Movement. That, too, is silly. But to deny its cultural and political impact reveals an ignorance of the realities of governing and societal norms in the United States of America prior to 1953.

Violence can be effective in promoting submission, but any hegemonic shifts incurred through violence must be maintained with violence. Violence sentences one to become increasingly more violent. I understand that those who are violent will on occasion be able to enforce my compliance or even assert their positions onto me given my unwillingness to return their aggression. Yet, still, I'd rather be the one who resists violence because I don't enjoy being with myself when I am consumed with violent thoughts; and violent thoughts don't play nice with my other more worthy thoughts. I'd rather not suffer in this way. So, in the final analysis, I have very selfish motivations for taking the position that violence is a nonstarter. Violence doesn't make me more effective in my argumentation, and it doesn't feel good to my soul.

*****

The very understanding that artful teaching is indispensable if we are to achieve Equity in education brings about a fundamental change in how one views the craft. To develop students with the capacities for intelligence and understandings, the educator themself must be engaged in the work of philosophizing, and this means remaining open to new learning and the difficult work of navigating issues of culture and identity and all the tribal distinctions we humans place upon ourselves.

NOTES ON ARTMAKING: LAYERED METHODOLOGIES

I'm a big fan of photography—especially street photography. (The Instagram hashtag #streetphotography is a go-to source for incredible shots!) I enjoy images of people and scenery and interactions in city spaces. I think, when done well, they have the potential to say much about the human condition.

I also enjoy visiting photography galleries. (Shout-out to the SOHO Photo Gallery and Aperture in New York City, the Photographer's Gallery in London, and Foam in Amsterdam!) I have many favorite photographers, and I encourage you to google them all, but the works of Gordon Parks, Don McCullin, Annie Leibovitz, Ernest Cole, and Devin Allen are particularly moving and insightful. Many of the images they capture are so powerful that they seem to hold more action in one still frame than some feature-length films! Their pictures have a way of informing of the human experience on a level even more visceral than language.

Like many, I fancy myself as quite deft with my smartphone camera (which is a more *powerful* image-capturing device than anything Dorothea Lange or Ansel Adams ever used). I try to take one good picture every day. Having the intention to get a clear and interesting shot with my camera phone keeps a part of my brain alert all day. I am more open to seeing that which might have escaped my perception when I set this goal as a daily intention.

Figure 3.1 is a picture that I took of my morning vanilla latte sitting at my preferred table for writing at Pablo's on 6th, one of my favorite coffee

Figure 3.1 My morning cup of vanilla latte at Pablos' on Sixth coffee shop (Denver, Colorado)

shops in Denver, Colorado. The image is of a cup with the letters VL handwritten on it in marker, sitting on the edge of a very distinctive ring etched into the table. But beyond this foreground, there's a background plane that holds a white trash can splattered with stickers just in front of the exit through which someone is about to fully cross its threshold. There are also plants placed along the protruding window ledge which give the image an additional sense of depth and perspective.

One of the compositional qualities that photographers talk about is layering. *Layering* refers to the stacking of attention-worthy elements in a photographic image across different depths of field and on multiple planes across the frame. An excellent example of layering can be found in the works of Rebecca Norris Webb and Alex Webb. You can see on their Instagram page how many of their images hold the eye by creating interest throughout the image, foreground to middleground to background.

Equity in education is also a multilayered construct with significant elements on multiple planes that contribute to its meaning ranging from up close and personal in the classroom spanning all the way out to the structural inequalities that shape the American opportunity landscape. For teachers, our students are in the foreground. We see them in high-definition detail. And every moment in any one of our individual students' lives is a kind of composite sketch of the events happening on multiple planes of their existence from their close network of relationships all the way out to the cultural groups from which they inherit psychological tools for making sense of the world. Similarly, every understanding—if it is really understood—incorporates multiple dimensions of knowing from the intellectual to the emotional and the shaded hybrid areas in between. We teachers, it seems, are in the layering business.

When it comes to solving for Equity problems of practice, we limit our own capacities for artful pedagogy by thinking in terms of single planes, lone dimensions, and siloed disciplinary buckets. The root causes of the Equity gaps we see in American education are the product of myriad pedagogical, social, cultural, economic, political, or even biological influences.

Thus, for we teachers who want to *do* Equity, it is impossible to conclude that any classroom outcome is caused by a single element of culture, genetics, hormonal activity, childhood trauma, parenting events, peer-group association, condition of socio-economic status, individual disposition, or social background. These are all layered and interacting and can't be understood apart from the others. The second you invoke one type of explanation, you are de facto invoking them all (Sapolsky, 2017).

Every concrete problem of practice in teaching is embedded in a complex, locally contingent frame; and any cause of events can only be properly understood in its specific context. Equity problems of practice require nuanced understandings of the persons and surrounding circumstances. This level of nuance is rarely found in extreme positions. The dearth of nuance is an indicator of a lack in rigor, which is an obstacle to our Equity work.

On my journey as an educator, I have found there to be a wealth of insight available to me within education scholarship but also in other fields, as well. I have come to admire works in the fields of cultural psychology, neuroscience and cognitive science, learning theory, and biology, in addition to the social sciences of anthropology, sociology, and education studies along with my long-held passions in the humanities, most specifically art, history, and literature. The boundaries we impose on our own inquiry are hindrances to our potential for facilitating empowering learning opportunities in our teaching. My point is that when we are talking about something as complex and consequential as teaching, we are unwise to constrain our interests into single discipline categories. No one discipline addresses more than a small fraction of the total range of considerations that fall into our purview.[9]

To best serve in our role as facilitators of understandings, we must be intentional curators of information. We teachers should model the kind of attention, intelligence, and humility that we hope to develop in our students through our own interdisciplinary philosophizing. We should favor content and sources that present many sides of an issue rather than just one or two. We can teach our students to recognize complexity as a signal of credibility. We can fight our tendency to accept simple binaries by asking what additional perspectives are missing between the extremes. So many of the great advances in human history have been the product of borrowing the innovations and outputs of the intelligences of others.[10] For all of these reasons, I am encouraging you to pursue the opportunities to layer your thinking about teaching; and I am further making the claim that Equity in American education isn't possible until (and unless) we collectively do so.

CHAPTER NOTES

1. Impaired development of this mentalizing mechanism can have drastic effects on social learning, seen most strikingly in the autistic spectrum disorders (Leslie, Friedman, & German, 2004).

2. Those "racial" categories with which we are most familiar capture only about 7% of the total genetic variation in our species, which reveals that racial groups are nothing like the subspecies found in other primates (Henrich, 2016).

3. *Economic inequality* refers to the unequal distribution of income, wealth, and revenue opportunities among different groups in society, which is known to have direct correlation with patterns of performance and achievement in schooling.

4. Similarly, repeatedly show subjects a picture of a face accompanied by a shock; soon, seeing the face alone activates the amygdala. "Fear conditioning" occurs faster for *other*-race than *same*-race faces (Kubota et al., 2012). Amygdalae are prepared to learn to associate something bad with *Them's*. Moreover, people judge neutral *other*-race faces as angrier than neutral *same*-race faces. So, if Whites see a Black face shown at a subliminal speed, the amygdala activates. But if the face is shown long enough for conscious processing, the anterior cingulate and the dorsolateral prefrontal cortex then activate and inhibit the amygdala. It's the frontal cortex exerting executive control over the deeper, darker amygdaloid response (Delgado et al., 2008; Sapolsky, 2017).

5. Frontal cortical activation during an interracial interaction could reflect: (a) being prejudiced and trying to hide it; (b) being prejudiced and feeling bad about it; (c) feeling no prejudice and working to communicate that; (d) *who knows what else*? Activation merely

implies that the interracial nature of the interaction is weighing on the subject (implicitly or otherwise) and prompting executive control (Sapolsky, 2017).

6. The lead author of the article is Mica Pollock, who is also the editor of *Everyday Antiracism: Getting Real about Race in Schools* (2008). I have regularly recommended this book as an excellent resource for school-based professional development and discussion. I like it as a text for schools because it focuses the attention of anti-racism on the tasks and outcomes of instruction.

7. Cognitive gymnastics also occur when our negative, homogeneous view of a type of *Them* must accommodate the appealing celebrity *Them*, the *Them* neighbor, the *Them* who has saved our ass—"Ah, this *Them* is different," no doubt followed by a self-congratulatory sense of open-mindedness (Leyens et al., 2000; Sapolsky, 2017).

8. In Chapter 9, I discuss the topic of culturally responsive assessments as those performative measures that allow students to leverage their cultural fluencies in the interest of showing competence. Here, it is also important to note that assessments must consider the local context or it cannot be said that they serve the goals of empowerment. The development of universal measures may not be feasible or conceptually sound given that the processes and outcomes of empowerment are context- and population-specific and should include relevant aspects of perceived control and knowledge of causal agents in socio-political context in order to be considered valid instruments of data collection (Zimmerman, 1995).

9. Some of the most creative scientific work is done by harnessing findings or methods in one field to problems posed in another. A classic example is the importation of chemistry into biology to create a succession of new disciplines—physiology, biochemistry, and molecular biology. Social Learning Theory, for example, sits at the interface of an impressive number of academic disciplines. How many other concepts could boast being central to both social anthropology and human evolution and also core material for experimental psychologists and

theoretically minded economists too? I am especially fond of the methodologies used in the fields of cultural psychology and anthropological research—particularly the behavioral and experimental economic "games" that are used to measure social dispositions and norms (e.g., cooperation) within societies and social groups such as the ultimatum game, the common pool resources game, asymmetric matching pennies game, the public good game, and the dictator game, to name just a few.

10. This represents one of the more important understandings for us to hold on to as we move forward in this discussion. Very few (and quite possibly none) of the ideas that inspire and influence artmaking of any form can be said to be completely original. Influence and inspiration can come from anywhere at anytime and is unrestrained by labels and human-made categories. The artists who are widely recognized for their innovations draw from a range of source material pulling from many frames and perspectives.

CHAPTER 4

Artmaking—As an Equity Issue

"Art divorced from life has no great significance. When art is separate from our daily living, when there is a gap between our instinctual life and our efforts on canvas, in marble, or in words, then art becomes merely an expression of our superficial desire to escape from the reality of what is. To bridge this gap is very arduous, especially for those who are gifted and technically proficient; but it is only when the gap is bridged that our life becomes integrated and art an integral expression of ourselves."

—Jiddu Krishnamurti

WHAT DOES IT MEAN TO UNDERSTAND?

Time for another thought experiment. Think about this: When would it be appropriate to use each of these terms? Do these all say the same thing?

Thanks

Thank you

Thank you very much

Thanks a lot

Many thanks

Thanks ever so much

Thanks for everything

Thanks a million

How can I ever thank you?

I can't thank you enough

All of these phrases are verbal expressions of gratitude, but they don't all say exactly the same thing. I prefer to compose in coffee shops, and it so happens that on the morning of my writing this sentence, I was served what may be the perfect cup of vanilla latte. My mood upon my first sip was one part delight and another inspired. I knew right away that this was quite possibly going to be the greatest cup of vanilla latte I have ever enjoyed. (I get emotional when it comes to my caffeinated beverages.) Though I was inclined, I held back from locking eyes with the barista while gently and genuinely saying to them: *How can I ever thank you?*

Each of these terms is a concept, a category of instances in which its use would be an appropriate fit for the moment in context. The concept of *Thanks* is related to but different from *Thank you very much.* They reveal different intent and point to how the situation may be read by its participants. Depending on tone and timing, *Thanks a lot* could be construed as sarcastic or even hostile, while *I can't thank you enough* may be interpreted as an invitation to friendship as much as a signal of appreciation. We will see in this chapter that whenever we do something as simple and pedestrian as communicating gratitude, we are sending our brain into a subterranean tussle to determine what category of gratitude is most fitting for any given context and intent.

To know if these expressions all mean the same thing and when it would be appropriate to use these terms are more sophisticated understandings than it might seem at first glance. Before we go there however, we must clarify what it means to *know* because the key to our own capacities for artful pedagogy is largely a function of our own clarity for what it means to understand.

The concept of ❤

What is this? ❤ What is it called?

Many of us would refer to this as a symbol of a heart or a heart emoji. Others might see it as shorthand for *love.* Though even if the symbol is argued to be a representation for *love*, it is still a visual image of a heart standing in for the meaning of *love.* In which case, it's first a *heart* before it can be *love*—and so we shall call this symbol a "heart"; but what does *heart* mean?

What I intend to show is that *heart* is a concept, and like all concepts, it's culturally and situationally fluid in meaning; and this carries tremendous implications for both our philosophizing and our craft. It behooves me to first define the term *concept* as it is central to this unifying theory that culturally responsive pedagogy is a useful approach for closing Equity gaps.

Though, defining *concepts* is not such a simple task. But here it goes: A *concept* can be generally defined as information, and information can be taken to mean what is commonly referred to as an idea, knowledge, belief, value, skill, or attitude (Barsalou et al., 2003; Richerson & Boyd, 2008). *Concepts*, as we shall see further in the second half of this chapter, are acquired and modified by social learning and affect both behavior and perspective; but our attention here is turned to the nature and utility of concepts like *heart* in our everyday lives. How do we learn concepts? What role do concepts play in thinking? How do concepts influence identity?

We might be tempted to minimize the significance of concepts in our thought lives because the dictionary seems to objectively define them with such ease. For example, the dictionary has a definition for *heart*; in fact, it has several. But as we shall see, these definitions only scratch the surface of meaning, and the meaning for the concept *heart* is loaded with subjectivity that drives our interpretations.

Heart can be defined as a noun, a verb, and a proper noun. A quick review of dictionary definitions shows at least six noun uses of the concept *heart* including:

heart (noun)
\'härt\
1a: a hollow muscular organ of vertebrate animals that by its rhythmic contraction acts as a force pump maintaining the circulation of the blood
1b: a structure in an invertebrate animal functionally analogous to the vertebrate heart
1c: breast, bosom
1d: something resembling a heart in shape
2a: a playing card marked with a stylized figure of a red heart
2b: hearts plural: the suit comprising cards marked with hearts
2c: a game in which the object is to avoid taking tricks containing hearts
3: personality, disposition

4a: the emotional or moral nature as distinguished from the intellectual nature, such as a generous disposition: compassion

4b: love, affection

4c: courage or enthusiasm especially when maintained during a difficult situation

5: one's innermost character, feelings, or inclinations

6a: the central or innermost part: center

6b: the essential or most vital part of something

6c: the younger central compact part of a leafy rosette (such as a head of lettuce or stalk of celery)

Heart may also be defined as a verb as in:

heart (verb)

transitive verb

1a: love

1b: to like an online post, comment, and so on, especially by clicking or tapping a heart-shaped symbol

And there are multiple proper nouns that are also referred to as *Heart*, including but not limited to:

Heart (geographical name)

a river in southwestern North Dakota flowing 200 miles east into the Missouri River opposite Bismarck

Heart (band)

an American rock band formed in 1967 that has sold more than 35 million records worldwide and whose members were inducted into the Rock and Roll Hall of Fame in 2013

The Heart (television series)

a television series that follows the journey of a district attorney's rise to become a formidable political candidate for President of the United States and is based on The Heart Series, a collection of nine novels written by Iris Bolling

There are, however, many more ways in which we can understand the concept of *heart*. We could also define *heart* with an analogy as in:

engine:car::heart:body (engine is to car as heart is to body)

This analogy might be said to be an advanced representation of the concept considering that it defines *heart* by its object-to-purpose relationship to the concept of *body*—which would seem to be more sophisticated than the previously listed noun and verb definitions, and thus, requires greater intelligence in order to understand. But it is also true that this more advanced understanding relies in some way on the dictionary definitions in order to take meaning. The dictionary definitions are a kind of low-resolution seed concept for the more highly developed understandings; but most importantly for our artmaking purposes, the relationship between the two are abstract and dependent on our experiences and interpretations.

The Cognition Core Hypothesis

This raises important questions for us teachers: If we can assume that the ability to grasp the meaning of *heart* in both dictionary definitional terms and also in more conceptually complex ways is a demonstration of intelligence, then how does one learn to understand concepts like *heart*? And what does that tell us about the nature of human intelligence broadly?

In the anthropological sense, intelligence is the ability to learn that which is necessary for one's survival (Nisbett, 2009).[1] Generally speaking, intelligence is the cognitive capacity of pacing, tracking, and ranking in the interest of formulating causal models of how the world works. But that's not super useful for this discussion.

We need an operational definition of *intelligence* to ground our philosophizing. I am fond of the Cognition Core Hypothesis that offers a useful construct for conceptualizing cognition—which we require in order to clarify our ideas for how we *do* Equity. We cannot know what it means to operationalize equitable learning opportunities for students if we haven't level-set a definition for *intelligence*.

And so, conceptually speaking, intelligence is the ability to put one's finger on what counts in any given situation; it is the repertoire of categories acquired through one's native language and culture, and the manner in which this repertoire tailors one's ways of locating the essence of something (Hofstadter & Sander, 2013).

I'm a big fan of the work of physicist and cognitive scientist Douglas Hofstadter. In his book with Emmanuel Sander, *Surfaces and Essences: Analogy as the Fuel and Fire of Thinking* (2013), they define *intelligence* this way:

> Intelligence, to our mind, is the art of rapid and reliable gist-finding, crux-spotting, bull's-eye-hitting, nub-striking, essence-pinpointing. It is the art of, when one is facing a new situation, swiftly and surely homing in on an insightful precedent (or family of precedents) stored in the recesses of one's memory. That, no more and no less, is what it means to isolate the crux of a new situation. And this is nothing but the ability to find close analogues, which is to say, the ability to come up with strong and useful analogies.

Thinking, then, is an abstraction-seeking process that entails identifying the essence of a situation and then bouncing back-and-forth between the actual situation and the essence that one found (Hofstadter & Sander, 2013). In defining thinking, analogies and concepts occupy featured roles; for without concepts there can be no thought, and without analogies there can be no concepts. Thinking is a type of perception, and while we perceive through our sensory organs, our perceptions that inform what we may call thinking are filtered through our concepts. In other words, we perceive not just physiologically but also conceptually.[2]

The ways in which we understand concepts objectively depend on our senses—since our concepts would be quite different if our sensory experiences of them were also different. It's also true, however, that our perceptions depend on our repertoire of concepts because our concepts filter the stimuli in our environment before any sensory stimulus reaches our consciousness (Hofstadter & Sander, 2013). So *heart* doesn't merely mean one thing, and its meaning depends on the context and circumstances in which it is evoked because it's through context and circumstance that analogues come forward into conscious thought. Categorization, the organizing of concepts, is the purpose of cognition, and analogy-making is the driving force behind all thought.

Analogy Is the Engine of Thinking

Do you remember the first time you learned of the concept *heart*?

At some point, you have likely heard that first impressions are important. But why? Why are first impressions so powerful? When we can clearly recall our first impression of something, we are revisiting the origin story of a conceptual understanding, our initial introduction to a knowing. A first impression is a kind of conceptual prototype for what to expect from a person, place, event, or thing.

Quite literally from the moment of birth, we humans are incessantly amassing concepts—each of which depends on antecedent, underlying concepts. Our thinking and understandings are constructed on an edifice of previously acquired concepts that can re-engineer and/or expand itself. The relative ties connecting concepts old and new are layered, blurry, shaded, reciprocal, and multidirectional. Thinking then, can generally be said to be a continual process of conceptual chunking and refinement (Hofstadter & Sander, 2013). As novel concepts emerge, they evolve the previously existing categorized conceptual schema that enabled them to come into being; in this way, newer concepts are incorporated inside their "parents" as well as the reverse. We are forever thinking, extending, reinforcing, and revising our concept categories because the strictest form of individualized, literal learning (i.e., total rote cognitive recording and interpretation of each and every instance requiring a unique interpretation and assessment) does not allow any resemblances to be noticed, and thus, excludes all categorizing which we could say is the opposite of intelligence (Hofstadter & Sander, 2013).

Let's think about a few other *heart*-related concepts. The meaning that can be drawn from concepts like *heartthrob* and *heartache* are dependent on dictionary definitions of *heart*, but they are also a function of the contextual, circumstantial, and cultural influences on our interpretations in any given moment.

Much like the expressions of gratitude listed at the start of this chapter, the concepts *heartthrob* and *heartache* are understood through a conscious and nonconscious process of categorizing and analogizing. The concepts heartthrob and heartache are densely stitched together categories of individual instances that share some similarity, some common essence. We understand them through cognitive comparisons, as in—this thing is like this other thing. When you consider an instance of heartache, for example, you are really comparing the event with other events either that you have endured yourself, or that you have witnessed in others, or that you have otherwise inherited in a cognitive niche. Your mental category of "heartache" is thus the outcome of a long series of analogies that builds bridges between entities (objects, actions, people, situations) distant from each other in both time and space. Every time we have an encounter with the concept of "heartache" the category of instances is expanded because no two "heartaches" are exactly the same even though they fit under the same conceptual label.

This-is-like thinking is ubiquitous in our cognition. Analogy-making is the perception of common essences between two things. "Analogies happen all the time for no purpose. They're fleeting, and transient, they appear and go away—often with no purpose. Our minds are filled with them" (Hofstadter & Sander, 2013). Analogy is the motor of the car of thought; it is the interstate freeway system of cognition. Quoting Hofstadter and Sander (2013):

Analogy-making is the cornerstone of this faculty of our minds, allowing us to exploit the rich storehouse of wisdom rooted in our past—not only labeled concepts such as dog, cat, joy, resignation, and contradiction, to cite just a random sample, but also unlabeled concepts such as that time I found myself locked outside my house in bitterly freezing weather because the door slammed shut by accident. Such concepts, be they concrete or abstract, are selectively mobilized instant by instant, and nearly always without any awareness on our part, and it is this ceaseless activity that allows us to build up mental representations of situations we are in, to have complex feelings about them, and to have run-of-the-mill as well as more exalted thoughts. No thought can be formed that isn't informed by the past; or, more precisely, we think only thanks to analogies that link our present to our past.

Culture, Context, and Personal Cognitive Styles

Concepts are chunked in the mind to create larger, more complex categories of related instances of a general thing. This manner of thinking is such an automatic process that we hardly even consider it cognition. It is so central to human consciousness that we can't easily discern the edifice of lower-level or more primordial concepts on which newer concepts are constructed. Consider these phrases and the meaning that can be drawn from them:

> a broken heart (to be overwhelmed with sadness)
> from the bottom of one's heart (very sincerely)
> in one's heart of hearts (in one's innermost feelings)
> wear one's heart on one's sleeve (make one's feelings apparent)

What do these phrases mean? How would one know? How might we explain the meaning of these phrases to someone who is altogether unfamiliar?

These are all concept categories, and each began as a single-memory category in our often unremembered organizing mental schema. The concept of *a broken heart*, as just one example, has been pieced together over time and through experience. This concept (and every other) is categorized, refined, and updated through individual experience, direct instruction, and all sorts of social and cultural learning.

No brain operates in a culture vacuum. We "see" as much through the cultural constructions of concepts as we do through the physiological photoreceptors that turn light into electrical signals that travel from the retina through the optic nerve to the brain. We use analogies to think and act in situations that we have never encountered. Situations are often social in nature. Our ability and process for arriving at understandings is accomplished by registering what is happening around us, at appropriate levels of abstraction, and this entire process is coded, aided, and influenced by the norms, knowledge, skills, and information shared by social groups—or culture (Hofstadter & Sander, 2013).

The crux of perception—even for a very young child—is an act of concept categorization that allows invisible qualities of objects, actions, and situations to be "seen." Categorization gives one the feeling of understanding a situation by providing a kind of conceptual blueprint for perspective on it. We learn to categorize situations by drawing heavily on social learning and cultural inheritance. Each one of the phrases—*a broken heart, from the bottom of one's heart, in one's heart of hearts,* and *wear one's heart on one's sleeve*—is a situation label. To understand these phrases, we are processing them by thinking: "This situation is like other situations in which I've heard people use the phrase. . . ." We learn much about these heart concepts by making inferences of our observations of the experiences of others. Luckily, that means it is possible to understand the concept of *a broken heart* without having to come into possession of one through the personal experience of individual learning.

Each one of our students has a personal cognitive style, and it depends on their entire repertoire of concepts built up over the course of a unique lifetime. At the heart of this personal repertoire is a rich and expansive inventory of concepts, which having linguistic labels and symbolic references, is shared in the context of social and cultural learning. A student's interpretation of meaning is a function of the essence perceived considering the social context and their frame of mind at a particular time. I will return to this later in this chapter, but for now we should bookmark this reference point: social context and culture have a tremendous influence on categorization and can inform how our students perceive even the most familiar of concepts (Hofstadter & Sander, 2013).

Concepts evolve over our individual lifetimes and also for our social groups.[3] The meaning of a concept is not entirely subjective nor can it be solely defined by objective criteria because concepts are living and evolving entities. The experience of a cardiac event, for example, while based on objective criteria for understanding, changes one's concept of *heart*. Similarly, a passionate romantic relationship changes one's concept of *heart*.

This business of concepts matters a lot because so much of how any individual exists is a function of the conceptual repertoire that shapes how they think and thus, heavily influences how they compose their perceptions of the world. We teachers must regularly return to this matter of concepts and thinking because to gloss over it creates the conditions for the conflation of difference with deficit. Our theories of learning guide the pedagogical choices we make moment-to-moment in the classroom. This matters to us teachers because it requires something of us.

I've picked the concept of *heart* to illustrate the Cognition Core Hypothesis that I find to be useful for the consideration of what it means to think and understand. We are all a kind of product of our concepts, and we learn our concepts via social learning in the cognitive niches in which we learn how to *human (v)*. At every moment, we are simultaneously faced with an indefinite number of overlapping and intermingling situational contexts, and our understandings are guided by the cognitive capacity (i.e., intelligence) to see the essence of any given situation for the purpose of identifying an analogous conceptual peer (Hoftsadter & Sander, 2013). "Behind any word, phrase, event, or entity of any kind (no matter how casual and simple it may seem) there is a non-verbalized concept category, sometimes simple and sometimes subtle, based on an implicit perception of sameness—which is to say, based on an analogy" (Hofstadter & Sander, 2013).

*****

In the first part of this chapter, I've presented a summary of the Cognition Core Hypothesis. In doing so, I seek to outline a model for what we can refer to as *thinking* because it is students' thinking that we seek to influence with our teaching. In the second part of this chapter, we will re-center the topic of culture to consider further the role that culture plays in thinking. To end the chapter, I will re-connect the craft of teaching to the work of Equity in education, which I argue is ultimately intended to empower students in rigorous and engaging learning experiences.

THE ROLE OF CULTURE RELATIVE TO ACHIEVEMENT

Let's re-set and return to the conceptual framing with this book's central thought-experiment: You're a teacher, and you want to be equitable. What does Equity mean *in* your teaching? How do you *do* Equity?

Cultural Identity

To *do* Equity, we're going to have to be able to tap into the sociality of all our students. Humans are a social species, and culture is the primary mechanism through which our sociality is activated. As such, you and every human you know is a cultural being with a cultural identity. In Chapter 1, I referred to a definition of culture as human knowledge, skills, and any kind of mental state—conscious or not—that can affect individuals' behaviors. One's cultural inheritance is acquired or modified through observation, imitation, inferencing, direct teaching, and other forms of social transmission. There are many ways that a human can be described, and one of those is by the cultural fluencies they hold. *Cultural Identity* can be described as the balance of those fluencies. It's the feeling of belonging to a group. It's part of a person's self-conception and self-perception and is related to race, ethnicity, religion, nationality, language, gender, class, generation, locality or any kind of social group that has its own distinct cultural features.[4]

Intelligence is the repertoire of concept categories acquired through one's culture(s) that facilitates the ability to put one's finger on what counts in any given situation, and the way this repertoire shapes one's ways of pointing to the essence of something. Though you are an individual with a unique cognitive style and capacity for thinking, feeling, and behaving, your sense of self is also defined in many ways by the understandings you share with others who have been similarly culturally indoctrinated. This has a profound effect on your cognition and intelligence. Your analogy-making mental machinery is developed in a social context. The culture of your social groups informs the ways in which you interpret the essence of things. These shared essence-understandings are the actual substance of the social bonds that you experience with other members of your cultural group(s).

Cultural Identity can be thought of as a composite of the various socio-ethnolinguistic subgroups with which one has cultural fluency. If you are like most human beings in the Western world, you download cultural variants from the cultural repertoires of multiple social groups.

One way to think about Cultural Identity is as if each of the social group buckets in Figure 4.1 was a kind of identity think tank where matters of existential and performative interest are deliberated by the group's cultural insiders. One's own fluencies within the domains of cultural learning comprise the intelligence that allows us to share meaning and norms with other members of our social group(s) by locating the essence of things. This is ultimately what it means to identify with a group. Even when we as individuals hold differing experiences and beliefs, we

Figure 4.1 Cultural Identity Bubble Map

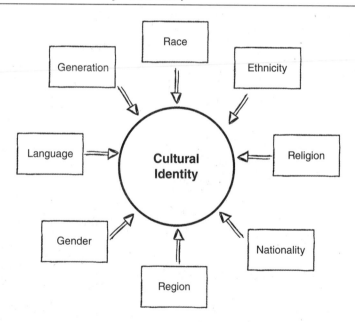

generally know how our cultural groups are likely to process philosophical questions regarding the natures of reality, knowledge, reasoning, and value as in:

Who are we? Who are they? What is the nature of humanity? What is knowledge? What are the limits of knowledge? How are language and communication used to convey meaning? What are the general expectations associated with problem-solving practices? What is good and right? What is wrong and bad? What is the nature of beauty? What is the nature of ugliness? Etc. . . .[5]

Culture is a package of adaptations, technologies, and social norms that allow for social groups to exist cooperatively under the constraints of the environment and other local contexts. Anthropologists and cultural psychologists describe the social-psychological real estate in which cultural adaptations take form as the *domains of cultural learning* which include:

Food preferences and quantity eaten
Mate choices (individuals and their traits)
Economic strategies (investments)
Artifact (tool) functions and use
Suicide (decision and method)
Technological adoptions
Word meanings and dialect
Categories ("dangerous animals")
Beliefs (e.g., about gods, germs, etc.)
Social norms (taboos, rituals, tipping)
Standards of reward and punishment
Social motivations (altruism and fairness)
Self-regulation
Judgment heuristics (Henrich, 2016)

In most of the classrooms I visit, I see a rich tapestry of racial, ethnic, language, and cultural backgrounds. It's not uncommon for a teacher to have 30 students and more than two dozen identity groups represented among them. It's important to resist the urge to compile simple categories of socio-ethnolinguistic groups and rather to view cultural identity as a kind of index that influences people's psychology as well as their outward expression of social practices and normed behaviors. Except in rare instances, all of us (our students included) download cultural variants and repertoires from multiple identity-group streams—which means that we are all, in some manner, multicultural beings.

As teachers, we are responsible for recognizing the role of culture in our philosophizing ways. Our own personal philosophizing is deeply influenced by our socialization. When we philosophize, we are drawing on the motifs and indoctrinations that we have acquired through social learning and the participation in cultural spaces. Our cultural identities are a reflection and function of the social philosophizing that defines our group identities. These ways of knowing allow us to make sense of the world.

Most importantly, it's critical that we all recognize and respect the intelligence necessary to gain fluency within *any* social-group's repertoire. Cultural fluency is useful for navigating and expanding cognitive niches and reducing risks of emotional and physical threats in the environment. This is not a matter of trivial personality adjustments. "Cultural learning reaches directly into our brains and changes the neurological values we place on things and people, and in doing so, it also sets the standards by which we judge ourselves" (Henrich, 2016). The acquisition of culture altars aspects of human psychology and endows individuals with new cognitive abilities (Boyd & Richerson, 1983; Henrich, 2020). It doesn't take a particularly fancy brain to learn how to motorically, say, throw a punch. But it takes a fancy, socially malleable frontal cortex to learn culture-specific rules about when it's okay to throw punches (Sapolsky, 2017).

A Note on Gene-Culture Coevolution/Dual Inheritance Theory

I, for one, find it utterly fascinating that our species has evolved to depend on culture to facilitate gene expression. Though Gene-Culture Coevolution is beyond the scope of the central arguments in this book, it's important that I give a brief overview so as to be clear about how evolutionary theory informs our understanding of culturally responsive pedagogy. But before I provide that overview, there are some reservations I should share first. Entering this space comes with great risk for us teachers. It's risky because it's easy to conflate the levels of analysis that are relevant to our task. Teachers work with students—and every student is a unique individual. The theories of Gene-Culture Coevolution (also referred to as Dual Inheritance) deal with macro-level population questions. We, however, need philosophizing tools that allow for the highest resolution analysis at the level of the classroom. I will return to this point shortly, but now for the 30,000-foot view of Gene-Culture Coevolution.

Culture plays a starring role in the story of humankind. We are a cultural species unlike any other on the planet, and our very survival as groups and individuals is dependent on our capacities for acquiring the large bodies of information that are accumulated nongenetically over generations. We use this information for everything from finding food to childbirth. Despite our large brains (and our hubris), humans could not survive without the specialized cultural information that has allowed us to thrive in nearly every ecosystem on the planet.

To understand the evolutionary success of humanity, culture should be seen as a semi-independent inheritance system operating alongside genetic evolution. That is, our adaptations for cultural learning are genetically evolved. In the field of genetics, populations are the unit of study as theorists seek to understand how (and why) traits are distributed throughout societies and over time. Social science notes how different populations exhibit persistent variation in language, social customs, moral systems, practical skills, devices, and art (Richerson & Boyd, 2008). It is now generally regarded as more plausible than not that culture is an active contributing agent in the shaping of our species not only in terms of social practices, but also in terms of our genetic and anatomic development. "The coevolutionary dynamic makes genes as susceptible to cultural influence as vice versa" (Boyd & Richerson, 1985). This is referred to as the Theory of Gene-Culture Coevolution or the Dual Inheritance Theory.

The story of Gene-Culture Coevolution goes something like this:

Long before the emergence of anatomically modern humans, probably over a million years ago, members of our evolutionary lineage began learning from each other in such a way that groups were able to accumulate and pass on ideas and know-how that increased their chances for survival. The earliest iterations of cultural evolution may have produced the abilities to manage fire for safety and cooking, and things like stone tools for cutting and processing food. The consensus among anthropologists and evolutionary biologists is that fire and cooking likely became, in effect, a kind of externalized digestive system shortening our colons and allowing our stomachs to shrink while simultaneously changing other aspects of our physiology, changes that would have freed up more energy to evolve larger brains, giving us greater dexterity for making and using tools. Over time, brains increase in capacity to acquire, organize, store, and re-transmit cultural information. That is, culture both shapes and is shaped by the evolved information-processing properties of human brains.

Cultural evolution then could have produced more knowledge for developing tools, and other techniques useful for survival which would have created genetic selection pressures for better cultural learners, and then eventually a cognition that allows us to acquire and store all this knowledge about different kinds of plants and animals in the specific environments in which different human groups lived. Culture has influenced the genetic evolution of our bodies and has contributed to an extended juvenile period, and a longer post-reproductive period. This interaction between culture, genes, and environment drove our species down a novel evolutionary pathway not observed elsewhere in nature, making us very different from all other species. (Henrich, 2016)

Some adaptive cultural variants, including psychological dispositions, spread and others diminished, leading to evolutionary processes that are every bit as real and important as those that shape genetic variation. Genetic evolution created selection pressures favoring psychological tendencies for cooperation, coordination, and the forming of social institutions, thus allowing the cumulative evolution of complex cultural adaptations. Over time, norms emerged, including those contained in languages, which influenced a vast range of human action, including ancient and fundamentally important domains such as kin relations, mating, food sharing, parenting, and reciprocity.

Over the evolutionary long haul, culture has shaped our innate human psychology. To ensure learning the best norms for their own groups and avoiding the dangers of hostile interactions with others, humans preferentially used marker traits like dialect and phentoype to identify potential models and then preferentially target their cultural learning and social interactions toward those who share their marker traits (Boyd & Richerson, 2008).

Genes are not deterministic blueprints that specify one's adult characteristics irrespective of culture or the environment—as in, one gene says you are tall, the other bald, that type of thing. Genes are like investors who are responsible for setting up a blind trust. On behalf of the trust, the investors leave brokers a set of initial instructions, which cannot subsequently be changed or canceled. In an unpredictable environment like the stock market, rather than give their brokers detailed instructions about which stocks to buy and sell at each future time, the better strategy is to give their brokers a flexible set of instructions. For example, they might specify that a certain proportion of the trust be held in blue chip stocks, some in speculative stocks, and so on, with the overall specification that the broker try to maximize revenue within these constraints (Richerson & Boyd, 2008).

The point I seek to make here relative to my larger arguments around brilliant teaching and artful thinking is that Gene-Culture Coevolution Theory is both beyond the scope of this book and also a limiting lens because of its focus on macro-level population characteristics. Quite often, I find that educators seek shortcuts to their questions regarding behavior and engagement issues in schools by attempting to use culture as a tool for predicting the behaviors of individual students. They want to know what strategies are most likely to work with [fill in the blank social group] students, but this is nearly always the wrong question to ask.

Let me illustrate the point another way. All the plant enthusiasts reading this will recognize Figure 4.2 as fern leaves. Ferns are a great example of fractals. Fractals are a sample of a larger entity, each part of which has

Figure 4.2 What kind of leaf is this?

Source: Christine/Adobe Stock

the same proportional features and characteristics as the whole. We teachers see students differently than administrators and policymakers if for no other reason than our micro-level positions relative to their experience in school. Teachers know kids not by their socio-ethnolinguistic identifiers. We know them by their stories. And when a teacher knows the story of a single kiddo, you know that their unique sense of self can never be accurately reduced to any stereotyped expectation of their character or interests.

Each person we have ever had in our classroom is something profoundly more than a caricature or cardboard cutout of a larger social group. When you know classrooms, and when you know students, it's difficult to consider them as fractal members of larger people groups—in fact, that manner of categorizing is ultimately harmful to our most vulnerable students who especially need to be uniquely seen and valued for them to be able to perceive the opportunities of school as worthy of their investment.

Trying to understand the evolution of human anatomy, physiology, and psychology without considering Gene-Culture Coevolution would be like studying the evolution of fish while ignoring the fact that fish live, and evolved, underwater (Henrich, 2020). But we aren't studying evolution; we're studying teaching and learning. When viewing patterns of students' engagement and achievement with a macro-level lens, it is easy to be tempted into believing that there are group characteristics that are predictive of individual dispositions and behaviors. Culture is, however, an evolving product of populations of human brains, and at the macro-level, culture is interwoven with genetics and environment. To ask whether behavior is determined by culture, genes, or environment is a dangerous oversimplification which easily leads down the ill-fated road of limiting stereotypes. Thus, the key to understanding how humans learn lies in an appreciation for the process, not in the products of that process (Richerson & Boyd, 2008; Henrich, 2016).

The task of teaching in the 21st century is to facilitate learning experiences that students perceive as responsive to their interests and identities. The classroom spaces in which this task is to be carried out are rich in racial, ethnic, linguistic, and cultural diversity. Culturally responsive teaching that closes Equity gaps is devoted to designing opportunities that invite the cultural fluencies of students in ways that do not disadvantage some relative to the advantage of others.

Instead of thinking about the specific group features of culture, it's more useful to ask what culture does. To understand how cultural fluency serves the individual gives much greater insight into the ways in which culture can be leveraged in responsive learning environments. This requires a depth of understanding that will invariably include heightened proficiencies in the interpretation of social-group cultural frames of reference— but what is most useful is a nimble capacity for recognizing how culture informs and influences the human experience broadly. An emphasis on the specific features of a cultural group may inadvertently result in stereotyping of individual students. It's easy to stereotype when searching for the predictable according to cultural edicts and folklorish ways of thinking. The understanding of what culture does is more useful for the artful design of opportunities to learn which empower students to draw from the funds of knowledge and cultural fluencies available to them. We owe all our students the opportunities to learn that draw on their identities both as members of people groups and also as unique and individual people.

All Learning (and Intelligence) Is Cultural—What's Worth Understanding?

In the first part of this chapter, I asked: *What does it mean to understand?* But given the role of culture in the human experience, and specifically, its relation to thinking and intelligence, another (possibly more relevant) question we are required to consider is: *What is worth understanding?*

This question—*What is worth understanding?*—brings together the issues of intelligence and identity because the answers to this question depend on the cognitive niche and cultural inheritance of the individual.

It's good to flesh this out.

Thinking allows for learning. The ability to learn is what we may call intelligence. For our teaching purposes, we can draw from the model of the Cognition Core Hypothesis and say that intelligence is the capacity for locating the *essence* of a situation or a thing, and thinking is the analogy-making process that allows for identifying that essence.

We learn to think in the social spaces where we learn to *human (v)*. We negotiate our identities in the social spaces where we seek shared understandings through collective conceptual schema and experiences with others in our cultural groups. Our identities as learners and teachers are impossible to disentangle from our cultural identities. And so, all learning is cultural. For that matter, all teaching is cultural too. Still, we can unpack this further.

First, a quick review of neuroplasticity—the process through which the brain rewires itself so that it can be most efficient in the storing and retrieval of information necessary for survival. Starting from birth, as information travels from the environment into the newborn brain, some neurons fire together more frequently than others, causing gradual cognitive, neurological, and anatomical brain changes. These changes in developing brains amount to higher complexity as neural connections are tuned and pruned so the brain can effectively perform its primary purposes of managing the body's basic budgeting needs and steering clear of dangers in the environment. Taken together, this continuous organizing, reinforcing, and reconfiguring of neural networks so that the brain can efficiently function as a single, massive, and flexible unit is what is generally referred to as *neuroplasticity* (Barrett, 2020).

Lisa Feldman Barrett (2020) describes our highly complex brain network of 128 billion neurons as something like an airline's network system for routing flights. Most major airlines organize their flight schedules using a hub network system, or more accurately, a hub-and-spoke system (see Figure 4.3). A hub is a central airport that flights are routed through, and spokes are the airways that planes follow out of the hub airport. Many airlines have multiple hubs that expand the scale and increase the capacity for meeting travelers' demands for air traffic. The hub system is flexible and scalable, and it forms the backbone of domestic and international travel. It allows all airports, even the tiny ones, to participate in the global network of airports. Your brain network is organized in much the same way. Its neurons are grouped into clusters that are like 128 billion airports networked through hubs for maximum efficiency.

Figure 4.3 A hub network system is flexible and scalable.

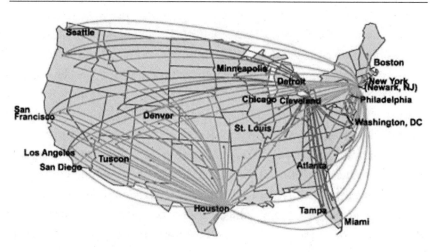

This hub analogy is helpful for understanding a cognitive science concept called *degeneracy*. *Degeneracy* means that the same cognitive outcome can be reached in multiple ways (Price & Friston, 2002; Seifert et al., 2016). A brain doesn't store memories like files in a cabinet—it reconstructs them on demand through electrical and chemical reactions. The retrieval of memories and understandings is really assembling. Your brain assembles each instance of retrieval with a different combination of neural-chemical reactions much like alternate flight routes to the same destination (Barrett, 2020). Every time we take a cognitive trip to our memory bank, we are uniquely assembling based on the context in which the memory was formed and also the specific moment in which the memory is retrieved. Further, every person assembles their memories and understandings of even the most mainstream, broadly known concepts with a different neuro-combination of electrical and chemical reactions than anyone else.

Emotion functions similarly (Barrett, 2020; Gendron et al., 2020). Each time you feel happy, for example, your brain could be creating that experience of affect using different combinations of neurons—likewise for every instance of sadness, fear, and every other emotion you've ever felt. Even when two instances feel the same, they aren't necessarily constructed in the same way.

This hub analogy is useful for a couple of reasons. First, degeneracy tells us something about the nature of the brain. It means the foundation for memory (and understandings) is the conceptual imprint of the experience of learning and not simply the rote recall of information (facts, dates, details, algorithms, etc.). We can say that we know something not merely because we can recite information associated with the learning target, but rather because we have integrated the information into a conceptual understanding that is shaped and colored by affect and personal cognitive style. The conceptual imprint of an understanding, integrated with emotion and information, is accessible through more connection points than the mere memory of facts, dates, details, and algorithms alone.

But let's take this hub analogy even further: Thinking is like air travel because thinking leads to understandings—the destinations we seek. A rewarding travel experience is worth the trouble because it offers up the potential for experience that is meaningful to the traveler in some way. Too often, the strategy teachers adopt in engaging their most vulnerable and/or reluctant learners is to make the flight path easy to follow by prescribing every step along the way. This, however, deprives students of the experience of thinking, which makes the destination decidedly less memorable. The experience of the destination is most valuable to our students when they are able to use their own flight routes to make the trip. They are best able to appreciate the *essence* of the space, event, persons, or landmark when they've reached the destination by making the connections to their cultural fluencies and inheritances so that they aren't dependent on others to schedule their travel plans.

Degeneracy reminds us that brains wire and rewire themselves constantly; therefore, we aren't teaching *the path* to the understanding (as if there were only one way). Rather, we're teaching students *how* to make flight plans. We're teaching students how to forge pathways by enlisting their own cognitive niches and cultural repertoires.

Intelligence is the cognitive capacity to perceive the essential, and social learning is the inference-making process of discerning meaning from the behaviors and artifacts within specific social spaces and cultural niches. Through shared attention and social learning, we are able to determine which parts of the environment warrant our attention; and by extension, knowledge and ways of being flow efficiently from generation to generation. Thus, intelligence is a relative feature of humanity—not in terms of some people being more or less intelligent than others, but that intelligence is relative considering the environmental and cognitive niches in which intelligence is developed and performed. Mentalizing capacities can be said to be part of a cultural inheritance—as in, having been sufficiently indoctrinated in a given social space provides access to some inferencing and essence-finding abilities that are uniquely applied among those group affiliates. It is more important in some social spaces than others to understand concepts in particular ways.

Within any cultural group, intelligence is based on the shared norms, concepts, and references that are the content of cultural repertoires; and fluency is intelligence with material value to the individual. The individual leverages their cultural intelligence along with their personal cognitive style in order to understand and/or to convey understanding within the social context of the group. Cultural fluency affords opportunities to cognitively engage in social spaces that are otherwise not possible. Since these fluencies are developed in specific niches, we can say that there are tendencies in how members of social groups are likely to process certain information; but there are also individual dispositions within the groups that further delineate the variety of pathways for thinking and understanding.

Thinking leads to understandings. The better the quality of the thinking, the better the quality of the subsequent understandings. We teachers seek to tap into our students' cultural repertoires in order to activate the connections that bridge what they know with the understandings we want for them to learn. I argue that the goal of brilliant teaching is to instruct students on *how* to think and not *what* to think. In this hub analogy, to teach students *what* to think would be like handing them a flight plan that outlines the path and transfer points to reach a destination, but to teach students *how* to think requires that they be empowered to reach the destination via a flight pattern of their own design.

Culturally responsive teaching *isn't* just good teaching because it isn't possible to teach well with a willful cultural ignorance without privileging some students relative to others. Our pedagogy is neither impartial nor unbiased because all learning is deeply cultural. Our concepts, the information which comprises our understanding of the world and all meaning in every way, are developed in the context of our environmental, cultural, and cognitive niches.

So, we require some conceptual framework for what it means to think and also what it means to understand; and further, we must be able to articulate and justify from the perspective of our students *what is worth understanding*. The best way to answer that question is to use your understanding of culture to design learning experiences with many possibilities for the conceptual pathways that students may assemble in coming to relationship with the essence of the understandings at the heart of your instruction.

We can ask: *What does it mean to understand?* But we should also be asking: *What is worth understanding?* This question considers intelligence and identity because *What is worth understanding?* is a relative question. Who you are as a cultural being is a function of what you have been socialized to believe is worth understanding. What makes you human are these socially developed, culturally motivated learning targets. Hence, all learning, and all intelligence for that matter, is cultural.

Integrated Understandings

When we teachers operate with a deeper sense of how culture influences students' thinking, we can better design learning experiences such that their cultural fluencies are useful to them in their engagement, which is a more empowering way to learn. We can more regularly create opportunities for our students to think while drawing on their assets and cultural inheritances when we teach for integrated understandings and not just specialistic knowledge.

An integrated understanding is an amalgamation, an arrangement of concepts that leverages intelligence at least as much as the *intellect*; and as I've attempted to show in the first part of this book, intelligence is a culturally relative construct—and further, culture is an influencer and arbiter of intelligence.

I think there are important distinctions to be made between intelligence and intellect. To merely cultivate the intellect, which is to develop specialistic knowledge, does not in and of itself result in intelligence. Intelligence values the capacity to feel as well as to reason; it is the integration of logic and affect. The intellect is satisfied with theories and explanations, but intelligence is not.

When I think of intellect, I think of specialistic knowledge. What is specialistic knowledge? A dictionary definition of *specialistic* is:

1. of or related to or characteristic of specialists
2. showing focused training; developed or designed for a special activity or function

Specialistic knowledge favors the technical. It's the ability to list and delineate the components of a multipart whole—but generally in fragmented terms. Specialistic knowledge tends to denote a focus primarily on a particular subject or activity, a finely tuned skill in a specific and restricted field. Knowledge that isn't integrated is specialistic. The accumulation of facts and the development of specialistic skill—which some think of as education—is, however, deprived of the fullness of integrated understandings because the whole cannot be understood through the part.

What is an integrated understanding?

An integrated understanding acknowledges the whole. An integrated understanding is useful and durable. An integrated understanding incorporates reason and affect. An integrated understanding is relevant within a range of schema and content areas. An integrated understanding connects, relates, and unifies concepts in various situations. An integrated understanding is performative and can be demonstrated by exploring, identifying, organizing, and synthesizing ideas and information to describe and solve problems. An integrated understanding is empowering because it is accessible through a range of cultural fluencies. An integrated understanding illustrates relationship with other specialistic parts of the whole. An integrated understanding expands self-knowledge. An integrated understanding clarifies one's mental models for solving problems. An integrated understanding is meaningful and provides traction for further understandings. An integrated understanding is life-changing.

Figure 4.4 is a brief comparison of the attributes of integrated and specialistic thinking/understandings:

This is not to say that specialistic knowledge is without value, but the value is incomplete outside of the context of integrated understandings. While most fields require a knowledge of facts—the Periodic Table comes to mind—it is most important to facilitate and assess what students know how to do with those facts (Luquet, 2015).

The highest function of education is to bring about individuals who are capable of integrated thinking and thus dealing with life as a whole. Integrated understandings produce the kind of comprehension to know one's

Figure 4.4 Integrated vs Specialistic Thinking.

INTEGRATED	SPECIALISTIC
1. artful	1. algorithmic
2. adaptive	2. technical
3. rigorous	3. difficult
4. nuanced	4. obvious
5. whole	5. segmented
6. theme	6. summary
7. comprehend	7. remember
8. improvisation	8. repetition
9. eras	9. dates
10. contextual	10. absolute

ignorance and how one's patterns of thought and actions inform as well as prejudice understanding. It develops self-knowledge, the learned skill of self-consciously questioning our understandings and ways of thinking in order to advance them. The more you know yourself, the more clarity there is. Concepts that can be understood through reason alone offer a limited understanding until and unless they are married to affect, the soft tissue of understandings, the part that shifts in tone and degree in order to match context. It is at this level of thinking that one's intelligence allows for the grasping of a full, meaningful comprehension, for an understanding that's worth the effort in coming to know.

The Equity Case for Culturally Responsive Education

> "The pressures of daily life require us, force us, to talk about events at the level on which we directly perceive them. Access at that level is what our sensory organs, our language, and our culture provide us with"
>
> (Hofstadter, 2007).

In Chapter 2, I reviewed Equity's origin story and named its three major pillars (i.e., measured by outputs, quality and effective opportunities to learn, and differences do not equal deficits). Equity is neither a new idea nor one that is passively defined. Equity is a concept with roots in the very essence of the American ethos. One could say that Equity is a product of social philosophizing, the result of much deliberation at many levels of abstraction. Most importantly in terms of the arguments of this book, Equity is the guiding principle for American education. And so the question is: *What does Equity require of schools?*

There is Equity work to be done at the policy level, for sure. Those who are responsible for executive-level decisions at the school, district, regional, and state level are all accountable for contributing (good or bad) to the practice environment in which teaching and learning occur. My own view is biased by the profound respect and appreciation I have for the teachers whose work is so immediate and pivotal for students. I am fully aware that the classroom conditions for teaching are impacted in all sorts of ways, directly and indirectly, by administrator-level decisions made in superintendent cabinet and school board spaces. But I think it's important to be reminded that any given student enrolled in an American public school district can go through 13 years in the system and never know the superintendents' or any board members' names, but there will be 50 or so people—mostly teachers—who can influence and empower that kiddo incalculably. The question for policymakers is how can the systems and structures evolve to match the support needed for teachers to meet the needs of our students? Whatever we are able to discover to more equitably affect the experiences of children will need to be implemented by teachers.

The center of gravity of Equity work must be teaching or we risk missing the whole point. I would argue that the point of Equity work in education is to provide learning opportunities for students that are responsive to them as individual people and empowering through fair and meaningful opportunities to draw on the fluencies and funds of knowledge shared by their social groups. If schools are to empower students, students must be empowered through actual learning. Students are cheated when they don't learn the tools to prepare them for the world that awaits. An empowering education positions communities—all communities—to profit from the talent within.

Culturally Responsive Education (CRE) is a mental model that is useful for identifying themes and tools of practice for closing opportunity gaps. The CRE mental model isn't a prescription, but rather a heuristic device that allows for the centering of students in the design of instruction while emphasizing rigor and other principles consistent with the most current understandings of culture and neurocognitive human tendencies. It's also a kind of interrogative apparatus for philosophizing in the context of planning classroom learning experiences.

Though firmly based in cognitive and social science principles, CRE resists simple formulaic approaches, which is why I think of it as an art. CRE is not a laundry list of strategies, nor is it a program specific to any particular population of students. It's an approach that takes cognitive science, learning theory, cultural psychology, and sociology of schooling into consideration in order to support teachers in designing rich and meaningful opportunities for students to learn. Our artmaking pedagogical task is to create opportunities for students to think, to employ their intelligence toward learning experiences in which they can bridge and expand their conceptual schema in meaningful ways. An empowered learner can use their intelligence—which by definition includes their cultural fluencies—in the interest of building and demonstrating their competencies in school.

There is an artistic sensibility in the spirit of teaching that is indispensable for the closing of opportunity, performance, and achievement gaps among students, and that sensibility is time-, space-, and audience-specific. Our classrooms are spaces where students are learning about content and also learning about the processes of learning. When our students are impacted by both the content as well as the experience of learning, they become motivated to learn more because they have the tools to do so. Knowing the process of learning allows our students to use their cultural fluencies to extend their thinking, to make real-world investigations of the concepts learned, to problem solve and consider multiple conditions of the skills and concepts, to apply their thinking in nonroutine manipulations across content areas and with multiple sources (Hess et al., 2009). In a culturally responsive classroom, it is nearly impossible to predict all the different combinations of understandings that may emerge.

Pedagogy that is intended to be equitable leverages the awareness of culture, race, ethnicity, gender, (dis)ability, and other social identity markers that shape the perceptions of educational opportunities in order to design learning experiences that empower students to draw on their backgrounds, identities, and cultural fluencies (Stembridge, 2019). To understand anything deeply is a function of culture. I don't think the meaning of things is entirely subjective, but I do think nothing is understood without the lens of culture. *Opportunity* is the *product* of Equity, and the *craft* of Equity in education *is* culturally responsive teaching.

NOTES ON ARTMAKING: COMPOSITION

To learn from any work of art, one must investigate its composition. By *composition*, I am generally referring to the arrangement of things, and the ways in which they are assembled for the purpose of creating an experience for the audience. *Arrange* is a word that stands out in how composition might be explained. It speaks to the design of the piece to be intentional in how the various elements relate to the others within the larger context of the whole. I am a fan of many sorts of artistic expression, and I especially enjoy spending time with brilliant paintings. There are, of course, many elements of paintings and many ways to appreciate them, but I often advise people to begin their inquiry by noticing the artist's use of line, form, and color. I'll look at a painting and give thought to what is initially calling for my attention? What are the artistic choices? Are there deep, pronounced lines that give shape to some recognizable (or unrecognizable) form? Are the colors bold or muted? Does the piece project a particular mood? What technical skill is entailed? What historical influences are evident? What is the relevance of the subject? I might try to imagine what the first touch of the brush to the canvas was. Was it some strong distinctive line? A short, colorful stroke of the brush? These are all elements of composition that give us insight into the artist's mind and their intent for the piece.

I want to ask similar questions about the composition of learning experiences. How do teachers arrange the pieces for an effective learning experience? What tools do they use? What is the emotional tone of the learning experience? How does the instruction create and sustain momentum? How might we define the aesthetic of the learning experience? *What is the relevance of the subject?*

Teachers re-envision, re-pattern, and re-purpose—just like the artist. The central premise of my argument as it pertains to pedagogy is that where brilliant art is made with paint or unmolded clay or cameras or through story-telling or song, brilliant teaching makes art through the medium of experience. Teaching that is artful is intentional in terms of style, process, subject, and opportunities for students to leverage their cultural fluencies. This is the essence of artmaking and brilliant teaching that has the potential to close Equity gaps.

CHAPTER NOTES

1. This is worth mentioning now, and we'll return to this in greater depth in Chapter 9 where we discuss assessments. We must be clear about what our definition of *intelligence* entails because assessments should give us authentic evidence that the education students are receiving is, in fact, furthering their abilities to survive in the modern social, political, and economic environment. An education that does not prepare one to survive is not only of poor quality, but the time and effort spent acquiring it amounts to a kind of opportunity cost (i.e., the students would've been better off had they allocated their resources toward developing the actual abilities which are relevant to their material lives).

2. Although jumping up the ladder of abstraction rung-by-rung may, in some cases, be a sign of intelligence and fluid thinking, if it is taken too far, it becomes a vacuous and frivolous game—and playing such a game with even the wisest of proverbs reveals an impoverished and superficial understanding of it. Indeed, in the end, an excess of abstraction winds up being similar to an excess of literality (Hofstadter & Sander, 2013).

3. We pluralize single-entity concepts, we combine concepts, we employ conceptual frames of reference, and we bridge concepts to extend and create new concepts. Although concepts expand by seeing new instances, some concepts are single instances, and yet they can still spread and blend into other conceptual spaces:

"Lebron James is the Michael Jordan of today's NBA."

"Pablo Picasso is the Michael Jordan of modern art."

4. For the purposes of the arguments I make in this book, I am focusing on culture and cultural identity as defined in terms of socio-ethnolinguistic group fluencies. This is not to imply that the categories listed in Figure 4.1 are exhaustive. These are, however, the socio-ethnolinguistic categories of cultural identity that have been the focus of most philosophical debate regarding opportunity in education. It's also true that these are the groupings that have been the focus of most study and analysis in student performance and achievement outcomes.

5. Other categories of considerations for the philosophizing of social groups may include:

The nature of reality: What is the nature of ultimate reality? What is the nature of humanity, and what is the human relation to ultimate reality?

The nature of knowledge: What is knowledge? What is truth? What are the limits of knowledge? What is the relation of knowing to that which is known?

The nature of corrective reasoning: What are the prevailing models and premises for deductive and inductive logic? How is language and communication used to convey meaning? What are the general expectations associated with problem-solving practices? What are the pathways to critical inquiry?

The nature of value: What is good and right? What is wrong and bad? What is the nature of beauty? What is the nature of ugliness? (Tesconi, 1975).

PART TWO

THE CULTURALLY RESPONSIVE ARTMAKING TEACHER (IN) YOU

"If you teach, you know that you gain as much from the interchange as do your students. . . . It allows you to draw energy from young minds filled with potential. It gives you a role in shaping the next generation of art. It keeps you alive. Teaching is part of the process of being an artist."

—David Bayles and Ted Orland

CHAPTER 5

12 Days
of Instruction

"The role of an artist is to look at the world as it is and to imagine alternate possibilities but also to heighten what actually is. What can I do as an artist that hasn't been done before? Look closer."

—Kehinde Wiley

SEATING CHARTS, VOLCANOES, AND DIFFERENT GLIMPSES OF THEMSELVES

Raucous might be a good word for it. Certainly not a single student was even acknowledging the attempts to get the class started. The noise rolled into the hallway. Turning to a student with a calm and measured tone, Mr. Derain asked: "Is this what it's always like in here? Is this what we do? Just ignore the teacher?" The question wasn't intended to be taken literally. He wasn't expecting a response. Rather, he was musing aloud as he looked over the classroom, taking stock of the situation and pondering his next move.

And there was a lot to take stock of. . . . Mr. Derain was filling a gap. Having started the year in the role of teacher-leader with one prep and coaching responsibilities in the science department, he'd been excited to teach two sections of 8th-grade physics and use the rest of his time to coach his team of eight colleagues. The teacher who had been teaching this section of chemistry, however, took a leave the week before—which felt from the first mention to be something more permanent than that. Rather than have this class be exposed to a rotating cast of subs and teachers pulled from their planning periods, Mr. Derain volunteered to cover until the end of the semester when the most appropriate solution for going forward could be decided.

This grade 6–12 public school was, like every school in the district, in the midst of a year unlike any other of recent memory—the first school year following a global pandemic. The tasks of teaching proved especially challenging, and Mr. Derain was not immune to the vexations of the situation. What's more, Mr. Derain's building presented an additional layer of complications. Many teachers spoke of feeling unsafe in the building and a lack of confidence in the school's administration. Several students from the district had been shot on or near campuses in the previous weeks, and just a few days prior, the school had been placed on security lockdown while the parking lot was searched for weapons, which raised tensions among students and staff.

At that moment, of the 28 students in the classroom, exactly none were moved by Mr. Derain's fervent attempts to gather their attention. The first Tuesday of December, Mr. Derain had been with this group of 10th graders for a grand total of five days. They had ignored him the same way his first day with them. There had been several productive days since, and he thought they had taken a step forward—but there was no evidence of such progress now. Nothing. The teacher who would claim to be disaffected in these scenarios is either lying, checked out, or altogether delusional. It's frustrating to be ignored when you're trying to teach.

To Mr. Derain's surprise, the student responded to his question about ignoring teachers: *Yeah, usually. You've gotta be meaner, stricter.*

AD: You mean, like a seating chart?

Wanting to recant his answer, which is not to say it was anything less than his most truthful response, the student attempted to backtrack, *Uh, yeah, but not for my table. For everybody else.* But Mr. Derain was already moving toward his desk.

AD: So I go to the front of the room, and I'm not saying anything. My laptop is projecting on the screen so I pull up the seating chart maker, and I start making a seating chart. And it's got their pictures on it, but so many kids haven't taken a picture since like the 6th grade so it's got their little kid pictures up there, and that grabs their attention; and so they're like, *Ohhh, look at so and so. Oh that's you!* So they're paying attention to the board, but I'm still not saying anything.

Through the utter chaos of students' cross-talk, shouting, and near total disregard for the presence of Mr. Derain, one solitary voice rang out above all the clamor: *What's he doing?* Another voice pierces through the cluttered sound in response: *He's making a seating chart!*

And almost in unison, an adolescent chorus of *Awww, man!* sang out across the room.

AD: And so I keep making it, and they're still commenting on each other's pictures. Then I get up, and I just start reading off the seating chart. Ok, this person, you're sitting here. This person, you're sitting here. I start going through it. Partly to my surprise, they start getting up to move, kinda grumbling—but then I'm like (extending his arms, palms facing outward) "Orrrr!" And they all freeze. "You can keep your spots, stay where you're seated, aaaand you can listen to me and take the notes."

Yeah, yeah let's do that!

AD: "Alright. So here's what we're gonna do. We're gonna set up this experiment. You're gonna copy it down, and if we can listen to it, we can keep our seats." AND THEY DID IT!

AD: So I start talking a little bit, and some kids start talking, and I'm like, "I don't know. . . ." To which students then begin the cross-talk again, but this time, it's *Shut up! Listen. We want to stay in our seats. Stop talking.*

AD: We get through the mini-lecture, they're taking their notes, again a couple of times kids start talking, I kinda stop and look and wait, and other kids shush them.

AD: So I write down: How does _____ affect _____? And the kids are like: *What do we write in the blanks?* I'm like, "That's what we're gonna get to. Just write a blank line." And they're looking at me like, *This is stupid,* but they're doing it.

AD: "In these two blanks, you're going to write down your independent variable and your dependent variable, IV and DV." And they're like *What's that?*

AD: "Just write it down."

They do.

AD: "What we're thinking about today is how the ingredients affect a volcano and its products." And they're like:

Are we making volcanoes?
AD: "Yeah."
Today?
AD: "Yeah, I've got the materials right behind me."

In all of the commotion, none of the students had noticed that Mr. Derain had prepared the experiments.

AD: "But we need a T-chart. Our independent variable, the ingredients, go on the left. Our dependent variable, our products, go on the right. So let's write down our three independent variable ingredients, baking soda and vinegar, our first IV. Our second IV is baking soda, vinegar, and soap. And our third IV is vinegar, soap and water."

With near incredulity, the students ask, *Are we doing three volcanoes?*

AD: "Yeah. Each table gets to do three volcanoes." These are sophomores and they're jacked. Super excited!

Mr. Derain had already observed for himself that this group had very little bandwidth for lectures of any kind, but he found that they could engage well with hands-on activities.

AD: I know from my own science upbringing that 99% of the procedures are "follow this experiment exactly," which makes sense in, ya know . . . vaccine trials. But if we're trying to learn how to actually do experiments, then that kind of thinking isn't served by DOK 1 procedures. So, I designed the experiment purposefully for this.

As much as we teachers would like to think that our students will hold on to our every word, it's more likely they will remember the emotional experience of the classroom and the connection with their learning process. Mr. Derain wanted to get his students hooked on the thrill of science discovery, and so he needed his students to have a strong feel for the concept of experimentation (Luquet, 2015; Keller et al., 2014).

AD: All right, we need to get them to experiment. So my plan was to get them introduced to the basic structure of a science experiment which for me is, you have a question: *How does blank affect blank?* and then you've got your T-chart. And once you've got that, you can start. Because normally, science instruction is (lifting his hands in the air in an expression of exasperation), you have to have your hypothesis, and then you write your procedures, and then you deal with design details, and it's boring! And it's not really applicable to everyone in life. So I wanted them to see that once you've got your variables and your T-chart, you can start collecting data. I also wanted them to see that once I listen to Mr. Derain, cool stuff starts happening. So I had a super short experiment setup and mini-lecture. But none of them have their notebooks. So I also want to get them taking notes, you know—develop some basic classroom routines.

This isn't exactly one of those Hollywood happily-ever-after movie endings where the students are transformed into perfect scholars by the experience of making volcanoes—changed forever after having learned to incorporate the concepts of independent and dependent variables into their schema for making scientific inferences. In the reality of Mr. Derain's classroom, the struggle to engage this 10th-grade chemistry class continued through the end of the semester, at which time the students were separated and dispersed into other sections. On this day, though, the classroom was utterly consumed with engagement.

AD: They're into it. They're having fun. And at one point, a student says to me, *Can we do more stuff like this?*, which is kind of a theme for this class. Like this isn't groundbreaking stuff. We're not synthesizing DNA, but they're into it because this isn't something that they've been getting for at least the last two years, ya know, with last year being remote. . . . So we go from not listening at all, just complete disregard for what's going on in here, to everyone is engaged, making their volcanoes, feeling like scientists.

Only one week after the volcano experiment, however, Mr. Derain started the class off successfully with a hands-on activity. Students were engaged, on topic, and the mood was high throughout the room. But when he tried to shift their attention to a mini-lecture, he got nothing! No engagement. No attention.

AD: It got rough for that one. That was pretty discouraging. I don't know if *discouraging* is the right word, but it kind of shook me a little bit. Which is funny in retrospect because now I can see we had the beginnings for good stuff. But at the time, I was really discouraged and almost . . . a little resentful. It was a struggle. The students aren't meeting me halfway here. They liked the framing experience, but we weren't getting anywhere with the content connections.

But there were clear victories. Just one day of volcano making and many students were able to get a different glimpse of themselves in relation to school.

AD: And, I wrote this down. One of my kids whom I'd seen have an extremely antagonistic relationship with the previous teacher came up to me at the end of class and said, *Mr. I did a lot of work today!* He was excited about it and proud about it. And I said, "I saw! You did!" Because he had been making sure he got everything filled out and working through everything. He recognized that he had done a lot of work compared to what he used to do.

WEEK 1: PLANNING (STRUCTURE AND PROCESS)

In addition to picking up a section of 10th-grade chemistry, Mr. Derain committed to take the two sections of biology that had also been part of the previous teacher's schedule; this teacher would go on to resign to take another teaching position out-of-district, one of ten teachers to leave the building before the end of the school year. With the decision to add these additional preps, Mr. Derain would now have three: 10th-grade chemistry, two sections of biology (11th and 12th grade), along with the two sections of 8th-grade physics that had been his classes from the start of the school year. Twelve days of instruction over 3 weeks, between Thanksgiving and the end of the calendar year—with one teacher work day, and one day when Mr. Derain had previously scheduled to be out of the building to attend to a medical procedure of a parent, and not counting the very last day before winter break, the day on which grades are due. Three preps, five sections, one planning period. It felt something like a high-wire act.

AD: So the Friday before Thanksgiving break, because again, I was supposed to be teaching only two classes at that point, I took the whole afternoon and sat down, and kinda outlined the storyline for each unit. To teach the way I wanted to, I knew I would basically have to outline a whole year, and then I'd have to think about where this unit would fit. So I got some information from the kids about what they had hopefully covered so far.

I was able to think through the rest of the year in 10-day chunks. So really, we've got a standard for this chunk of time, and then we've got four per quarter. . . . So even though I'm only teaching these classes for just 3 weeks, really 12 days, I need to know what they covered so far. Not what have they covered . . . Where are they in the story? And what's still coming in the story for me to be able to plan a unit? And you know, it sounds like a lot—it was deep thinking—but it didn't take that much time. Then I had to think with those big ideas and write a story within it.

When planning for the two sections of biology, in particular, Mr. Derain recalls: "Here were a group of students that were willing to learn and wanted to learn after a pandemic year, a year and a half, two years at this point . . . and there was gonna be no instruction, a complete lack of science instruction for a month."

Figure 5.1 CRE Mental Model.

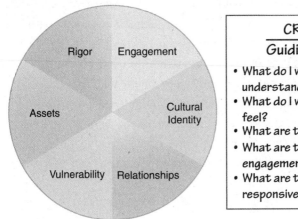

Rigor   Engagement

Assets   Cultural Identity

Vulnerability   Relationships

CRE Planning
Guiding Questions

- What do I want students to understand?
- What do I want students to feel?
- What are the targets for rigor?
- What are the indicators for engagement?
- What are the opportunities to be responsive?

Stepping in to teach these classes, Mr. Derain returned to his go-to method for planning, which is described in *Culturally Responsive Education in the Classroom: An Equity Framework for Pedagogy* (Stembridge, 2019).

AD: And then what I do for each unit is I have my CRE questions, my assessments, and my unit outline. So I had this vision of a 10'ish day unit. What I've landed on is a responsive hook slash launch [i.e., framing experience], and then kind of a two-phase experiment part. There's a mini-lecture that goes with that responsive hook slash launch and then an assessment. And then there's an experimental portion of the unit. The first one is teacher-directed so there's a chance for some direct instruction—kind of like modeling, but it still gives the kids a chance to do the experiment. I also get to talk about experimenting and the scientific process within the standard, as well. And so I kinda give them the baseline of the experiment, and then they get a second round. I tell them, "Here's how the formal science part works. And now I want you to remix it, and make it your own." So it sets them up to experiment within the big concept that I want them thinking about. After we do the more concept-based experiments, there's a second portion where

Figure 5.2 CRE questions.

CRE Questions
What do you want students to understand?
- The challenge of design is to optimize within constraints
- Constraints often drive design

What do you want students to feel?
- Hopeful
- Empowered
- Eager

What are the targets for rigor?
- Create DOK4/Understand DOK4
  - Synthesize information across multiple sources or texts
  - Relate mathematical or scientific concepts to other content areas, other domains, or other concepts

What are the indicators of engagement?
- Cognitive
  - processing multiple factors and possible explanations
- Affective
  - excitedly communicating ideas for explanations
- Behavioral
  - completing work within allotted time
  - lower phone use
  - striving for higher achievement in tasks

What are the opportunities to be responsive?
- Students explaining cause-and-effect relationships
- Students explaining a complex situation with multiple factors
- Students explaining someone's behavior or decisions

I'm re-teaching concepts based on what I know that students are missing from the responsive performative assessments, and then we get into more iterative practice around the concept. So that's the overall structure.

Living My Best Life

The NGSS (Next Generation Science Standards) standard for the biology unit Mr. Derain is teaching is: Use mathematical and/or computational representations to support explanations of factors that affect carrying capacity of ecosystems at different scales.[1]

Figure 5.3 Assessments.

Assessments
- Recurring questions
  - What do I need to live my best life? How can I get it?
- Products
  - Sequencing or prototypes and measured results

Six facets of understanding (Wiggins & McTighe, 1998):
1. EXPLAIN . . .
   Different graphs depicting the interactions with constraints/limiting factors
2. INTERPRET . . .
   Tell the story of the factors impacting the populations/success of the design
3. APPLY THE UNDERSTANDING BY . . .
   Design multiple iterations of something and display the results as a function of the constraints
   Observe the interactions of limiting factors on a real-world population
4. SEE FROM THE POINTS OF VIEW THAT . . .
   Describe the "positive" and "negative" impacts of limiting factors and carrying capacity
5. EMPATHIZE WITH . . .
   A specific member of a population interacting with limiting factor
6. OVERCOME THE NAIVE OR BIASED IDEA THAT . . .
   Constraints are static

Beginning within that content standard, Mr. Derain searches for what he calls the *life-changing understanding*—the kind of insight that allows one to see and understand some part of the world in a paradigm-shifting sort of way. He then seeks to build course-long storylines into which he can incorporate unit-focused essential questions.

AD: I wanted to find the storylines within the standards just for me because there are storyline progressions out there. NGSS puts that out there. But I wanted ones that came from me with my knowledge of the kids. My favorite CRE planning question has always been "What do I want students to understand?" because I really like to pull out that essence-understanding. And so I was thinking, what is the essence of this type of science? Basically, it's optimizing design within constraints, the idea that constraints often drive design within environments. There's limiting factors within our environment that determine the populations of living things that can live there. And then those things interact.

Mr. Derain's big-picture storyline for biology is: *How do I live my best life?* Or really: *How does any living organism live its best life?* In addition to planning for the life-changing, biology understanding, Mr. Derain also has goals for the emotional composition of the unit-long learning experience.

> AD: I want them to feel hopeful, empowered, and eager, like they can look at a complex situation, and look at constraints, and feel like *I can make this work*. For rigor, we'll be synthesizing information across multiple sources or texts. They'll be looking at multiple factors giving them information about situations within any given ecosystem.

In Mr. Derain's planning, he conceptualizes his assessment strategies by considering what Wiggins and McTighe called the "six facets of understanding: explanation, application, interpretation, perspective, empathy, and self-knowledge." Before he plans out the technical details of how his students will demonstrate their understanding, he brainstorms what the various dimensions of students' understandings might look like. His goal is to expand his students' opportunities to show their competence rather than restrict them unnecessarily.

What Would You Do?

Mr. Derain showed a *What would you do?* (WWYD) video from YouTube and had the students answer the following questions in small group discussions and gave raffle tickets to the most thoughtful responses that made the connection between constraints and decision making:

What would you do?

What are the constraints in this situation?

How do the constraints influence the decision?

He used the discussion to set up his first mini-lecture of the unit in which he defined *constraints* and linked it to design. He wanted his students to know that without constraints, design is often severely limited.

Figure 5.4 Week 1, Day 1 Mini-lecture notes.

Mini-lecture
- Purpose of Bio
- Big Question we are thinking about
- Defining *constraints*
- Quote about constraints leading to creative solutions
- Practice together with the WWYD
- "Without constraints, design cannot happen."
- "The first stage of the design process is often discovering which constraints are important."

AD: There's *WWYD* scenarios. Same three questions. And then I want them to pull a scenario from their life where they had to make a decision with a constraint.

Mr. Derain wanted his students thinking as much as possible about how constraints affect decision making in specific environments, and he wanted his students to be able to draw from their cultural repertoires and life experiences in doing so because their capacity for finding the situational analogies is the substance of an understanding. As such, he moved his students progressively from thinking about *WWYD* scenarios to situations in their own lives and ultimately into scenarios they might conjure up from nature. All of this was a precursor to the first experiment of the unit, a virtual simulation of limiting factors and carrying capacities in action. The simulations ran across two days with mini-lectures on constraints, population-limiting factors, and carrying capacities woven throughout the discussion and experiments.

AD: The cycle, the heart of all the experiments, is collecting the data, and then some reflection on what kind of patterns you see. What's the cause-effect relationship that you're noticing? And what are you observing? What did you see in your experiment or in your data that makes you think that?

So there's this NetLogo bank of simulations, and it's really good for data interpretation. So you can literally mess with the limiting factors, run the experiment, and it will show you the population graph.

This one was wolves, sheep, and grass, and it will run the experiment. I told them to mess with the settings, and see what happens—which is what you wanna do with these things anyway. Write down what you've changed and what you felt like the effects were, what you observed.

WEEK 2: SUPERPOWERS, NOT HACKS...

Three days into these 3 weeks (12 days) of instruction with his biology students, Mr. Derain was feeling good but not great about how his classes were going. In particular, he struggled with not feeling like he was able to get his students to produce classroom work that could be used as evidence of their growth toward understanding. He could attribute this, in part, to still getting to know his chemistry and biology kiddos, but he also had similar feelings about his current physics unit, and he'd had those students since the beginning of the year. While he felt somewhat clear about his targets for high-rigor thinking, he wasn't sure that the activities he was assigning in class were useful in matching the students' tasks with the life-changing understandings he was hoping to facilitate.

His Sunday morning reflection entry speaks to the challenge he was experiencing.

12/5

AD Project

Weekend

Sun

AM—feel like I need to focus on the products of student thinking + how I capture it. That might be the intersection of the behavioral and cognitive engagement I'm struggling w/. Getting students to produce evidence of their thinking has been a behavioral struggle + outlining the cognitive progression has also been a planning struggle. Maybe a progression of questions that let me spreadsheet their answers? Which just cycles back to behavioral engagement. Like what I found in a portfolio, but the management of that takes a lot of scaffolding for non-school proof kids. And time. Ugh, I feel discouraged.

AD: Biology is a lot of memorization . . . cause I was talking to the other teacher, and she said you gotta memorize all these cycles, but then you have to be able to apply higher level thinking and interpret these biological cycles. Also, I was watching this video of Nandi Bushell, she's this 10-year-old drummer, and I was watching her have this conversation with the drummer of the Red Hot Chili Peppers and this other drummer who has worked with Ringo Starr. I think she's 10 or 11 or 12, and she's having a high-level conversation about drumming with these two experts. The goal is getting kids to a level where they can have a conversation with an expert of the craft, and they can leverage their personal experiences to have those conversations with the expert—which is the whole point of CRE, I suppose . . . I got stuck on the technical details. I was like, how is this setting me up to lead the kids to a place where we're learning all these extra technical DOK1 facts and details to support the high level conversations we would have? And I wasn't quite seeing the connection, and it was bugging me!

But by the afternoon, Mr. Derain had begun to uncover a more visceral observation regarding his technical questions. The purpose of activities, he would surmise, is about bringing alive an understanding in the context of a rich instructional moment. To remain clear about the larger goals for instruction makes it easier to identify the steps along the way.

12/5

AD Project

Weekend

Sun

PM—figured out the central question for this unit has to work both for the content + for the kids' lives. It functions as the bridge between the responsive moments to the content understanding + also must push their stories of self forward, everything feels higher stakes because of my 3 prep situation

AD: And then I figured out that there are these three things: there's a framing experience, there's a students' experience, and then there is the content kind of understanding. And I realized that the central question of the unit has to connect those three things. I need to design that question in a way that lets me ask it about the framing experience, I can ask it about the kids' lives, and I can ask it about the content. And so this helped me really refine the way the *life changing understanding* needs to show up every day in the lessons in that one big question that I can ask about all three of those things.

The essential questions are a big part of what creates opportunities for the teaching and learning to be dynamic. They make space for the pedagogical lunges that build behavioral, affective, and cognitive engagement.

AD: Then a whole bunch of stuff made sense to me in retrospect. I thought about activities that have worked really well, and this dynamic was at play. What I thought was working about the activity, really it was the question that I could use to mine that activity. . . . So now it got less scary, I guess. I felt more confident we can get to the big understandings if I've got that question.

The possibilities for rigor are increased when the most important thinking can be routed through a shared experience in the classroom, the content, and the students' own cognitive niches and cultural identities.

AD: The essential question of the unit is a thing that connects the framing experience and the opportunity to be responsive and the content understandings all together. And so that question becomes a thing that I gotta ask over and over and over. So I think that's what was circling around in my head, that idea of wanting the kids to unlock deeper parts of the content but also being able to do the same thing in their lives. That big question, which is like a DOK3 or 4 question—it has to work in the framing experience, it has to work in the kids' lives, and it has to work with the content as well.

So when you look at the evidence and outcomes for this 8th-grade physics content standard: construct and interpret graphical displays of data to describe the relationships of kinetic energy to the mass of an object and the speed of an object—really what they want students to know is that kinetic energy is mass times velocity squared. The deeper understanding is the relationships within that equation, whereas kinetic energy and mass can have a proportional relationship, and kinetic energy and velocity are gonna have an exponential relationship because velocity is squared. I want students to understand that relationship in terms of a phenomenon and in a graph. So I want the students to understand a multivariable relationship, actually to be able to understand representations of multivariable relationships. I want them to be able to look at a graph or a figure and feel satisfied, like they're able to understand it. Satisfied, centered, clear-headed . . . the way that I want them thinking is to develop a mathematical model for a complex situation.

And so what I realized is if I can turn that storyline into a *you* question, it connects the content standard, and the framing experience, and the opportunities to be responsive. Using *you* then taps into the kids' internal storylines. So, I had to adjust my physics question a little bit. Instead of my original question of "How do you hack the universe?"—which is really: "How do you break the rules?"—And [laughing] that's not a road we want to go down in middle school. They'll figure out that plan on their own. So the question instead became: "How do you get superpowers?" You can build a narrative around that. It's almost like these elemental human narratives, like: "How do you level up in life? How do you gain the ability to do things that you couldn't before? How do you get better or faster or stronger?" That's something people want to do. That's a story you want to be a part of. And I hadn't quite figured that out like I thought. I was close when I thought about hacking the universe, but that implies taking shortcuts, cheating. I can ask: "How do you get superpowers?" in lots of ways. "What is it? How does it work? What are the rules? What can we control or influence? How can we make it work for us?" All the derivatives of that are much more propelling questions. The big question is what my unit questions are derived from. The big picture question in chemistry is: "What are the recipes for the universe?" You are figuring out how to make anything in the universe. It's very empowering.

And then for biology, "How to live your best life?"—again still a useful analogy. But really the question that we're thinking about with carrying capacity is: "What limits your success? What are things that are limiting your success?" You're living that out every single day. It's almost like you're kind of compelled to answer that question. You can't not think about that. That's one of the big questions of humanity. And so from that question, I can ask about the content, I can ask about the framing experience, I can ask about kids' lives.

To Cull or Not to Cull?

Mr. Derain's clarity about the purpose and function of his essential questions led him to want to revise his biology students' framing experience so that he could repeatedly ask them to consider in multiple ways what limits their success. The framing experience is a pedagogical practice that closes Equity gaps because it lessens the disadvantage of differential cultural inheritance or personal experience in accessing references for learning and understanding. It creates a common context for social learning from experiences shared in the classroom.

AD: So today [Monday, Day 4 of 12] we did a build, the paper book support challenge, where you get four large pieces of paper and you have to get it to hold as many textbooks as you can. This one is fun because at first there's disbelief and someone starts to figure out, *Oh, let's roll it into cylinders*, and then gradually that kind of idea spreads, and you'll get various arrangements of it. And then you test it with textbooks and eventually someone will get a really nice setup and you'll get 20 or 30 textbooks. So we did this and they're really into it, you know, they're building. Talking trash to each other but like in a positive way. There are four pieces of paper, and they build up the stack of books on it, and then at some point the limiting factor kicks in and it collapses just like a population does.

So they had that experience today, and tomorrow we're gonna get into a deeper connection to the content. So those questions—"What are the key factors for your or the organism's success? What is limiting your or the organism's success?"—are kind of humming around in their brains. Those questions work for the framing experience, they work in connection to the content, and they work in the students' lives. And the use of *you* I think is important in there. It kind of directs the students' thoughts inward. It keys into their personal lives and pushes forward their personal stories. And it's not just that the lessons had high engagement, but also because I had this question in mind, I'm more responsive and in tune in the moment to have conversations with students around that question, looking for opportunities where I get to ask that question, push their thinking around that question. It keeps me more responsive and in the zone.

So it was a big aha. I was feeling really stuck and thinking about it over the weekend, and that kind of fell into place. And then not only did today's lessons go really well, but the next steps, the rest of the unit kind of unfolded in my head. So that was exciting, and we'll see what happens tomorrow.

Having defined *constraints* and *limiting factors*, and having planted the essential questions—"What are the key factors for your success?" and "What limits your success?"—we turn to the classroom discussions. Mr. Derain looked for a topic rich with potential for application of the big ideas so that students could have conceptual space for further integrating understandings into their repertoire of cultural fluencies and cognitive niches. He wanted his students to have the opportunity to practice thinking about the concepts in a real-world context.

AD: I wanted students to have the experience of me asking "What is limiting your or the organism's success?" over and over because that's what triggers that thinking over and over. We're doing a real-world example slash application of the concept where we can build on the questions and also apply these concepts to a controversial local or relevant phenomenon—a situation where we have to think about the ethics of something.

Over the past several years, Mr. Derain had been following the issue of the increasing population of geese in his own neighborhood and the local parks where he and his family regularly visit. It occurred to him that the topic was also controversial and had the potential for eliciting a range of perspectives.

AD: At this point, we've got the big idea introduced, we've connected it to all three domains, but now we need time to make further connections with it and process it, and use it to create something, and that's where the topic of geese culling comes in. For my biology class, I was thinking about population examples, and I wanted to pick a local one. And I remembered in the last few years, the city culled something like almost 2000 geese.

Last year I found John Green when I was mining for content for remote teaching, and I'd been reading his book, *The Anthropocene Reviewed*. The whole point of the book is that he's reviewing different aspects of humanity—the Anthropocene, the current modern human era—on a five-star scale. So it's a semi-humorous series of essays that go into deep reflection of things going on. He had a whole chunk in there about geese and about how part of the reason they've exploded so much is that we have increased the carrying capacity for them with all the Kentucky blue grass, and parks, and lawns, and they love ponds where there's not high bushes around it so they can see. It's just a perfect habitat for geese. But now we're saying it's too much; and so now we're trying to impose an artificial carrying capacity. We're introducing limiting factors. And it's kinda messed up, right? We caused this problem, and now we're slaughtering these geese who are just doing what they're supposed to be doing. And that was the big idea of limiting factors and carrying capacity. Limiting factors themselves are not particularly complex or rigorous, but what makes it rigorous is that we are the only species that can really make decisions about carrying capacity and limiting factors, and that was one of the themes in John Green's essay about geese.

I was thinking about different perspectives—which connects to the six facets of understanding—and that reminded me of this thing I used to do years ago: pose a question to the kids, and then put a spectrum of *yes* or *no*, and then have them write something on a sticky note and go post a note on the spectrum with what they think.

So we did. "Should we cull the geese or not?" They discussed it in groups, and every group took a stand on that. They presented different items for the class to consider, and that circles back to the big idea of carrying capacity and limiting factors. You have to have an understanding of limiting factors. You're literally asking should we limit the success of the geese? And so there's a couple different factors there. There's that conceptual connection, and then two, there's something about the positioning of *you* in the question.

So, I posed the question. I showed them a news clip about the geese; and then I compiled a bunch of resources like some graphs on goose-related things. And we watched a clip about this orange kind of drone thing called the Goosenator to try to scare them away, and we looked at graphs. Every goose trajectory curve is exponential, there's no indicator that it's hitting the carrying capacity. So, we've got this question, should we cull or not cull? Which is not the big question. The big question is: "What limits your success?" But it's a real-world application of the big question.

Carrying Capacities and Limiting Factors

AD: At the start of the next class, I asked them, "Did anyone see any geese? If so, how many?"

Yes, and I took a picture!

The students were noticing the geese in their environment differently now in relation to their growing understandings of the biology concepts of carrying capacity and limiting factors. They were literally, neurocognitively changing their perceptions; their brains were responding differently to the sight of geese, which Mr. Derain saw as an opportunity for responsiveness.

AD: And I'm realizing that this is one of those things where for the rest of their lives, they're going to remember the class, carrying capacity, limiting factors—this is one of those life-changing understandings. There's a chance that my bio students are never gonna be able to look at a goose again and not think about this class.

The students were connecting this science content understanding in the context of their own life stories. When a student is compelled to take a picture of something that before then was distinctly unremarkable, it means that their neurocognitive architecture has been reorganized in recognition of the meaningfulness of a concept learned in school that relates to the circumstances of their own environmental and cognitive niches. It's fair to say that Mr. Derain's biology students hadn't previously been in the habit of looking at a goose and thinking about the possibility of its demise given the limiting factors being imposed through culling. Now, however, their thinking about the situation of geese in the environment can draw on a rich and dynamic schema for understanding not just geese, but so much more that is conceptually analogous to any situation in which carrying capacity and limiting factors might apply. This is an understanding that is likely durable, and thus, possesses the possibilities of further integration into other understandings.

AD: On Tuesday [Day 5 of 12], I wanted to get more specific about carrying capacity. I gave them feedback on their first simulation experiment, explaining to them that what I really want to hear is an explicit explanation of the cause-effect relationship. How are those factors affecting the wolf population? And then the rest of the unit is just a further connection to these two concepts, carrying capacity and limiting factors.

Then Day 6 is Wednesday. So now that the ideas are coming together, now the design part is coming into play. Looking at this from multiple angles: What are you learning about biology? But also what are you learning about how to learn about biology? So we set up our note-taking process and look at our sources and think about our big questions. And I want them thinking about what does that source make you think about the big question?

That John Green article was originally a podcast, and we had listened to that podcast. And I put all the resources I'd given them on Google Slides, and I had them look through it, and then we read the three-page podcast script together, which is really like an essay; but I could play John Green's voice cause it was a podcast. And the first time we read it through—I felt I was sneaking in some English instruction—I had them underline stuff that stood out to them, anything that was interesting. And they added it to their annotated bibliography, and they did their mind map, and they did their first draft. I told them: "We're gonna take this and I want you to outline for something to publish, whether it's an article, or a YouTube video, or a podcast, or a series of TikToks . . . any kind of thing you're gonna publish about this."

So, we were reading this as a whole class and annotating to add to their notes. I'm doing it in two-minute chunks. "Okay, what grabbed your attention? Underline it. Mark up the text."

"OK, look through these resources and make a simple T-chart. What's the source? And then, what does it make you think about the big question? Yes, no, maybe, and why." So, after we make T-charts, we make rudimentary annotated bibliographies, and then I had them mind map it; and then at that point, it was still just their opinion— and I did not say the words *claims, evidence, reasoning* cause I don't want to go down that road, cause it's got so much negative connotation and terrible instruction around it. But basically, more or less, they put their claim in the middle and their evidence and reasoning around the sides from that.

Mr. Derain wanted his students writing like scientists, and so he had them create mind maps, the format and intent of which he explains this way:

AD: So, handwriting them on a blank piece of paper. . . . You put your answers in the middle and then connect your item and a detail for the item. "What's your answer? What are three items that connect somehow that made you think that? And what's a detail from that?" And then, I wanted them to continue their thinking: "Now where does this content fit in? This stuff we've been thinking about? How does that fit in there?" So, we just started with putting our answer to "Should we cull or not?" in the middle, at least three items around it, and then details from those items that are connected to your thinking.

Mr. Derain was worried, though, that his students weren't getting it, and that his instruction may have strayed from the big ideas.

AD: "OK, now you need to add the two big concepts, carrying capacity and limiting factors. Where do those fit into this mind map?" And, I was starting to get a little concerned. It wasn't coming back like I wanted it to.

And so then, yesterday, one of the kids says: *Mr., I can't figure out how carrying capacity and limiting factors fit in?* And then it clicked with me. The question is coming back! And I was like: "Well, really what you're thinking about is what is limiting the success of populations. What's limiting the geese's success? What's limiting human success?" And he was like, *Oh I get it!* And that happened multiple times in bio.

And then I think of asking that question again, connecting them back to the framing experience we'd done. And I had them think about what led to a success in your life, and it's like, *Oh, I see where it fits in!* And it helps them connect those big concepts, and so that was pretty cool seeing this full connection the kids are making—the connections to the concepts and their background experience.

WEEK 3: FROM COMPLIANCE TO AGENCY

On the first day of the third week, Day 9 of the 12 days of instruction, Mr. Derain provided an opportunity for a grade-check/make-up day. His goal in carving out class time for this is to further prepare students to be able to navigate school spaces through managing their assignments in the online grading portal used by the district.

AD: So Monday I did a grade-check slash make-up day. Part of this is just practical thinking because grades are due this week, and I've always thought the grading system can be weird. I've always felt like this is a tool for students. One, it's a communication tool; and two, it's a tool for students to experience agency. And then three, for them to learn how to navigate that world. What I want them to get out of these make-up work days is to realize, *if I'm present and engaged in class, I can get this stuff done.* I want to shift them out of the mindset of completion and compliance to that feeling of agency. I wanted to facilitate conversations about how *this is doable work.* Like, I think some students' resistance is about *Oh, it's too hard, I don't wanna do it.* But I want them to realize it's doable work.

It's weird cause I taught these three weeks like I get to keep the kids forever. I don't know . . . that's just the best way for me to show up as a teacher. And so if I had them for another unit, they'd recognize the structure of it, and then the work we'd be doing, and the thinking we'd be doing, and they would start to get that kind of rhythm and agency. Like, *Oh, I can do this. I don't have to disengage with my phone or my friends.* . . . So even this make-up work day is intentional to try to build the students' sense of agency in school.

So, I can go through and write down what grade they got and what they wanna redo or stuff they were missing that they wanna complete, and the kids were into it, across the board. And then it also kind of reconfirmed that storyline because it was there throughout all their make-up work. I was able to have mini-conversations with kids about the essential questions. Doing the make-up work, they still had to do the thinking I wanted them to do. So, even though it was a make-up workday, because of the deeper level planning, it wasn't just busy work. It was facilitating some little conversations where I can correct misconceptions—that kind of thing. Even though this is a make-up workday, I get to have the conversations with students where the big ideas just keep coming back.

As one of the students was turning in her stuff, I asked: "Was that helpful?" And she said: *That actually helped a lot. Most of the teachers are just, like, go do the missing work. But we don't know what it is so we just sit there.*

I want the students to learn the content, and I want them to connect it to their lives. I also want to give them skills they can carry forward to help them be successful should they choose to continue down the academic road—including how to use [the online portal] and see what their grades are. How to track their own data, their own growth more or less.

Mind Maps and Proposals

The constraints of Mr. Derain's situation limit the options for assessment. He knew, however, that he wanted his students to be able to relate their understandings by being able to reference their own cultural fluencies, cognitive niches, and communication registers.

AD: And I told them, "You know, scientists when we talk to each other, it's like, *Here's the data and here's what I think* and we argue about it. But that's a terrible way to communicate these things to the general public, and so we as scientists have to learn how to communicate our ideas in a more human way. We have learned some simple structures for scientific writing before, but now we're looking at professional structures."

So, we reread the John Green article, and I pointed out the structure to them of how first, he introduces the topic, and then in his second section he starts saying *you* and connects the audience to the concept, and then in the third section he tells a personal story so he's bringing us in even deeper cause we're looking at it from his perspective. And in the fourth section he's dropping the big ideas he wants his audience thinking about. Whatever you're creating has to have those four elements. They don't have to be in the same order. I'm not telling them to just copy John Green. But you have to have all four of these elements somewhere in there.

We have two days left in the semester, and I know we're not going to get to a full-on publication. So between physics and biology, I realized that instead of it being a publication, we're gonna do a proposal. We're gonna have your mind map, a draft/outline of what you want your publication to be, and I ended up adding a proposal summary sheet to it.

Mr. Derain's plans for this model going forward include production weeks in which students form teams to build their proposals into projects. A truly performative assessment where kiddos are authentically composing the evidence of their understandings.

AD: My dream, if I could keep the kids, is they're all gonna have these scripts, these proposals. And so I wanna put them in production teams where they select a proposal. I see this just getting more rigorous, and more real-world, and more performance-based. For the students who will go into a hard science future, the kind of traditional scientific assessments will be important to them. But I'd argue that the cycle of being able to take understandings and put them in the context of real-life is still gonna be important to them. One, to be able to communicate with nonphysical science majors, but also to understand the meaning of what they're studying and why it's important. And it sets them up for all kinds of future jobs. If you want to be a doctor, great. You can do the science experiment data collection part, but if you wanna do anything else, you at some point are gonna be producing some kind of published content, where you collaborate with a team and think about how you're gonna put this out there.

Mr. Derain sees the Equity issue here as being about scientific curiosity, as in: *Who gets to be curious?* All too often, science classrooms seem to center the curiosity of persons talked about in textbooks in faraway places and long ago times, but Mr. Derain believes that an equitable science learning environment should focus on the present and future interests of the students being taught. Their discovery is the point of the whole endeavor.

AD: I don't want the students to reproduce the scientific concepts on a test. My real measure of understanding is *How deeply can you think about the concepts?* What connections can you make to them? How fluent are you with pulling concepts together to compose a new thought? Because, to me, that's what I'm looking for when I'm thinking of scientific literacy. Not, can you regurgitate the correct analysis of this physics problem? But, how can you put this together in the context of real life?

The *you* questions in the storylines of artfully designed instruction feature students as the protagonists. If there's no *you* question in the storyline, there's fewer opportunities for students to draw on their own categories and concepts, no opportunity to reshuffle the seat of inquiry. A responsive assessment has to empower students to demonstrate what they've done with their story, the learning that they've pursued in their story, the depth to which they can think about the concepts.

AD: The importance of the mind map isn't so much the mind map itself, it's incorporating all the stuff that's leading up to the mind map. We basically did prewriting, we did research, looked through different sources, and then built a mind map around the central question. Answer these questions using these resources, and then add a layer of these concepts we've talked about, and then add a layer of the writing structure. So I'm looking for those kinds of connections. Do they make sense? And the second part of this—turning it into a publication—is asking can you think about this in a way that you can communicate it to another human being? What kind of structure would work to communicate this to someone else? What would an audience need to hear to understand?

The mind maps and proposals are meant to give Mr. Derain's students agency by amplifying the tools of intelligence that help organize and track their thinking. This is consistent with the principles of Culturally Responsive Education because it provides fairer opportunities for students to create their own flight patterns to the destination of understanding by drawing on their cultural fluencies and personal cognitive styles in demonstrating their competencies in school. And since no brain operates in a cultural vacuum, the opportunities to leverage the content of their cognitive niches in coming to understand scientific (or any) concepts expands the potential for analogy-making and categorizing, which as was discussed in Chapter 4, is the essence of thinking (Hofstadter & Sander, 2013).

Differences in cultural frames of reference do not equate to deficits. Equitable teaching emphasizes the opportunities for students to build on those cultural variants and ever-evolving concepts that live at the heart of all that we know. The point of assessments is to measure as directly as possible the quality of learning and the effectiveness of teaching. Most importantly, Mr. Derain wants for his assessments to measure his students' understandings, which require opportunities for all his students to be able to communicate what they have come to know while drawing from their cultural inheritance. The goal is to assess without privileging any one cultural repertoire over another.

> AD: What really became clear to me was seeing the difference in the questions I was able to ask about the mind map. This became a really key assessment. Seeing this mind map and how they made connections was a level of insight into the students' thinking that I had not been able to get to before in previous units.

Dopamine Loops

If science instruction is to be engaging, it has to emphasize something much more than specialistic knowledge and rote memorization (though there are surely some things which are important to memorize). What is most engaging about science, or any school-based learning experience for that matter, is the opportunity to acquire integrated understandings that expand our sense of selves and the possibilities for who we can become. A tremendous challenge in 21st-century teaching is motivating students to put forth the effort necessary to learn. To expect that every student will enter school with the same motivational calculus to justify the investment in learning is not reasonable. Brilliant teaching in science or any subject requires that the instruction presents the thinking itself as the reward for the effort. This means that the skill of incentivizing the cognitive engagement of students is a pedagogical requirement in a way it has not been in any past era of American education. (I return to the topic of incentives in Chapter 8.)

AD: Yeah, I think the foundation of my understanding of incentives is just that dopamine is a fact of life. I took a neuroscience class a bunch of years ago, and they talked about, you know, dopamine is so prevalent. You want this thing, you get this thing, and it releases dopamine; and then that gets more and more embedded in your brain. So much so that even an indicator of that thing can release dopamine. Whereas you got the opposite where we avoid stuff that causes stress and cortisol. At the very basic level, like I think of incentives and that sort of thing, especially with students who have different concepts of school or less than a great relationship with school. Which is why I never understood the *I-want-my-kids-to-learn-from-intrinsic-motivation* teachers. That's great. Are you going to lecture them about that? Because now you're starting to attach more cortisol to their school experience.

Mr. Derain seeks to create the opportunities for these *dopamine loops* in which his students can marry their own cultural fluencies and intellectual interests with experiences that confirm the value and validity of the difficulties involved in coming to learn anything of substance.

AD: I just really kind of do everything I can to deepen that neural connection; and so that's kind of the thought process I have around incentives. I know that my activities and the things that we do in class ultimately have to be dopamine releasing activities so it's almost like more of a philosophy.

If you're building a relationship with something, we don't want it to be like this is something I have to do. That was my relationship with school. I never really liked school for the vast majority of my, you know, kindergarten through college, grad school. Most of my classes I didn't like. It was just something I had to do for delayed gratification. Delayed gratification is great, but it's not gonna work well if you're not already bought into that cultural construct.

And if that cultural construct is flawed, then I don't know that it does anyone much good! So that's kind of how I see it connecting. It's that surface and essence thing. On the surface, it's just as simple as giving a kid a chance to win a bag of chips; but on a deeper level, it's modeling the kind of relationship we want students to have with learning. Not just the kind of relationship we want them to have, it's modeling the way we want them to think about school and teaching and learning. That when we design learning experiences, this is something that's going to give my students something worthwhile and valuable and essential. Not something we do just because we have the test coming up.

I wanted students to have a chance to present their proposals because part of it is that I want them to get more comfortable with public speaking. So I had them talk with the people at their table. "Share with them what you've got so far, and what you like about their proposals." I told them, "We're no longer at school, we're at a fancy science conference." So, I played Stan Getz's *The Girl from Ipanema* album on Spotify. We had this French jazz thing going on, and they were sitting and chatting with each other. It had a good vibe. They're talking about their stuff, they're giving each other feedback. And then they finish up, and they can incorporate that feedback into their proposals; and I asked if they wanted to turn the jazz off. *No,* [laughs] *keep it on. Keep it on!*

The proposal was a real-life way to sketch out and submit their ideas. It mirrors the real world, gives them another pass at their thinking. So, it sets me up for another dopamine-elevating experience that fits with the visions we see for ourselves in the future. That's where the proposal seemed to work better than just this paper you turn in to me, I grade it, and then we're done with it kind-of-thing. This serves the same teacher function but has much cooler student function.

And a proposal lets me *yes-and* a lot more because a kid could propose something that we could never do, but I can say, "Yeah go for it! Write a proposal for that." Even though there's no way we could do this. "Well, maybe not. But right now, just propose your dream!" That also lets kids pull out any kind of idea, any kind of thing they want to. It lets me step around the constraints of time. So, I can get a whole huge diversity of ideas. And students can bring any kind of fluency and experience to express their thinking and I get to *yes-and* it, and build their thinking up with a proposal format versus the final product format.

"SOMETHING HAS TO WORK BETTER . . ."

Mr. Derain spent a lot of time talking with me about the types of lessons that work, and so I asked him what kinds of lessons don't work well for his students?

AD: I guess, like, what I grew up with mostly was lecture, lecture, worksheet, lecture, worksheet, and test. I've even seen diminishing returns with *I do, we do, you do*. Actually, I didn't really see great returns on that from the get-go. Real formulaic lesson plans, any kind of curriculum that if you just take it straight out of the curriculum and go from that, any kind of hyper structured—any kind of structure written or designed without your specific group of students in mind isn't gonna work. They're not just gonna fit into a predefined structure and go with it. It's gotta be customized, tailored to go with them.

This is an artful approach to thinking about the design of learning experiences. An artmaking mindset for instruction is useful to Mr. Derain in planning more cohesive units and sequences of units.

AD: Teaching has to be better. Something has to work better. How can art and television and movies capture our imagination and even iPhones and technology? How could that work so well, and we struggle so much in classrooms to engage the same human beings?

One of my goals taking over these three classes was, I saw two roads: one was they just have a roving band of subs, and students' personal narratives get further and further apart from school, and they have more and more negative experiences with school. At the very least I thought, we can give the students opportunities to think and feel like biologists and chemists and physicists. And also attach positive associations with thinking like a scientist.

The work of teaching is extraordinarily complex—and it is also possible. Teachers should know, the work will stretch you. It requires great vulnerability. To make art and to teach is to court heart-breaking failure with enthusiasm.

AD: I think this seems to be a part of the creative process. Something is not working, and I need to fix it, and there's this feeling of "Does this ruin everything? Am I making a mistake here?" What's weird is that both times that happened, I had a great day the next day based on the adjustments that I made. In these three weeks, there were two really bad days, and both were when I was on the edge of something new. In retrospect, neither one of them felt like wasted days.

I think that's part of the struggle—the tension, the disappointment of the bad days. It's like you want it to be where I can plan it out, and I know exactly what's going to happen on those bad days. I want to be able to plan it out. I've heard that really good quarterbacks like Peyton Manning or Tom Brady can ask the receiver "Where do you want the ball? Do you want it a little lower or higher?" And they can make that adjustment on a throw 60 yards down the field. I want to be that good. But this is a different kind of a thing.

NOTES ON ARTMAKING: ORDINARY RESURRECTIONS

Like all of us—you, me, and everyone you have ever known—Mr. Derain is a fusion of contradictions and multiplicities. I am hoping to make three points with the telling of Mr. Derain's philosophizing over three weeks. First, it is possible to design learning experiences that support our students in even the most challenging of school environments. We are wrongheaded to double-down on inadequate pedagogical models of the past that were never intended to be responsive to a culturally diverse group of students. Second, it is unsustainable and woefully inappropriate to expect that teachers will be able to teach effectively, much less responsively, in environments in which their efforts seem to require heroic feats to circumvent unsupportive systems. In the telling of this story, I've chosen to focus on Mr. Derain's intentions for supporting students, but there were many criticisms he and I had for both the school's and district's policies and practices. Some of the more important systemic questions to ask in the reading of this account are less about Mr. Derain's methods and rather about the obstacles to his methods. Many rightfully ask: *What can teachers do to better support their most vulnerable learners?* Another equally pertinent question, however, is: *Why is it necessary for teachers to seemingly work against the system to better support their most vulnerable learners?*

Last, and most importantly in my mind, is the matter of the well-being of teachers themselves. Teaching has never been a simple task, but it's complicated in ways now that were nearly unimaginable when I began my career in what now seems like the distant era of the 1990s. The point that I make to teachers is that you are responsible for your own resurrections. I make no proselytizing reference with the use of that word, though the resurrections that I am thinking about are no less spectacular than the ones written about in religious texts. I'm talking about the *ordinary resurrections* that define the commitment that countless teachers make every day to pick up the tools of the craft and return to what may often feel like a thankless task.

And yet, I've spoken to students all over the United States, the very ones whom I've witnessed derail lessons with defiant and ostensibly unprovoked disruptions. Away from the eyes of their peers, once I've established a feeling of safety and even surface rapport, they nearly always tell me that they don't want their teachers to give up on them. To take care of them, teachers must take care of themselves. Use your tools. Practice a healthy thought-life. Consciously attend to your philosophizing. The most magnificent resurrections are witnessed on the mornings of school days all over the country when teachers show up full of the verve necessary for our craft.

Who Is Mr. Derain?

André Derain (1880–1954) is an artist who is most regularly associated with the Fauvists, a group of French Post-Impressionist painters who made radical use of color and form in their paintings. His work is featured in some of the world's most important museums, including The Metropolitan Museum of Art in New York City and the Tate Modern in London. My favorite Derain painting in The Met's collection is titled *Regent Street, London* (1906). In *Regent Street, London*, like many of his other Fauvist paintings, color takes on different qualities than what we'd typically expect. Derain wields his brush with colors in ways that give them new meaning. His paintings reveal something even more realistic about the image than the traditional use of colors might accomplish.

My other favorite Derain painting (in truth, I have many) is a self-portrait in the Tate Modern collection titled *The Painter and His Family* (c. 1939). It's easy to walk past this painting without taking its layered meaning and craft into consideration. Self-portraits are always a kind of statement for the artist. They are communicating their own perceptions of their essence in the techniques and use of symbolism. In Derain's *The Painter and His Family*, he is telling us of his own commitment to his craft through the depiction of his suited attire and facial expression—brow furrowed, gaze concentrated. He is squarely in the tradition of the brilliant artists who have preceded him with all the appropriate convictions in tow. But Derain is also showing us his place relative to the supports and relationships that give him the foundation for his painting, and we see them in poses and with props that represent Derain's awareness of context and historical significance.

We chose André Derain as the pseudonym for the teacher whose philosophizing has been profiled in this chapter because of our admiration for his work, but also because Derain himself faced an artistic crisis in his own career, having destroyed much of his catalog of paintings sometime around 1910 when he had succumbed to the belief that his work was useless and unappreciated. It's largely unknown what may have led Derain to such drastic actions—and I don't know that I should even feel entitled to inquire. What matters most to me is that he resurrected his passion for his craft. It may have been that this was a daily rebirth and that *The Painter and His Family* is an homage to the tools that enabled the rediscovery. Derain is one of my favorites not only because of his craft, but also because of the model he provides. His paintings light up my brain and lift my spirit—which is also what I feel when I'm in the presence of teachers who are brilliantly committed to their work. So, thank you, Mr. Derain. Every artist is necessarily vulnerable every time they step in front of a blank canvas. Thank you for sharing your own vulnerability with us.

CHAPTER 6

Improvisation

"We are all improvising all the time. We all enter each encounter and our every moment with a general sense of what might happen but rely heavily on the degree of empathy, knowledge, language, and social skills that we've obtained over the course of our lives to negotiate those moments."

—Pat Metheny

Time to re-focus things with this book's central thought-experiment: You're a teacher, and you want to be equitable. What does Equity mean *in* your teaching? How do you *do* Equity?

MAKE IT INTO A MELODY

There's nothing cooler than when a class is clicking . . . when every kiddo is locked in, thinking. And then the moments I love the most, a student takes the concepts, switches it up, makes it their own, followed by that unmistakable look of *I get it!* It makes my teacher-soul happy . . . especially when I'm right there to meet them with the perfectly-timed affirming response—or pause, or question, or smile, or fist bump, or transition, or whatever teacher move I have at the ready. Can you relate? At one point in my career, I thought those moments were magical—as in, there was just a mystical alignment of the stars that somehow dropped the opportunity to improvise, thus drawing students into closer relationship with a big and meaningful understanding. I used to see it as something beyond my control. I just had to wish for the best, I thought, and hopefully, the chance for the perfect improvisational teacher-move would materialize before me. But now I know that I can set these moments up and be prepared to take full advantage of them.

So where does one begin in improvising? Well, the answer isn't sexy, but it's real. All those dope improvisational moves that pull students into a profound experience of engagement start in planning.

First, a definition of *improvisation* is in order. While improvisation is used at times in comedy and dramatic stage performance, and other music forms, it is most pronounced in jazz. According to Wikipedia:

"Jazz improvisation is the spontaneous invention of melodic solo lines or accompaniment parts in a performance of jazz music. It is one of the defining elements of jazz. Improvisation is composing on the spot, when a singer or instrumentalist invents melodies and lines over a chord progression played by rhythm section instruments (piano, guitar, double bass) and accompanied by drums."

That's an accurate if not somewhat technical definition.

Improvisation in a culturally responsive classroom is the co-coordination of students' opportunities for discovery and connection with the content inside the feeling of relationship and community. It's the call-and-response, the sharing and extending of a thought so that everyone can partake in the making of an understanding. Improvisation is a discovery act that goes beyond the application of a pre-existing technique. It aims to leverage students' assets and identities in such a way that an integrated understanding is within their conceptual grasp. Improvisation has a versatile and interactive nature; a performance can be modeled and adapted to different circumstances (Luquet, 2015). Just as musical improvisations are modified and adjusted in relation to the conditions of the performance, the adjustments in teaching involve feedback and incentive loops consisting of real-time answers to the events of learning.

To improvise in a jazz performance, one must be able to hold on to the melody and also depart from the composition. The skill is in finding just the right opportunity to extend beyond what's ordained by the written note. It's an experience created out of and extemporaneously responding to the living learning environment before you (Fink, 2014). It's in the improvisation in a jazz performance that learning takes place for the individual players involved. They use what they have learned to learn more, and subsequently, the players learn with and from each other (Luquet, 2015). Just like in musical improvisation, we teachers present the understandings that live in our content and try to push the composition boundaries into new forms to give it different dimensions and expanded feelings. And while improvisation does have elements of traditional teacher-centered methods, the goals of instruction are quite different. The whole point of improvisation is to hand off the center-stage spotlight so that students can share in the discovery.

The first step in improvisation is making the understanding you want to teach into a melody. In Mr. Derain's biology unit from Chapter 5 on carrying capacities and limiting factors, his essential question—*What is limiting your success?*—which is a kind of storyline—is *also* a kind of melody.[1] Just like a melody holds a tune together, the melody in your instruction is the essence of the understanding you teach. This melody forms the core structure to the integrated thinking Mr. Derain seeks for his students. These are the refrains to which he and his students can regularly return, to re-center themselves in the conceptual infrastructure of the understanding; and every time students revisit this chorus, Mr. Derain gives them opportunities to extend, remix, and personalize for their individual cognitive style. We are saying to our students: take this melodic phrase, repeat it, and make variations on it. In a culturally responsive learning experience, improvisation invites students to develop self-efficacy with the material through their own cultural fluencies.

UNCERTAINTY

Too often, would-be artmakers problematize their artmaking by imagining artists to be certain. But, in truth, there is no such thing as a certain artist. Making art in any medium is chancy. It has to be so. To think like an artist doesn't mean to be without uncertainty or above the fears that pause the rest of us. Rather, the artist embraces the tension of artmaking because the artist knows it is central to the task. To think like an artist first and foremost requires the will to look squarely at one's own uncertainty with the full knowing that without it, art isn't possible (Bayles & Orland, 1993). In teaching, uncertainty is the essential, inevitable, and all-pervasive companion to brilliant teaching; and the teacher's tolerance for uncertainty is the prerequisite to responsive learning opportunities for the student. Both the problems and the opportunities for improvisation are sourced by uncertainty, and so shedding the dependence on certainty is necessary for artful teaching. Without risk, the return is muted.

Even as we realize the necessity of uncertainty in our craft, we are still fully capable of caving in under its immense pressures. Brilliance is a process, and to be brilliant, we must realize that uncertainty is an asset. Vision precedes execution—and uncertainty is an inevitability from which all artists (artmaking teachers included) must learn. Vision is always ahead of execution, and thus, uncertainty is a virtue (Bayles & Orland, 1993). Artmaking is a generative endeavor; it seeks to broaden the range of possibilities for brilliant teaching rather than seeking the most narrow possible pathways. Process, when too narrowly defined, may serve to constrict rather than expand one's capacity for brilliance.

The uncertainty we encounter about our designs for learning experiences are compounded by legitimate concerns including pandemics, school shootings, and any number of observable obstacles to teaching and learning. Our students have needs like never before, and there's lots wrong with our systems. For that matter, there's lots wrong with society in general. Still, the opportunity inside of the uncertainty is also the invitation to improvise. There is, then, a necessary cognitive dissonance that must be accounted for in artmaking—a reconciliation of the doubt with a conviction drawn from purpose. The artmaking teacher knows that their doubts will never be satiated, and yet their artmaking efforts continue. We engage with doubts about our capacities for producing, and we know that to engage the tensions of our craft is elemental in artmaking.

We, too, make a kind of music with our teaching. Our melodic phrases are the integrated understandings we seek to teach our students. Our job is to help our students develop their own feel for and relationship with the integrated understanding. In jazz terms, a *lick* is a stock musical phrase that can be incorporated into a solo to improvise a melody. In pedagogical terms, a *lick* is like a teacher-move that can be big (e.g., a re-designed framing experience to reset an entire unit) or small (e.g., a well-timed turn-and-talk), but it's an intentional effort to provide the opportunities for students to play with the melody.

IMPRINT THE MEMORY

Just like a jazz musician, one of your jobs is to show your students the song. *But what do you show them?* Imagine you and your favorite people have taken an all-expense paid, two-week vacation to your favorite destination, and it was PERFECT! But you didn't just take a holiday. You discovered something on the excursion that has had a moving effect on you, and now you are changed. Fortunately, you had a professional photographer document the entire trip from start to finish, and the pictures make you very nearly feel the same transformative joy and connection you experienced while on the journey. When you show those images to whomever you choose to share them with, you will want to present them in a way that the meaningfulness of it all will be appreciated. It would be a shame to see the photographs and not also see the larger conceptual context they represent.

We need to do something similar with our content. Ask yourself, what do I believe about the learning target? What makes it groovy? How am I changed by knowing this? What does this understanding allow me to see and do differently than before I understood? Ask yourself, what do I have to show for the understandings to be appropriately recognized by my students? What are the various vantage points from which the integrated understanding could be considered? How can the students be led to play with interesting parts of the overall concept so that they can see the various intersections and contributing elements?

An integrated understanding has a feel, an emotional state, a character. *Show,* don't *tell,* your students about the understanding and why it's worth coming into relationship with. It helps to consciously focus on the feel of the melody. Give it an emotional description. Your improvisational teacher-moves will be informed by your own connections to the understanding.

I think of the six themes (engagement, cultural identity, relationships, vulnerability, assets, rigor) as the vocabulary of Culturally Responsive Education (CRE), and I think of the five guiding planning questions as the grammar. (See Figure 5.1.) The grammatical structure of the CRE Mental Model supports you in consciously and intentionally focusing on the feel of the understanding, which in turn, sends an instruction to your unconscious, which prepares you with the pedagogical sentences that match the emotional state. Taken together, the vocabulary and the grammar facilitate your engagement with the uncertainties for how to *do* Equity in your teaching.

Identify the conceptual elements in the understandings, those core pieces that your audience must hear to appreciate the melody. If your students trust you, your belief in the meaningfulness of the melody will compel them to engage. And if your students aren't bought into the learning, they will be more likely to invest once they are able to relate their cultural fluencies to the concepts at hand. When students feel that their cultural repertoires are useful in their thinking, the experience of thinking takes on deeper meaning.

My best advice to teachers for preparing themselves for the responsive, improvisational opportunities is to imprint the memory of the integrated understanding in your teacher brain. In the same way that a pianist, for example, has an imprinted memory of the scales in their musician brain, you need an instant picture of the essential understanding.[2]

In order to execute the lunges and departures that are necessary in improvisation, you have to make a good melody, and you have to know the melody well. The imprinting of the memory, which is necessary for making a learning target into a melody, is developed using the vocabulary and grammar of CRE. The CRE Mental Model can be used to transform the content standards and learning targets into melodies.

Melodic phrases are like sentences. For the musician, they first form in the unconscious, get put in the right order—matching notes with chords—and as they come into the conscious mind, they make their way into the world via the instrument. The goal of improvisers is to become fluent in this process. It is in the practice of the use of our "scales" that we build the awareness and preparedness that makes possible teaching that can be experienced as truly responsive to the cultural dispositions of our students. Once you have a melody, you can improvise by remixing it, by placing emphasis on its different parts. The words you use in discussion and description may be the same or close to the same, but the feeling and the rhythm of the flow of thinking change to match the context in which your students integrate the meanings into their own cultural fluencies.

And remember, in jazz, the ability to improvise starts with knowing the tune; but it's not enough to know it, you have to *believe* in the tune. You have to believe the tune is worth knowing. A student who is taught by a teacher who richly knows and loves the tune is greatly advantaged over one whose teacher is disaffected. Culturally responsive teaching is an artful mechanism—a conceptual approach that leverages our composition and improvisation. It allows the teacher-artist to be led to and surprised by new ideas without deviating from their own pedagogical principles (Saltz, 2020).

NOTES ON ARTMAKING: HAVE STUDENTS TRANSLATE THE MELODY

I'm defining *improvisation* in teaching as the artful departures that we take from the melody so that the essential learning targets are more accessible for students. One of the ways we can know that the teacher-moves we make are good risks is when students have opportunities to build *this-is-like* connections to the essential understandings. When students integrate what they are learning with the interpretive lens of their cultural fluencies, they come into more meaningful relationship with both the content and the learning community.

Our capacity for improvisation isn't limited to a particular instructional strategy. Mostly, I think about how students can have opportunities to filter information through the lenses of their social and cultural identities—which amounts to a sort of translation. In the classroom, *Gallery Walks* can be a great activity for students to have multiple rounds of investigating content and/or the work of their peers. With each round, they can be prompted to connect to and extend the themes and concepts represented.

I also like the *Think of a Time* strategy for eliciting multiple perspectives which is useful when creating those opportunities for sharing melodies. In *Think of a Time*, students are grouped into threes, and each student is assigned a role. The key here is to assign good roles! You'll need to find three distinct vantage points for considering a topic or prompt. The roles may be as general as participant, observer, and supporter, or the roles may be based in past time periods or political affiliation or regional background—or you might assign roles of a biologist, chemist, and physicist. . . . The roles may be something more or less specific to your content or topic, but they should be able to produce different viewpoints. Once your students get the hang of it, they can generate their own questions and other roles from which outlooks can be drawn. Think artfully in terms of what mix of perspectives is likely to bring about a wide-angle view of the concepts being taught. It's the students' investment in the roles that comprises the energy of the activity. Give your students time for a free-write response to a prompt so they can sketch their thoughts before sharing and comparing their accounts with others. In triads, students reflect upon what they know about the concept and what new insights they've formed since the process started. We want serve-and-return-and-volley exchanges. Our goal in support of improvisation is for students to have many opportunities to put the content-related concepts into their own words, which is, of course, a lot like what happens at a jazz set.

CHAPTER NOTES

1. As was discussed in Chapter 5, the NGSS standard for the biology unit Mr. Derain is teaching is: Use mathematical and/or computational representations to support explanations of factors that affect carrying capacity of ecosystems at different scales.

2. I recommend the Dream Exercise for finding the integrated understanding learning target in content standards. I write about the Dream Exercise in *Culturally Responsive Education in the Classroom: An Equity Framework for Pedagogy* (2019). The gist is, we give ourselves permission to dream of perfect circumstances for teaching and learning, and we ask: Three to five years from now, if my students learn this thoroughly, what will they still know? Three to five years from now, what will my students be able to do? Three to five years from now, what will my students still value?

CHAPTER 7

Story

"What are we thinking about? What is our job here now? We've got the basics, the grammar and the vocabulary. Our job is to be a storyteller. This is what we do with our melody as we put together a solo; and it's a classic concept, developing a theme and variations. It's often referred to as you've introduced a thought, a little fragment of melody, and then your job is to do something with it—to show the listener what's interesting about it. Listeners want to follow you doing something. You as a storyteller want to, in fact, draw them in and hold their attention and build suspense and entertain them right up to the end of your solo. That's your goal as a soloist."

—Gary Burton

OUR JOB IS TO BE A STORYTELLER . . .

I listen to music when I'm in museums, and when I find a masterpiece painting I like, I'll study it carefully. It's a little brain game I play. I imagine the painting as a scene in a movie, and then I'll search my music catalog to see if I can find a soundtrack that makes sense to accompany it. I find that this exercise helps me to retain a conceptual imprint of the masterpiece and more memory of its detail. The music becomes one with the image in my assembling every time I think of the painting. Every masterpiece is a story unto its own, and melody or a song is something like a story even when it isn't paired with a masterpiece painting.

Story is the original human pedagogy. Our model-making brains are always looking for storyline templates in order to place pieces of experiences and emerging understandings into some familiar framework. Students construct stories—about what they learn, and about *who* they are in relation to *what* is being taught. Equity considers, "From what perspective is the story experienced?"

Brilliant storytelling provides for multiple access points. By making use of storylines, Mr. Derain seeks to increase the engagement through lessons and activities that place students in positions where they can draw from their backgrounds to relate some concept or principle to the science learning targets. Without that context, many of Mr. Derain's students won't commit to their engagement. They need learning environments that bring their own life experiences and cultural assets to bear, or they are unlikely to perceive the opportunities to learn as meaningful.

Mr. Derain thinks a lot in terms of relationships, and not just his own interpersonal relationship with students. He thinks in terms of students' relationship with school itself. His students are in various stages of relationship with school. Many who are in poor relationship with school hold drab and uninspiring narratives about their academic identities.

> AD: The ones who don't have identities that are in good relationship with school will often come to school, but they come to school to socialize, to see their friends, for a stable environment even if they're not conscious of that. But they're the ones that'll show up on the snowy days, and the last day of school. But when it comes to applying themselves academically, if I do a traditional lesson, even if I have a great relationship with them, they'll only go along for a little bit. I tend to think of them as the ultimate connoisseurs of my teaching because if something works for them, then I know it's good teaching. . . . So for that audience, what I'm kinda seeing is either they've got so much going on in their lives or they've had so many bad experiences in school to this point that they're not gonna give me any benefit of the doubt. It has to resonate for them somehow; it has to serve some need for them; it has to fit their lives . . . or else I don't get a pass. There's no freebies there. It's not like an antagonistic relationship; it's just we're not operating out of a cultural assumption that this is what we do, this is how school works, we'll just go along with it. It's hard, but I also kinda like it because I know for sure that if something works, it works! We're starting to rebuild their relationship with school, connecting their narratives to school narratives.

THE STAR OF THE SHOW

Our students along with each and every human being on the planet has a *Story of Self* that seeks to answer from a first-person perspective the questions: *Who am I?* and *How have I come to be?* The *Story of Self* is told in the key of culture and transmitted through social learning.

At a time of pandemics and social discord, it's easy to see how many students' personal narratives have become detached from the narratives in school; but in the interest of Equity, it is our job as teachers to re-intertwine them. When a student's narratives are detached from schools', their academic success in school is largely dependent on transactional experiences and compliance, and true rigor and cognitive engagement are near impossiblities.

The power of story is in its relatability. The more relatable a story is, the more likely the audience will be able to find something meaningful for themselves. When a story is told well, even from the perspective of the first person, it allows others to feel empowered to also relay their own narratives. Your students have to be able to identify something within themselves that resembles or speaks to the essence of the storylines you're trying to depict. Your students have to insert themselves into the story. Story is a form of play that teaches us how to read our environment. How do I control the world when unexpected change happens? Who do I have to be in order to control it? What do I have to understand to be the star of my own show, the one who affects the story in meaningful ways?

The storylines we use to engage students with content should provide *multiple on-ramps* for students to use their cultural fluencies to center themselves as protagonists . . . otherwise we are asking them to audition for bit roles and not as the stars in their own biopics. Our teaching must offer opportunities for students to find their way into the story. We have to write a story that they want to see themselves in as opposed to *telling* them that this is a story that they should want to be in. When students are engaged in a good story, they can discover who they are, and who they can come to be. They can become more aware that engagement has consequences, and those consequences can be engineered with intention so that learning is purposeful.

The best stories star (as in feature) *YOU*. If our learning experiences don't tell the story of *YOU* to our students, then they are not empowered to draw on their cultural fluencies. So, when Mr. Derain re-framed his physics essential question to *How do you get superpowers?*, he was opening a doorway through which students could enter equipped with all of their most valuable tools for learning, their cultural fluencies. This way, they will more likely be able to integrate what is being presented into their cognitive niche for how they *human (v)*.

AD: "How do you get superpowers?" This I can personalize into, "What's the superpower that you want to develop?" You wanna get really good at playing the piano? Or whatever? Physics can help you do that because it's all about developing superpowers. And so I think this question situates them in a protagonist role and helps me personalize the connection to the content for them . . . tapping into those deeper questions. That's when I could see us starting to tap into the same kind of things that draw millions of humans to these billion-dollar Marvel movies. We can also tap into those same fundamental story-making neurons in our brains to engage students. And it answers the questions *why*. It helps me personalize, to set opportunities for students to bring their cultures, their lives, their identities, and their assets into the *why* question.

THE STORY UNFOLDS AS A QUESTION . . .

The story must unfold as a question because if the story is already told then the experience is stagnant. If the experience doesn't have energy, our students won't be able to make it meaningful and it won't be worth their effort. We can't just tell our students how the story ends. We're not telling a story *to* our students. We're telling a story *with* our students. It must be composed with them as cast and crew. If the story doesn't unfold as a question there's nothing to garner momentum. We're handing these questions off to our students and that's what empowers them to both engage in the now and continue to be lifelong learners.

AD: Why are storylines more engaging? One, it helps me plan a more cohesive kind of unit and sequence of units which helps you know where you're going. But I think on a deeper level, I've come to understand that the structure of stories resonates with these deep internal questions that we have, and that's what engages us. . . . You gotta make a compelling storyline, otherwise, they're just sitting in the stadium seats observing someone else trying to live their best life.

Our students come to us with their own cultural superpowers that enable them to navigate social situations and environmental niches. In order to answer these storyline questions, students are more likely to draw from their backgrounds, their identities, their cultural fluencies in the interest of learning the content.[1]

NOTES ON ARTMAKING: THE POWER OF STORY

By making use of storylines, we seek to increase the engagement through learning experiences that place students in positions where they can draw from their cultural inheritances to relate some concept or principle to their own lives. Without the larger context, many of our students won't commit to much of any engagement. They need learning opportunities that bring their own cultural assets to bear—or they are unlikely to perceive the opportunity to learn as meaningful. This makes social learning a much more powerful mechanism for students' experience in thinking about content.

You will determine the best approaches given your own philosophizing. I have seen success with KWLs, mind maps, and "Would you rather—?" type activities to inspire students' thinking. I also like the *Give One, Get One* as an experience for students to spend their cultural inheritances and share their thinking. You should develop a rich prompt which can be answered in multiple ways. When students have different answers, they can trade, but after a few rounds, students will meet with partners who have similar ideas, and they should be encouraged to co-author new responses. This is often a fantastic time for spotlighting not just the students' responses, but also the pathways taken to them. I look for the opportunities to say something like: "Oh, okay. I think I see what you're doing there, but can you tell us a bit more about how the two of you came up with that response."

I especially enjoy assigning classroom TED Talks. I've found the key in selling this to your kiddos is a vibrant description and modeling of an excellent TED Talk. The point of a good TED Talk is to inform and inspire with an original twist on an observation of significance. You want for your students to feel motivated to find the unique take that compellingly connects their life with the content.

In the *Interview You* strategy, students are told they have to play the part of both a journalist and an expert who is being interviewed on [fill in the appropriate content topic]. The students will feel the difference between low- and high-rigor questions when they provide responses in the role of the expert. It's hard to give interesting answers to low-rigor questions. When students are able to find the more interesting ways of interviewing themselves about the content, it's generally because they've been able to make a connection with the topic and their own individual, shared, and identity-group experiences. I have students record their interviews, but I've found it's advisable to place stipulations on the production, otherwise the focus of students' thinking can be misapplied to the technical components of making videos. We want our kiddos to be thinking about the types of questions and the nature of the responses those questions are likely to evoke. When their thinking is focused appropriately, it's a beautiful thing to see how empowered our students can be when extending their understanding of concepts with the cultural references and storylines cherished by their home communities.

CHAPTER NOTE

1. A note on working with pre-packaged curriculum: I meet many teachers who feel saddled by more-or-less scripted curriculum that paces and specifies classroom lessons. I've been in the business of teaching long enough to see that these curriculum packages have come a long way in terms of quality of design, and yet, they will never know your students as you do. They will always have a last mile delivery problem. The "last mile" in the supply chain journey of any product faces the greatest exposure to the most combustive elements in the delivery environment. On one hand, I can see the value in a carefully

considered curriculum, but these alone cannot tell us what and how to teach. The questions of what and how to teach arise in concrete situations loaded with particulars of time, place, person, and circumstance. I prefer to think of the curriculum packages I see in districts across the country as a resource and not actually curriculum. To the artist, resources are like fundamental particles: charged, but indifferent. If you answer the five guiding planning questions with the CRE vocabulary, your thinking will be more artful, and you will be able to use the resources as a tool among others in your toolkit.

CHAPTER 8

Audience

"I think there's a lot of people that are neglected in art."

—Jean-Michel Basquiat

A CAPTIVE AUDIENCE

A big difference between brilliant teaching in a classroom and brilliant music performed in a jazz club or a brilliant painting exhibited on a gallery wall is the art performed in brilliant teaching is generally performed before a captive audience. Everyone who walks into a jazz club or museum, even the people who enter begrudgingly, presumably have some choice in being there. But, if given the option, some (maybe most) of our students who are the hardest to engage would choose to be somewhere else, and so our audience requires a different kind of incentive in order to buy into the story and to hum the melody along with us.

In Chapter 4, I made the argument that our pedagogy is neither impartial nor unbiased because all learning is deeply cultural and our concepts—the very entities that comprise our understanding of the world and all meaning in every way—are developed in the context of the social and cultural spaces in which teaching and learning occur. Our methods shouldn't neglect the social assets of our students. Indifference is inequitable. We must appeal to our students' learning sensibilities with opportunities to consult their cultural knapsacks. Brilliant teaching actively seeks out opportunities to cognitively engage its audience. We are responsible for providing our students with the tools for participating in the motivational infrastructure of our learning experiences, or the opportunities to learn are neither artful nor equitable.

There are many classrooms filled with students who are effectively made "school-proof" by the circumstances of their lives. The single most reliable predictor of students' achievement in school (as measured by high-stakes standardized testing) is zip code, which suggests that socio-economic status is at least as important as quality and effective teaching in student outcomes (Au, 2010; Turner, 2019; Khushal, 2021; Cushing, 2022).

But it's not just that some students have material advantages over others that explain the differences in school performance. In this case, it's appropriate to think in terms of social ethnolinguistic groups. *Social learning* is defined in Chapter 1 as "learning that is facilitated by observation of or interaction with another individual or the products of other individuals' learning" (Hoppitt & Laland, 2013). Social learning allows for those with less experience (i.e., naive learners) to develop their own cultural fluencies which, in turn, influence theirs and others' behavior through inferences and observation. Social learning is both a more efficient and less costly process for acquiring valuable information than individual learning.

Some students have the advantage of learning how to *human (v)* in social spaces where the cultural repertoire is closely aligned to the cultural variants (i.e., information, norms, symbols, values, and narratives) that are conceptually centered in the policy and practice environment of schools. In addition to being less burdened by the effects of systemic inequalities, students in the more affluent zip codes are more likely to enter school with social learning tools and cultural fluencies that schools tend to favor and hold in high esteem. Students who have developed intellectually in a cognitive niche that mostly encompasses the same language as the predominant style and social prose of schools require less cognitive demand than those who have to both learn the academic content lessons and also translate the cultural value of what they're learning. I refer to students whose social backgrounds are largely consistent with the cultural repertoires of affluent zip-code communities as school-proof. It doesn't mean that individual students from these communities can't and don't perform poorly in school. It means, however, that an individual's poor school performance is less likely to be a function of the social, political, and economic inequalities that have a detracting effect on students in the socio-ethnolinguistic groups not residing within affluent zip codes.

I'm biased in this way, but I prefer working with the students who are not school-proof. They're so interesting! Plus, they teach me a lot about my craft. They bring cultural fluencies that are tailor-made to serve them in their home communities. Their cognitive niches differ from their socially advantaged peers. They are differently motivated in their learning. They are more likely to depend on the instruction to provide evidence of the value of their investments in learning. In Chapters 6 and 7, I argue that improvisation and story have to be developed to match the social context in order for us to say it is an equitable learning environment. To close Equity gaps, we must apply our artful thinking and philosophizing in ways that center the classroom as a social learning environment. One way we can view this is in terms of audience. Teachers know that, in these classrooms, when the audience tunes out (i.e., when they can't follow the music), they start following other things. So, the question becomes: How do we hold our audience's attention?

In effect, we're looking to create habits for our audience of learners. Habits *of* thinking, habits *for* thinking. Habits that are neither contained nor restrained by a particular content area, but rather habits of thinking that are generative in terms of building momentum for deeper and more expansive thinking. When we are clear about how we want our students thinking, and we design storylines and melodies with which our students can make *this-is-like* connections and *this-reminds-me-of* extensions, then we have potentially engineered a space where our understandings of the content, our pedagogy, our sense of students as cultural beings, and the processes of social learning come together to form a vibrant and responsive learning environment.

A GOOD CLASSROOM IS SUPPORTIVE OF NEW IDEAS . . .

I love being in classrooms. They are living and growing organisms, changing every minute. The atmosphere in a responsive learning environment is a charged space filled with feeling and the social texture of relationships. Our students make decisions to engage based in many ways on their relationships with the content and their interpersonal relationships within the classroom community. The hand-offs for students' thinking are essential because they develop spaces in which interpersonal relationships gain traction. This is needed for the basic levels of trust required even for what may seem the simplest types of social transactions in a classroom. Without at least some trust, our kiddos who aren't school-proof won't exchange much at all, for fear of being disappointed in the return on their investments.

This means that when exchange is risky and rare (i.e., engagement is low), you can increase it by building more and better interpersonal relationships.

A good classroom is supportive of new ideas. It works best when the audience is empowered to share ideas. Our minds integrate understandings in response to the world, as it creates and re-creates itself. When students take chances with the material, it changes their perspectives, expands their way of thinking, and allows them to be open to new ideas and learning experiences. When it's working, the students allow themselves to be changed by new understandings and experiences rather than being stuck in their old ideas (Freedman, 2003).

In a classroom supportive of new ideas, the goal of instruction is to hear something new. That's possible if we're teaching for integrated thinking (but less so for specialistic knowledge) because there are countless possibilities (think *degeneracy* from Chapter 4) for students to personalize the understanding in the social and cultural context of their backgrounds and identities.

I am regularly in classrooms with more than a dozen socio-ethnolinguistic groups represented. Our strategy isn't to leverage a particular cultural fluency, but rather to pose opportunities for rich thinking in which students will be inclined to draw from the cultural inheritances and cognitive niches that frame all that they know and can do. In classrooms that are supportive of new ideas, students do not learn in spite of their backgrounds but rather because of them.

Inference-making provides lots of opportunities for students to make use of their cultural fluencies. To make any inference is inherently a type of analogy making. Inferencing is a mental habit central to one's ever-evolving categories and concepts. It's also a mental activity that's ripe for building highly engaging learning experiences that can capitalize on a host of social issues and current events.

Improvisation in teaching starts with clarity about the intentions for learning and the presentation of information in artful ways that assist in discovering new ideas. Like jazz musicians, our learners should experiment with the information. They stretch it into new places, remix it, play with it, and take risks. Perfection is not the goal in jazz. New ideas based on old ideas that sound good to the audience are what is most important.

When the teacher gives the student room to "play" with an idea, the student further constructs a sense of "self-efficacy"—the belief that they have the capacity to perform a designated task—which is essential in the development of an academic identity that justifies the efforts needed for meaningful learning. When students play with the information, it's planted in relation to their cognitive niches to allow for not only the memorization of specialistic knowledge, but also the integration of understandings and the development of new tools and frameworks for learning. Through the iterative processes of consolidating and re-consolidating, new neural pathways are forged, and a conceptual imprint of the understanding is formed (Alberini, 2009; Kepinska et al., 2017).

But how? How do you invite students to engage with new ideas when they seem to be altogether disinterested? It's an inelegant question, but that doesn't mean it lacks merit. As in all human endeavors, it's a matter of motivation.

IN DEFENSE OF INCENTIVES

My position on incentives has taken a sharp turn since the first part of my career. I was once adamantly opposed to using incentives in my classroom. The idea that students should be given treats to motivate their engagement in school struck me as demeaning and likely to condition students to expect to receive trinkets for some of the basic behaviors necessary for their success and well-being. *Students should be intrinsically motivated to learn*, I would say. *We are teaching students to depend on outside forces for basic motivations that should be internalized*, I would say. *Our students need to learn how to motivate themselves without some external carrot to spur them on*, I would say. This was a position I held staunchly for years. Now, however, my thinking on incentives has evolved.

Let me pose my thoughts here in the form of a question: Is it possible for a student to be intelligent and not be motivated to engage in school?

I have found that most teachers would answer, yes. I, myself, have known many students to be bright and curious and yet not motivated to put in the consistent effort or seem to care enough to be successful in school.

If it's possible for students to be intelligent and not motivated to engage in school—and our task in terms of Equity is to design quality learning opportunities that are effective in bringing about achievement—then teaching requires not only that we make our content into a melody with storylines and relevant essential questions, but also that we support the motivations of students for engaging in the learning experience.

I advocate for incentives to be used to support motivation for cognitive (and not behavioral) engagement in order to provide a more culturally responsive learning environment—particularly in the classrooms where motivation for learning is low. The three points of my claim are:

1. All learning (and intelligence) is cultural.
2. The motivation for learning is a function of cultural inheritance: that is, motivation is a social construct—the result of fluency in a cognitive niche.
3. Culturally Responsive Education doesn't attempt to merely insert culture into the education, but rather insert education into the culture.

All Learning (and Intelligence) Is Cultural

In Chapter 4, I made the argument that all learning is cultural and that we learn by leveraging our fluencies—that is, that which is useful to us in our environmental niche(s). Human activity does not occur in a cultural vacuum. Any kind of human activity is *human* precisely because it is a function of human sociality and emotion. The capacity for designing fair opportunities for students is channeled through the clear understanding that all learning and our perceptions of intelligence are a function of culture. In the discussion of social transmission (Chapter 1), we saw that cultural variants spread through social spaces in ways that assist adept cultural learners to be successful beyond the innovative capacities of a single individual. This is true, however, only to the extent that naive learners can identify the cultural variants that benchmark successful models for learning, imitation, observation, and inferencing. Equity in education seeks to give every kiddo the chance to build and confirm their emerging understandings in community where they have opportunities to access multiple avenues of social learning. It adds to the potential for rigor and increases the likelihood that all learners will have a chance to find their way to the integrated understandings that we want them spending time with.

Some would say that incentivizing engagement is similar to training pets. This is a common behaviorist analogy that many bring to mind. But this comparison is deeply flawed in significant ways starting with—human intelligence isn't about specific behaviors. When I discuss incentivizing cognitive engagement, I am referencing the literature on Social Learning Theory, and I am talking about something unique and specific to humans. It would be difficult to impossible with our current technology to measure the thinking of a dog or pigeon or most any nonhuman animal. Even our closest primate relatives don't "think" like humans much less leverage culture in the accrual of understandings anywhere near the extent of our species.

When using incentives with animals, we are measuring the efficacy of the rewards by tracking the variable of their behavior. This approach is insufficient for humans, however, given that behavior by itself offers only a limited view into the invisible mechanisms of the brain. Further, our pets aren't cultural species (or otherwise I'm pretty sure they would have united to unseat us, their overlords, by now). Our pets do not rely on social learning or cultural inheritance for their survival in the ways that humans do. Our pets are able to survive through *individual learning*, and this is why the strategy of incentivizing cognitive engagement is nothing like training your pet. Instead of using rewards to compel pets to potty outside or chew only on pet-approved toys, our incentives are to inspire students to think.

Intelligence in humans is a function of processing information in order to identify the essence or gist of a situation (Hofstadter & Sander, 2013). We humans have the capacity for language and learning through inference making in social spaces. We are able to anticipate the meaning of gestures and events by mentalizing, which along with emotion, may be the most quintessential aspects of the human experience. Problem-solving behaviors and the associated skills that extend from intelligence are developed within and in relation to human cultural repertoires and cognitive niches. There is no culturally neutral way of being intelligent. Further, all intelligence is developed inside of cognitive niches mediated by the social norms that govern interactions among the members of the social group.

I have been a long-time fan of the work of Deci and Ryan (2012, 2017), and I cite and appreciate the large volumes of research that inform Self-Determination Theory and related ideas. However, after taking a deeper dive into the literature of cultural anthropology and cultural psychology, I now have different suppositions and questions about the self-determination research. My philosophizing curiosities led me to read Vygotsky, Cole, Bruner, Bandura, Boyd, Richerson, Henrich, and others who have argued that the research models often used to study the psychological predications of human behavior cater primarily to a narrow perspective of the human existence. When the subjects of motivation studies, as an example, are predominantly college-educated persons and the studies themselves are conducted on majority White university campuses, we can assume that the sample population being studied is a relatively homogenous group with a particular background of social experiences, preparation, and cultural fluencies. These studies are conducted in starkly different circumstances and social spaces than the work of teaching in American public schools where dozens of racial, ethnic, language, and cultural groups may be represented in one classroom.[1]

The motivation for learning is a function of cultural inheritance: that is, motivation is a social construct—the result of fluency in a cognitive niche.

There is a large body of evidence and argument based in the research on human thought in the social sciences, the cognitive sciences, and specific fields of study, including cultural anthropology, psychology, and behavioral economics (among others) that motivation is a cultural construct (Anderman, 2020; Bandura, 1982, 1988, 1991, 2001; Dweck, 2017; Kinderman, 1993; King & McInerney, 2016; Maehr, 1974, Nolen, 2015; Osher et al., 2020; Roeser et al., 2009; Sage & Kindermann, 1999;

Turner and Patrick, 2008; Schunk & DiBenedetto, 2020; Usher, 2018; Wentzel, 1998, 2009; Wigfield et al., 2015; Yosso, 2005). We learn our frameworks for agency and our calculus for motivation in the same social spaces where we learn how to *human (v)*. We learn through our social and cultural indoctrinations how to achieve status and success within the social group. These knowings become the baseline(s) for our motivations. We develop our register for motivation in relation to that which we learn to be valued in our cultural niche. In the initial stages of our development, this isn't merely a calibration of preferences, it's a function of our survival (Barrett, 2020).

Culture shapes our worldview. We perceive not just physiologically but also intellectually. It's literally true that people from different societies vary in their ability to accurately perceive objects and individuals both in and out of context (Brown, 2004; Henrich, 2016). Cultural niches result in different cognitive abilities, perceptual biases, attention allocations, and motivations. Across societies, differing expectations and normative standards incentivize and mold distinct psychological conventions (Henrich, 2020; Turner & Patrick, 2008; Yosso, 2005).

This is one of the defining features of humanity. People involuntarily inherit the cultural variants modeled for them with or without incentives. This is a powerful mechanism for human understanding. We learn from and with other humans through individual and social learning habits like observation and inferencing. After the capacity for social learning has fully developed, one cannot keep people from learning what they have seen (Bandura, 1997). Incentives for cognitive engagement can enhance the conditions in which the opportunities for social learning are optimized. Importantly, the point isn't to motivate specific kiddos, but rather to bring attention to the kinds of engagement that are most celebrated in the classroom community.

Culturally Responsive Education doesn't attempt to merely insert culture into the education, but rather insert education into the culture.

The goal of culturally responsive teaching is not to insert culturally relevant references into learning experiences but rather to design opportunities in which students think rigorously and reference their cognitive niches.

In the words of Gloria Ladson-Billings (1995):

This notion is, in all probability, true for many students who are not a part of the White, middle-class mainstream. For almost 15 years, anthropologists have looked at ways to develop a closer fit between students' home culture and the school. This work has had a variety of labels including "culturally appropriate" (Au & Jordan, 1981), "culturally congruent" (Mohatt & Erickson, 1981), "culturally responsive" (Cazden & Leggett, 1981; Erickson & Mohatt, 1982), and "culturally compatible" (Jordan, 1985; Vogt et al., 1987). It has attempted to locate the problem of discontinuity between what students experience at home and what they experience at school in the speech and language interactions of teachers and students.

Incentives for cognitive engagement can be employed to acclimate students to the norms, values, and expectations that situate them to recognize and benefit from learning opportunities in school. This is most successful in the context of culturally responsive learning experiences in which students can draw on their cultural fluencies while thinking rigorously about content. Students are most likely to be able to reference their cultural funds of knowledge when led to investigations or applications in which they can reason and extend the academic concepts into nonroutine manipulations across multiple disciplines and a range of sources. This is something deeper than changing the names in a math word problem from Mary and Peter to Maria and Pedro. This requires that we value our students' cultural fluencies as having pedagogical value. Recall that a featured premise of Equity in education is that cultural differences do not equal deficits. To incentivize cognitive engagement further necessitates that we have clear targets for rigor in the design of learning experiences.

Rigor

I've taken the position in this book that culturally responsive teaching is best served with a conceptual understanding of intelligence as the ability to identify the essence of something in order to learn that which is useful and necessary for decision making and problem solving. The most meaningful learning experiences are those in which students are able to think rigorously in order to gain an integrated understanding of some skill or concept. By rigorous, I do not mean harder, or a greater quantity of work, nor am I referring to specific types of texts or content.

Rigor is a theme of CRE because it allows students to extend their understandings in rich and complex ways so that they can leverage their in- and out-of-school competencies in deep learning (Stembridge, 2019). Karin Hess's work on cognitive rigor is essential in order to support responsive instruction. In this definition, rigor encompasses the complexity of content, the cognitive engagement with that content, and the scope of the planned learning activities (Hess et al., 2009).

If you search the internet for "Karin Hess Cognitive Rigor Matrix" (CRM), you will soon find many subject specific versions that all follow the same format. The CRM superposes Bloom's Taxonomy of Educational Objectives and Webb's Depth-of-Knowledge (DOK) model. There are types of thinking described down the far left column and depth-of-knowledge levels listed along the top row. It is one of my go-to tools in planning. I use it to set my targets for rigor every time I design a learning experience.

Hess et al. (2009) explain:

Although related through their natural ties to the complexity of thought, Bloom's Taxonomy and Webb's DOK model differ in scope and application. Bloom's Taxonomy categorizes the cognitive skills required of the brain when faced with a new task, therefore describing the type of thinking processes necessary to answer a question. The DOK model, on the other hand, relates more closely to the depth of content understanding and scope of a learning activity, which manifests in the skills required to complete the task from inception to finale (e.g., planning, researching, drawing conclusions).

These DOK-level descriptions indicate the complexity of the content and the task given to students. On most versions of the CRM, the descriptors for the Depth of Knowledge (DOK) levels and the Bloom's types of thinking are very similar to:

DOK-1: Recall and Reproduction—Recall of a fact, term, principle, concept; perform a routine procedure

DOK-2: Basic Application of Skills/Concepts—Use of information, conceptual knowledge, select appropriate procedures for a task; two or more steps with decision points along the way; routine problems; organize/display data, interpret/use simple graphs

DOK-3: Strategic Thinking and Reasoning—Requires reasoning, developing a plan or sequence of steps to approach problem; requires some decision making and justification; abstract, complex, or nonroutine; often more than one possible answer

DOK-4: Extended Thinking—An investigation or application to real world; requires time to research, problem solve, and process multiple conditions of the problem or task; nonroutine manipulations, across disciplines/content areas/multiple sources

The Bloom's taxonomy categories speak to the processes and knowledge to describe educational objectives.

Remember—Retrieve knowledge from memory, recognize, locate (point to), identify

Understand—Construct meaning, clarify, paraphrase, represent, translate, illustrate, give examples, classify, categorize, summarize, generalize, infer a logical conclusion, predict, compare/contrast, match like ideas, explain, construct models

Apply—Carry out or use a procedure in a given situation; carry out (apply to a familiar task), or use (apply) to an unfamiliar task

Analyze—Break into constituent parts, determine how parts relate, differentiate between relevant-irrelevant, distinguish, focus, select, organize, outline, find coherence, deconstruct

Figure 8.1² Modified Cognitive Rigor Matrix with Question Stems

	DOK-1: Recall & Reproduction—Recall of a fact, performance of a routine procedure	DOK-2: Basic Application of Skills/Concepts—Use of information, two or more steps with decision points along the way	DOK-3: Strategic Thinking & Reasoning—Abstract, complex, or nonroutine; often more than one possible answer	DOK-4: Extended Thinking—Nonroutine manipulations, across disciplines/content areas/multiple sources
Remember—Retrieve knowledge from memory, recognize, locate (point to), identify				
Understand—Construct meaning, illustrate, categorize, generalize, infer a logical conclusion, predict, construct models	• What–Where–/Who is–? • How did–? • Which one–?	• How would you explain–? • How does – function?	• What about – is the same/different as–? • What are my own examples of–?	• What would happen if–? • Is – relevant or irrelevant? Why?
Apply—Carry out or use a procedure in a given situation	• What are the types of–? • What's the definition of–?	• Why did–? • What evidence or support is offered?	• What conclusions can be drawn from – information?	• What is my opinion? What evidence and/or arguments support my opinion?
Analyze—Break into constituent parts, determine how parts relate, outline, find coherence, deconstruct		• How can you organize this?	• What hypothesis or theory explains this information–?	• What would you change? Why? How might you change–?
Create—Reorganize elements into novel structures, hypothesize, design, produce			• Why did you change–? Did it work? Why? Why not?	• Why are we learning this?
Evaluate—Make judgments based on criteria, detect inconsistencies or fallacies, critique				

Source: Adapted from 2009 © Hess, K., Carlock, D., Jones, B., & Walkup, J. Presentation at CCSSO, Detroit, MI, June 2009. [khess@nciea.org].

Evaluate—Make judgments based on criteria, check, detect inconsistencies or fallacies, judge, critique

Create—Reorganize elements into new patterns/structures, generate, hypothesize, design, plan, produce

It sometimes helps to think of cognitive rigor in terms of the kinds of questions students will be led to consider. In planning, when we are clear about the types of thinking and the DOK levels we expect to see from students, we can incorporate question stems into the design of rigorous learning experiences. Figure 8.1 is a simple graphic of how questions can be developed in the context of setting targets for rigor. These are not intended to be exhaustive in any respect, but they point in the direction of how questions can explicitly and/or implicitly support students' thinking.

Rigor reinforces social learning by providing opportunities for degeneracy, the assembling of memories and thoughts with varied neuro-chemical and electrical combinations (recall the hub analogy in Chapter 4). Instruction that assumes that students will construct their understandings in a particular, predictable way (like retrieving files from a file cabinet) are flawed and inherently inequitable. We know that with multiple opportunities for routing of the understanding through neurocognitive pathways, the brain assembles memories differently according to the context in which the memory is being reconstructed (Price & Friston, 2002; Dodel et al., 2020). Cultural repertoires and cognitive niches serve as organizing principles for how concepts are understood. The cultural fluencies that students have learned through the participation in their social groups influence how they are likely to build their analogical bridges. These are the on-ramps that lead potentially to *this-is-like* understandings.

NOTES ON ARTMAKING: INCENTIVES ARE NOT THE REWARD

In my philosophizing, I've come to reason that incentives aren't actually the reward; rather, incentives are the commemoration of the rewarding experience of rigorous thinking. I argue that the reward for cognitive engagement is the experience of thinking itself. Learning experiences that extend students' thinking—the opportunities for students to remix and integrate their understandings—are joyful and meaningful. The incentives we use in our classrooms serve to memorialize a fulfilling experience of thinking so that the imprint of emotions, motivations, and emerging understandings are easier to access in the future. The goal in my use of incentives for cognitive engagement is to inspire the community of learners and not just one or two kiddos. There are many classrooms that do not need coaching for motivation, but I would argue that there are many more where the learning environment could be pushed to another level of rigor and cognitive engagement with the use of incentives.

When considering incentives, it's about the *being* and not the doing. As in, I use incentives to encourage my students to *be* curious, to *be* agents of their own intellectual growth. The goal is to provide the environment in which our students learn how to *be* cognitively engaged and not merely *do* the behaviors associated with successful engagement in school. This is not to say that incentives are a cure-all. In fact, in Social Learning Theory, reinforcement is considered a facilitative rather than a necessary condition because factors other than response consequences can influence what people attend to. When attention is drawn to modeled activities by the events themselves, the addition of affirming incentives does not dramatically increase observational learning. Again, the real issue is rigor. I am advocating for the use of incentives for cognitive engagement, which is the output of rigorous thinking. You must offer your students something rigorous that is worth thinking deeply about—and it must be clear that you want them to gather from their cognitive niches in doing so (which is what makes the learning meaningful). Without opportunities for truly rigorous thinking, it's unlikely that incentives will do much more than pacify antsy learners whose Equity needs will likely remain unmet.

I've found that the actual incentive itself can be almost anything as long as it resonates within the classroom community. Though I prefer not to give candy, I have. (I actually wish Takis weren't so effective because I personally think they're disgusting. Fruit snacks can be a big hit too!) I've had success with weekly raffles. I know teachers who purchase hoodies from their local Goodwill store for less than $10, hang them high on the wall, and make a big production out of a monthly draw for the winning ticket. (This has the added benefit of a free advertisement for the value of learning in your classroom when the winning kiddo wears the hoodie that everyone saw prominently displayed.) Almost anything can be an effective incentive, from monthly lunches with the teacher to showing up at a weekend soccer game to the waving of a *brain power wand*! (I have a picture of this in a Kindergarten classroom that will absolutely melt your teacher heart.) I wouldn't have believed it unless I saw it myself, but stickers work with kiddos pre-K all the way through 12th grade!

The key is to be clear about the targets for rigor (Hess et al., 2009; Stembridge, 2019), and to name the reason when issuing the incentive. Your incentives should only be given for thinking or students will rightfully learn that rule-following behavior is what's truly valued in your classroom. You should have a catch phrase and a nonlinguistic hand gesture. When I give incentives, I say "Oooh, you are making my teacher brain happy!" while I look at the student with my hands open, palms facing me, and vigorously wiggling my fingers. You will know that your incentives are working when your students tease you about it, as in: *"Brace yourself because your teacher brain is going to be super happy when you hear what I'm thinking!"*

CHAPTER NOTES

1. I understand and appreciate the arguments for PBIS (Positive Behavioral Interventions and Supports) models, but these are intended to incentivize behavioral engagement. I do not intend to refute PBIS claims as much as I would hope to promote those in favor of incentivizing cognitive engagement. It may be that the two can co-exist, but I would strongly encourage teachers to use altogether different incentives for the support of the behavioral goals of PBIS so students are less likely to conflate those with our expectations for their cognitive engagement.

2. Adapted from 2009 © Hess, K., Carlock, D., Jones, B., & Walkup, J. Presentation at CCSSO, Detroit, MI, June 2009. [khess@nciea.org].

CHAPTER 9

The Art of Culturally Responsive Assessments

"Exactitude is not truth."

—Henri Matisse

A CULTURE OF RESPONSIVE ASSESSMENTS

There is an art to culturally responsive assessment. When performed well, a classroom with a culture of responsive assessments not only provides a robust return of data useful for making those teacher-moves that best support students' learning outcomes, but it also enriches the sense of community and the opportunities for social learning. The art of culturally responsive assessment is the design of experiences for students to perform their understandings in a way that makes feedback available to them with ongoing opportunities to revise, edit, and adjust their thinking and the products that are intended to be the evidence of integrated understandings.

In terms of Equity, assessments are intended to measure the extent to which students have developed integrated understandings of the concepts at the heart of instruction and support students in further developing their intelligence through the experience of thinking. The art of culturally responsive assessment is to evaluate the quality of the thinking and the understandings about content in light of the social and cultural context in which the teaching and learning occur. In addition, culturally responsive assessments generate robust opportunities for feedback, which is the information about progress made in the efforts to reach a goal.

Performative assessments are rich teaching tools because they provide space, range, and scope for the types of feedback that students can perceive as useful as they seek to perform their competencies. From a culturally responsive perspective, feedback is an opportunity to share attention with students. Equity gaps are exacerbated the more we teach without assessing students' understandings because poor assessment models add to the likelihood that only our students whom are already proficient will be able to exploit the opportunities to extend their thinking. Robust feedback loops allow for our students to see, hear, and feel the layers and nuances of understandings that integrate into their own schema and cultural fluencies.

A performative assessment is an experience of demonstrating an understanding. Experience is the medium for the art of Culturally Responsive Education, and culture is the arbiter of experience in any social space. It's not possible to measure what a student understands when we cut off their access to the cognitive niches and cultural fluencies for knowing that are critical to their capacities for locating a conceptual essence. Neuroscientist Mary Helen Immordino-Yang's work (2016) on the intersections of culture, emotion, and cognition reveals a great deal about the ways in which affect gives form to thought:

> Our emotions and our relationships and our cultural experiences in the social world organize and shape the development of brain networks that allow us to learn. This is shaping, changing, and recruiting brain networks for memory and emotion that will not be recruited any other way. It is literally neurobiologically impossible to think about things deeply or to remember things about which you've had no emotion.

Teaching is profoundly human, and the cognition we seek to assess is enmeshed within affective and cultural contexts. I argue that high-stakes, standardized testing, as it is currently conceptualized and administered, offers only a partial and proximal view of the quality and effectiveness of teaching and learning. Standardized tests, even when used in the most appropriate ways, are intended to be measures and not the goals of quality and effective teaching and learning. So, when I'm asked if culturally responsive teaching will improve standardized test scores, I know whomever is asking has, at best, an ambiguous view of how pedagogy and assessments are supposed to work together. The question, "Will this improve test scores?" represents a fundamental misunderstanding of the goals of instruction relative to the goals of assessment. The better question is, "Will the test scores reflect the improvements in the quality and effectiveness of teaching and learning?"

WHY ARE PERFORMATIVE ASSESSMENTS MORE EQUITABLE THAN TRADITIONAL "STANDARDIZED" ASSESSMENTS?

If Equity in Education is the policy and practice directive to provide quality and effective learning opportunities so that background and identity are neither correlative nor predictive of student performance and/or achievement outcomes, and it entails attention to outputs (rather than inputs) as the primary metric for measuring fairness without conflating cultural difference with deficit—*then what are we trying to accomplish with equitable assessments?*

In terms of Equity, assessments are intended to measure the extent to which students have developed integrated understandings of the content. These integrated understandings are in relationship with specialistic knowledge though they need not be narrowly defined by it; therefore, we need responsive assessments that measure students' capacities for thinking without unnecessarily pigeon-holing the cultural expressions of what they know.

The goal of Equity is fairness, and so we can ask: What would a fair— that is, equitable—assessment entail? In other words, what does an equitable assessment measure? And how does an equitable assessment collect evidence of that which it seeks to measure?

A culturally responsive classroom endeavors to allow for social learning opportunities that encompass many cultural ways of being in assessments. If all learning is cultural then it stands to reason that the evidence of learning is also cultural. Therefore, we need to be intentional about how we think about who our students are as cultural learners and how we create opportunities for them to demonstrate what they have learned.

Traditional assessments like quizzes, examinations, research papers, and the like have been generally associated with teacher-centered models of instruction. These traditional assessments ask some variation of the same question: *Did you learn the lesson?* The culture of a responsive classroom, on the other hand, features many iterations of a different question: *Do you understand?*

We must carefully interrogate our goals for culturally responsive assessment because *Do you understand?* isn't the same inquiry as *Did you learn the lesson?* The goal of culturally responsive assessment is most certainly *not* to design classrooms that perfectly replicate lessons—not even in the case of those lessons that we think of as culturally responsive. The goal of culturally responsive assessment is to design classrooms that robustly and accurately deliver the evidence of quality and effective learning experiences. This is an argument I can make easily to teachers, but it runs counter to the central though generally unnamed premise of the high-stakes, *perfection-driven*, standardized testing paradigm.

Perfection versus Robustness

The arguments in favor of standardized tests are not completely without merit. The idea is that we must have a neutral arbiter that is easily referenced and systematically administered so that a comparative measure for quality learning outcomes can be evenly applied across the various levels—school, district, state, regional, and national. Further, the arguments go, current standardized tests draw items that present a composite scoring of reasoning abilities which can be applied universally across socio-ethnolinguistic groups.

Tests are called "high-stakes" when they are used to make major decisions about a student (such as high school graduation, tracking placement, or grade promotion) or schools based on students' scores. A standardized test is any form of test that (1) requires all test takers to answer the same questions, or a selection from a common bank of questions, and that (2) is scored in a "standard" or consistent manner in order to compare the relative performance of individual students or groups of students.

I agree that it is essential to assess the relative performance of students through measures of their achievements in learning, but I argue that the current high-stakes, standardized testing paradigm not only fails as a strategy for measuring quality and effective teaching and learning, and worse, it contributes to a culture in schools and classrooms that dis-incentivizes culturally responsive pedagogy. A valid assessment measures directly that which it seeks to know. A useful assessment for teachers is valid while also providing information that can be used to improve the effectiveness of instruction in supporting quality learning outcomes. The current models we use for testing do neither. I am not referring to diagnostic tests that can be useful for developing context for supporting students' learning. Rather, the state-administered, high-stakes standardized tests that shut down instruction for weeks throughout the school year cannot be tied to the instructional goals of a responsive learning environment—at least not in any way that a teacher can readily leverage to further build a rigorous and responsive classroom culture.

The goal of standardized testing is to perfect the methods for collecting the evidence of learning outcomes; but I say the goal of perfection is not the right goal—the right goal is robustness. In computer science, robustness is the ability of a computer system to cope with erroneous input and errors which may occur during implementation. A system is robust if it maintains stability and performance in some permissible range within non-standard and even disruptive conditions. Systems designed on the premise of robustness serve a different purpose than perfection-centered systems. Systems based on the premise of perfection assume that there is a perfect output that can be measured with perfect accuracy. The goals of education systems espousing perfection are to produce the same equally perfect outcome in every instance of teaching and learning; by contrast, the goals of a robust system are to produce quality and effective outcomes given the range of pedagogical contexts. We need assessments to measure the goals of a robust system. And, of course, we know that there can be no perfect system in the distinctly nonstandardized social, political, and economic (to say nothing of cultural) contexts in which teaching and learning occur.

Some would say that the goal of Equity—and not standardization in data collection—is too messy to imagine; and I say, of course it's messy, but we should still imagine. *What is the alternative?* Should we continue to promote standardization as a goal of assessment even as it compels standardization as a goal of pedagogy?

The instructional goal of standardized student learning outcomes is incompatible with the goals of both Equity and culturally responsive pedagogy. We should not be attempting to standardize the sameness of learning outcomes (as in all students will accumulate all the same academic skills and knowledge). Our most ambitious goal should be to provide all students opportunities to learn in rigorous and responsive learning environments. A responsive learning environment offers a quality and effective learning opportunity that isn't required to be the same in terms of topic or delivery. Instead of centering our assessment models around goals for standardized (i.e., equal) learning outcomes, we should be working to standardize the quality and effectiveness of students' learning experiences. If that were our goal, then our interpretation of the goals of standardization would change from standardized results to standardized methods for measuring student learning outcomes in nonstandard pedagogical contexts. Therefore, I am simultaneously making the argument that (1) performative assessments that leverage experience, real-world context, an emphasis on depth of understanding, and evidence collected over time are more reliable proof of students' understandings than static, traditional, standardized measures; and (2) performative assessments contribute much more to the teaching and learning environment in the way of a robust bounty of opportunities for responsive feedback loops. The messiness that's frightening to many and difficult to imagine is necessary—it is a feature of Equity and not a bug to be avoided. There is no such thing as a perfect understanding, nor is there a perfect way to assess.

The goal of culturally responsive assessment is robustness. By robust, I mean instruments and methods that can collect evidence of students' understandings in multiple forms and funnel it into data that can reliably inform both our systems- and classroom-level capacity for quality and effective teaching and learning. This is essential if we are to maximize the usefulness of assessment data for responsive instruction. Feedback is the product of a robust assessment environment.

The central premise of the high stakes standardized testing paradigm is a goal of perfection—to create perfect systems for standardizing the test and producing perfect reports of students' learning outcomes. But that perfection is not possible because we're dealing with profoundly imperfect circumstances including foundationally unfair circumstances in our society.

Our goals for assessment must be aligned with our goal for Equity, which is to develop systems and structures that support robust learning outcomes. We are not inclining our students to become automatons who think exactly like every other automaton, and therefore, robustness and not perfection is our most ambitious pedagogical effort. I argue that the premise of high-stakes, standardized testing is inequitable because the reduction of instruction to the goals of standardized learning is fundamentally incompatible with the goals of responsive pedagogy. Though Matisse was speaking about the virtues of Impressionist painting, his statement also holds true for the goals of assessments: "Exactitude is not truth."

Performative Assessments Empower Students

A major thrust of this book is to challenge insufficient views of culture because when we think of culture merely as the lists and labels of the foods, fashion, and festivities of other groups, we are at greater risk of inappropriately using our surface-level knowledge to marginalize and stereotype groups and individuals. Culture is much more complex than its symbols. Culture is the information in human minds that affects behavior and decision making; it is the software that makes the brain hardware operational. Culture is integral to our understandings and our expressions of what we understand. The understandings we seek to teach can neither be taught effectively nor fairly without attention to culturally responsive practices in instruction and assessment.

If our goal is to *do* Equity then performative assessments are inherently fairer than traditional high-stakes, standardized tests. Performative assessments are more equitable because the structures empower students to draw from their cultural inheritances in the demonstration of understanding. All of what they know and understand is more useful to a student in the context of performative rather than traditional assessments. High-stakes, standardized testing most reliably measures a certain type of socio-ethnolinguistic fluency. By that I mean, they most reliably capture the evidence of accumulated social learning in a particular environmental niche, benefiting from a specific brand of cultural fluency that is consistently found in predominantly White middle-class to affluent social spaces.

It is true that these fluencies can be learned along with content on standardized tests, but that would also mean that the tests aren't intending to measure thinking or understandings but rather one's familiarity with a particular brand of cultural repertoire.

The high-stakes, standardized testing paradigm is fatally flawed because it mistakenly positions measures in place of goals. A high-stakes, standardized test may measure an outcome of schooling, but it can't be said to definitively indicate either intelligence or understanding—and certainly not in a way that is imminently useful to students or teachers. The most valid measures of intelligence and understandings are collected over time and considered in the social context in which the demonstrations of intelligence and understandings occur.

In the matter of assessments of students' learning, from the Equity perspective, we can say that it's not a fair opportunity unless students can use their cultural fluencies to show what they know. It is the ability to draw on one's cultural fluencies that makes an opportunity to learn meaningful because it allows for traction in integrating an understanding into one's existing schema for knowing.

It isn't equitable to teach something in a way that doesn't allow some students to use their cultural fluencies in order to understand and then measure what they have learned with the cognitive handcuffs of assessments that ignore their assets. Students benefit from the opportunities to use feedback as part of the responsive assessment process. Assessment tasks should model and demand integrated thinking. Those tasks should recur so there are many chances to consider the big ideas at the core of the learning target from a variety of angles in light of multiple perspectives.

The current high-stakes, standardized testing paradigm, even if it could be perfectly implemented with fair test items, would require an overemphasis on specialistic knowledge (and not integrated understandings) in order to claim statistical validity in the measurement of quality and effective teaching and learning. This is mostly true because specialistic knowledge is easier to measure in standardized testing formats, but it's most useful in the context of integrated understandings. While a knowledge of facts is convenient in many areas of study, it's more important in the internet age that students know what to do with those facts. The over-emphasis on specialistic knowledge outside of integrated understandings is a failed strategy if we want assessment models that provide meaningful and constructive feedback on the efficacy of instruction.

Much of what we measure in traditional assessments isn't the type of learning that can be integrated thoughtfully into a larger context—which is the kind of thinking students need to successfully participate in an information-based economy. The assessments I most often see in schools, and certainly those administered through the state during testing season, emphasize the brand of specialized knowledge that fades into cognitive oblivion, unretrievable and functionally useless beyond the short-term ability to regurgitate in standardized-testing formats. What's more, the testing paradigms we currently abide by leave little to no opportunity for the leveraging of emotion in students' thinking. I would argue that the current models we use test students' resolve to endure bad testing practices as much as anything else.

MEASURE IT PERFORMATIVELY . . .

Performative assessments are bodies of systematically and purposefully curated demonstrations of how students think, question, analyze, synthesize, and produce evidence in one or more subject areas across multiple topics and/or pieces. Performative assessments are the integration of process and product, developed with an explicit purpose, according to predetermined criteria, in a specific time period. When I make reference to performative assessments, I am generally talking about three models: PBLs—which refer to problem-based or project-based learning experiences—portfolios, and capstones. It's important to define each of these with your students. Much has been written about these models. They all can display integrated understandings, but they do it differently: PBLs are experience-focused; portfolios highlight development of understandings over time; and capstones showcase depth in understanding. I offer brief definitions of the models here, but what's most important is for teachers to recognize how and why these performative assessment structures offer culturally responsive learning opportunities for students.

As assessment strategies are implemented in the classroom, thought should be given to meta-questions that can direct the design, such as: How does one learn to solve problems, or build portfolios, or complete capstone projects? What skillsets are you expecting for students to bring to bear as a baseline? How will students be able to perform their emerging understandings in the context of community? What is the cultural value of the assessment? (That is, how might the skills and understandings developed in this assessment be underscored by students' cultural fluencies?) What is the social benefit of the assessment? (That is, how do the skills and understandings developed in this assessment potentially expand and/or translate into other social and cultural contexts?) How do these structures draw from and incorporate the core principles, customs, values, and beliefs of our students' people groups? *These questions are excellent tools for philosophizing.*

You have options in your assessment strategy, and you must think artfully in terms of how you put them together. The strategies and approaches we take in assessing students' learning inform the way behaviors, beliefs, and norms are interpreted in the culture of a classroom. Assessments should not be painful. When students experience responsiveness in assessments, they connect to the learning and the classroom environment in much more meaningful ways than otherwise. Importantly, performative assessments that students perceive and experience as responsive provide opportunities to question and rethink assumptions and habits in the context of safe and supportive learning communities.

What Is *PBL*?

You are your most cultural self when solving a problem. By that I mean, we tend to return to our default settings for *humaning (v)* when we're under real or perceived duress. We humans inherit all sorts of problem-solving tools—both physical and cognitive. It's unlikely that most give much thought to this, but we regularly withdraw from our cultural funds of knowledge as we seek solutions to the problems before us.

Problem solving is cultural in the most elemental way because humans, the species, are unique among the entire plant and animal kingdom due to our capacity for social learning—facilitated by culture—that affords more knowledge than any one human could ever acquire through individual learning in a single lifetime. Culture gives us many of our most basic problem-solving devices, including colors, integers, and language mechanisms like grammar and pronunciation rules. Culture plays a leading role in the complexity and efficiency in learning. Joseph Henrich (2020) writes that these capabilities have evolved over time:

> Psychological evidence indicates that the contents of vocabularies and the rules of grammar, such as those related to color terms and integers, may alter our cognitive abilities, including both memory and perception. Western children now master their basic colors at a younger age than they did in generations past, suggesting that the cultural system is evolving to be better at transmitting this knowledge. Acquiring these products of cumulative cultural evolution—integers and color terms—shapes our brains and influences our cognitive abilities. More broadly, words are useful for thinking, so possessing a large vocabulary likely improves some kinds of problem solving.

I am defining PBLs as either *problem-based learning experiences* or *project-based learning experiences*. They are not precisely the same thing, but they are close enough that I am able to group them for the purpose of my observations here. A problem-based learning experience centers a specific problem and is intended to showcase the related understandings performed through hypothesizing, analyzing, and solution finding. This is also mostly true for project-based learning experiences, though the "project" aspect implies a more real-world focus yielding an application of thematic understanding. Problem-based learning experiences can be much more abstract in the nature of their design. I refer to both as PBLs because both focus attention on an experience with a problem—whether material or theoretical—and each is intended to evoke a suggestion which reflects understanding.

PBLs, like all performative assessments, are about both process and outcome, but for the purposes of culturally responsive assessments, it's the process that yields the richest opportunities for integrated understandings. When designing PBLs for students, be clear about the value of the actions embedded in the process. How do they support integrated understandings? How are cultural fluencies useful to learners as they carry out the process? In what ways are students likely to be able to take advantage of their cultural fluencies in developing and demonstrating understandings?

What Is *Portfolio*?

One of my favorite examples of portfolio is a 60-piece series of paintings by Jacob Lawrence (1917–2000) titled *Migration Series*. The masterpiece depicts one of the more significant population movements in American history—the Great Migration of approximately six million descendants of enslaved Africans from the largely rural communities of southern states into northern metropolis areas. One can analyze and appreciate the aesthetics of narrative and visual imagery in Lawrence's *Migration Series* without knowing much about Black people or even the United States; but to understand how and why the paintings so vividly represent this enormously significant development in African American history requires a wide-angle, integrated view of the social, economic, historical, political, and cultural factors in play.

The full collection of Lawrence's *Migration Series* is split between the Phillips Collection in Washington, DC, and the Museum of Modern Art (MoMA) in New York City. The images have all the drama of epic poetry. The series itself can be said to be both a product and depiction of the Great Migration since Lawrence was the son of parents who had taken their own journey north. The energy of migration captured the imagination of Black people for more than half a century. The descendants of enslaved Africans sought refuge from the cruel, codified, and violent systems of social, political, and economic White supremacy. Lawrence explains to his audience with paint and brush the centrality of the African American experience to the evolution of the United States in a way that historians have struggled to convey. These are images of Black people re-imagining the ethos of the American experiment. The people portrayed are engrossed in a mighty struggle against the legacy of chattel slavery. There is faith; there is sorrow. There is dignity; there is degradation. *A people on the move*. It's the heroic human story of hope gone viral, and it is apparent that Jacob Lawrence was in possession of an integrated understanding of his subject:

> I decided to paint this series—I wasn't thinking of sales or a gallery. I liked storytelling. I went to the Schomburg Library and selected events from the South and North. I think that the series alternates from South to North. I just got into it. I didn't separate it. I wasn't looking at it from the inside out or the outside in. This was such a part of my life. . . . In retrospect now, I think my central concept was "people on the move." I guess that's what migration means. . . . You think of trains and buses and people just on the move. Of course, I was doing research at the time. I guess it was both emotional and intellectual.

In the way that a photographer, painter, or sculptor might prepare a sampling of their work for an exhibition, a portfolio is a purposeful collection of student work that exhibits the efforts, progress, and achievement relative to a particular skill or understanding. The portfolio is a cumulative illustration of how students engage—cognitively, affectively, and behaviorally—with the big ideas at the heart of instruction. Through the portfolio structure, students' knowledge, skill, and dispositions toward the subject matter are selected and commented on by the learning community to assess progress in the development of a competency.

Portfolios showcase a number of snapshots, the narrative arc of knowing showing growth over time. The portfolio structure is more equitable than traditional assessments because it gives more opportunity for students to demonstrate multiple aspects of their understanding. Wiggins and McTighe (1998) describe an understanding as being multifaceted. These facets are different but related, in the same way that different criteria are used in judging the quality of a performance.

According to Wiggins and McTighe (1998), "the six facets are most easily summarized by specifying the particular achievement each facet reflects." When we truly understand:

- We can explain: provide thorough, supported, and justifiable accounts of phenomena, facts, and data.
- We can interpret: tell meaningful stories; offer apt translations; provide a revealing historical or personal dimension to ideas and events; make it personal or accessible through images, anecdotes, analogies, and models.
- We can apply: effectively use and adapt what we know in diverse contexts.
- We have perspective: see and hear viewpoints through critical eyes and ears; see the big picture.
- We can empathize: find value in what others might find odd, alien, or implausible; perceive sensitively on the basis of prior direct experience.
- We have self-knowledge: perceive the personal style, prejudices, projections, and habits of mind that both shape and impede our own understanding; we are aware of what we do not understand and why understanding is so hard.

I refer to these when I design culturally responsive assessments by considering how students who understand (fill in the integrated understanding that is the learning target here) should be able to:

explain . . .
interpret . . .
apply the understanding by . . .
see from the viewpoints of . . .
empathize with . . .
overcome the naive or biased idea(s) that . . .

This exercise is helpful in identifying greater range in the types of assessments, which is essential in terms of the goals for robustness.

To be equitable in our assessments, we must provide broad on-ramps for students to learn and also broad off-ramps for students to demonstrate what they understand. Just like culture, an understanding isn't static and can't be defined by a single interaction. Understandings evolve just as humans do, and the portfolio structure can give insight into how students' learning develops over time and from different vantage points. More importantly, given the goals of Equity, our students' cultural fluencies can directly contribute to the performance of an integrated understanding in ways not feasible with high-stakes, standardized tests.

What Is *Capstone*?

According to *The Glossary of Education Reform*:

A capstone project is a multifaceted assignment that serves as a course culminating academic and intellectual experience for students resulting in a final product, presentation, or performance. Generally, students are asked to select a topic, profession, or social problem that interests them, conduct interdisciplinary research across different domains of knowledge on a subject, develop a literature review, create a final product demonstrating their learning acquisition or conclusions (a paper, short film, or multimedia presentation, for example), and give an oral presentation on the project to a panel of teachers, experts, and community members who collectively evaluate its quality. Students' choice is a prominent feature of the capstone structure which tends to encourage students to connect their projects to community issues or problems and to integrate outside-of-school learning experiences, including activities such as interviews, scientific observations, or internships.

Capstones feature the depth of students' integrated understandings and provide rich opportunities for students to compile and compose an array of skills and understandings into a culminating social, academic, and intellectual experience. Over the course of the study, research, and preparation for presentation of a capstone project, students are utilizing their cultural fluencies and cognitive niches to develop and perform their understandings.

The element of choice in the capstone structure mitigates the likelihood of students being pinned into a single identity corner. Identity corners are disempowering because they cut off students' access to the full suite of their cultural repertoires. An empowerment orientation in assessment requires that students have an active role in both the design and the criteria-selection process (Zimmerman, 2000). There is a great deal of potential for cognitive engagement in a capstone project starting with the choice of their topic and methodology. Capstone projects synthesize subject knowledge with research and creative design integrating various pieces of an understanding into a unified whole. A well-designed capstone project provides students the opportunity to both reflect on their study experience and look forward to ways in which to apply the understandings.

NOTES ON ARTMAKING: "THEY WEREN'T TAKING CUES OFF OF ME."

In the previous chapter, I asked: Is it possible for students to be intelligent and not be motivated to engage in school? And if so, what responsibilities does this incur for the teacher? We could also ask: Is it possible for students to take on integrated understandings that may not be reliably quantifiable by traditional, standardized tests? If so, what responsibilities does this incur for the teacher when students may understand but don't have opportunities to perform those understandings in any culturally situated way? Some of the most profound evidence of cognitive engagement and integrated understandings is difficult to measure though no less significant.

Much of the criticism of performative assessments isn't about the intrinsic or potential educational value, but rather on the poor quality of implementation which reflects low academic standards that allow students to complete relatively superficial projects of minimal educational value. The process of engaging with performative assessments gives opportunity for students to be empowered through reflection and metacognition. It allows for students to interrogate their emerging understandings such that all sorts of sparks and intellectual connections become possible for them. They can thread new insights in with those inherited in their most precious social, cultural, and relational spaces by contemplating: *What do I understand? And how has this understanding come to be?* Thinking in this way reveals the trajectories of students' growing awareness of themselves as persons with cognitive agency, thinking humans who can use their intelligence in myriad ways. It seems frivolous to ask students to do *anything* that doesn't bring them closer to this kind of awareness. It's another kind of philosophizing. It's a different level of relevance. When our students can think deeply with a particular focus and see how their ideas and associated skillsets develop over time, they are better able to consider those age-old, deeply human questions: *Who am I? And how have I come to be?* These processes lead to life-changing, personal paradigm-shifting understandings.

I'm reminded of a quote by the photographer Annie Leibovitz, which I find to also be true for brilliant teaching:

> When I'm asked about my work, I try to explain that there is no mystery involved. It is work. But things happen all the time that are unexpected, uncontrolled, unexplainable, even magical. The work prepares you for that moment. Suddenly the clouds roll in and the soft light you longed for appears. (Mallon, 2009)

Assessments, rigor, cognitive engagement, social learning, culture, responsiveness, Equity . . . these are all tied together in ways that we teachers must artfully consider in order to meet the needs of our particular audience of learners. I, too, try to explain to the teachers with whom I thought-partner that there is no mystery involved; though I make no claims that any of this is easy—only possible.

I've found that integrated understandings take on an unmistakable look and feel of learning in the context of community in the classroom. The acoustics are different. The rhythm, the beat, the tempo, the buzz . . . it all hits differently when students are integrating their understandings in a learning community. In fact, it occurred in Mr. Derain's classroom when his chemistry students had their vibrant albeit slow-starting learning experience in experimentation with volcanoes. Nearing the end of the 64-minute class period of fully engaged thinking about T-charts, variables, and volcanoes, something pretty cool happened:

AD: They start cleaning up, on their own, going the extra mile to clean stuff up. (In his student voice) *Mr. How do we clean this out?* It was just sort of natural, it was a feeling of wanting to contribute to this. *I want to help clean up. I'm a part of this whatever is going on here.* It was kind of a caretaking, and this kept happening every time we did an experiment. They just all kinda got into it. There was no defiance. There was no messing around. I took it almost as a kind of thank you. Like a show of appreciation. Like respect for the materials and the space and what we just did. It was meaningful and important. The community vibe was definitely there. They weren't taking cues off of me. They were taking cues off of each other, and that's what I had to work with. So, I took that as a measure of engagement that I wasn't even expecting to see.

AFTERWORD

"Anybody can play. The note is only 20 percent. The attitude of the motherfu**er who plays it is 80 percent."

—Miles Davis

In this book, I attempt to make the case that teaching that closes Equity gaps is much more artful than algorithmic. Teaching is the art of empowering students with understandings. And further, the art of teaching is performed through learning experiences that position students in proximity to concepts such that their cultural fluencies are useful to them in integrating understandings into a schema of meaningful knowing.

I am neither formally trained in art history nor have I dabbled much at all in any form of painting or draughtsmanship (though I do fancy myself a highly proficient amateur "smartphone" photographer). What I have learned about art has been mostly gained through time spent viewing paintings as often as possible on the walls of galleries and museums. My interests in "fine art" are rooted in my relationship with *Hip Hop*. As a kid in the Bronx, I was fascinated by the graffiti on the 1980s subway trains. I would study street art to try to determine the motivation for and influences behind the spray-painted, montage-style images. Many of the pieces I studied were exquisitely composed—conveying an authenticity that eventually came to be the visual art expression of *Hip Hop* culture.

In 1996, Jay-Z released his first solo album, *Reasonable Doubt*. Like many dedicated fans of the genre, I listened to the album countless times and remember taking specific notice of a line in one song "Friend or Foe": "You draw, better be Picasso, you know the best." If I would've had a smartphone then, I would have googled Picasso to figure out exactly who he was and why he deserved such prominent mention in this Brooklyn rapper's lyric. I'd heard the name before, but then it registered in my consciousness differently. Over time, my interests in Picasso led me to others whose works are often exhibited in the same galleries as his, including Matisse, Moreau, Renoir, Cezanne, Monet, Manet, Bonnard, van Gogh, and many others. Later, I began to learn more about the modern artists that Picasso and his contemporaries inspired including Rothko, Pollock, and Basquiat (another favorite of Jay-Z).

Today, while still a fan of street art, I enjoy spending time in museums because I am a vested audience there. I almost always have a purpose when I enter a museum, either to see a specific exhibit or piece, or to deepen my own understanding of some particular artistic element. In my eyes, museums are inspiration warehouses. I use my time in museums to tap into my own insights so that I can better facilitate spaces and experiences in which insights are available to others. As teachers, we provide inspiration and influence through our craft. We have a responsibility (much like the artist) to retain a vibrancy in our approaches to practice. This is central to our work and also the cause of Equity, and we can learn much from artists in the effort.

So once more, let's re-set and return to the conceptual framing with this book's central thought-experiment: You're a teacher, and you want to be equitable. What does Equity mean *in* your teaching? How do you *do* Equity?

BRILLIANCE

Throughout this book, I ask: *What does the brilliant artist do?* I prefer the word *brilliance* over terms like *mastery* because brilliance both shines a light on and illuminates from within. A masterpiece is the handiwork of brilliant artistry. In museums, I regularly remind myself that every master-piece painting I see was once a blank canvas. The artist brings to bear tools and skill developed in preparation for the moment. Without the artistic frame of reference and the mental models that direct their awareness, the tools of the craft are inconsequential. Without the tools of the craft, the vision of the artist lays dormant. It is unwise to see art and craft as being in hierarchical relationship. They are interdependent. It is not possible to make masterpieces without the interplay of the two. Those museum mas-terpiece canvases I spend time with aren't special for some uniquely defin-ing characteristic of the canvas, and no level of artistic brilliance can be performed without the tools of the craft.

There are two observations I'd like to share here about brilliance. The first is simple enough: to be brilliant is to evolve. That's easily said, and yet, by definition, it takes a lifetime to achieve. It is the ultimate process goal. The second observation I can make about brilliance is that too many peo-ple have a profoundly false notion of what brilliance seeks. Brilliance seeks solutions to the problems that interfere with our capacities for brilliance. If you are like me, you want to be brilliant every day with your students. But there are lots of challenges to that goal in today's schools. Brilliance is not the search for entirely new inventions in craft. The goal isn't to find an *original* solution for your problems of practice. The goal is to find *effective* solutions. The worst possible interpretation of brilliance is that it can be obtained without drawing on the best ideas about the problems you seek to solve. *Invention* is not synonymous with *innovation*.

Brilliance is less about innovation than it is about the artful capac-ity for the recombination of ideas, insights, techniques, and approaches. In truth, this is the case for the entire history of humanity. Every major human inventive advance is actually the culmination of countless baby steps preceding the breakthrough—nameless persons re-visiting old ideas they've borrowed and inherited. Our artfulness is pivotal for us to be inventive in the interest of fairness, so that we can *do* Equity. As such, Equity and artfulness are inseparable entities; one isn't possible without the other.

BRILLIANT TEACHING IS PHILOSOPHIZING

There are so many ways to talk about teaching. I have my way, and I have learned from the ways of others. Readers may relate to some of the explanations I give, and others may hear something different from another source that resonates in a way that moves them. I say often that brilliant teaching in 21st-century classrooms is more challenging than sending a rover to Mars because the latter only requires a mastery of the principles of advanced astro-physics, quantum robotics, and space engineering which, once accomplished, can be replicated successfully by following the direction of previously successful missions. However, to brilliantly teach in an American classroom is a unique task marked with its own nearly limitless, distinct variables, each having the potential to affect others in all sorts of ways.

There can be no simple scripts for the complex tasks of teaching, but there are heuristics and mental models that inform thoughtful educators with the tools to mine their own insights in productive ways. Consciously or otherwise, all teachers (much like artists) have mental models of the craft. Mental models are organizing philosophical frameworks useful for vetting good ideas from bad ideas and better ideas from good ideas. Our mental models are not laws but tools to be taken up as the situation warrants, and these tools should be sharpened and revised so that they don't become dull and insufficient to the tasks at hand. To be useful, our models should be realistic, incorporating those factors that influence student engagement.

The art motif employed in this book is intended to be something more than a mere compositional device. I am hoping to make a point about the nature of our project and the responsibilities inherent in it. I am pronouncedly biased toward two things in my work: one is a bias toward the defense of public schools; and the other is a bias in perspective, as in I tend to take the vantage point of the teacher in understanding issues in education.

My argument is that teaching is an artmaking craft. The *artistic intent* of culturally responsive pedagogy is to create equitable opportunities for all to learn...that is, to design experiences in which our students can draw from their social identities, cognitive niches, and cultural fluencies to show their competence. Without artistic intent, you are performing an act of mimicry at best. You are likely copying someone else's craft, and your own is undefined. Without artistic intent, you are likely prioritizing your own comfort over the necessary effort of engaging the tensions of the historical moment in which you teach. Teaching in the 21st century is much more complex than copying even the most magnificent masterpieces. We are wise to draw inspiration from the brilliance of others—that influence is invaluable. True brilliance is a product of intentional philosophizing, the searching of ourselves, and the rigorous investigation of our craft.

To philosophize is to pay attention, to be alive, to be engaged in the events of our own existence. To philosophize is to identify what is meaningful inside of what appears immensely ordinary. To philosophize is to perceive the transformative, to be aware of and inspired by what we can imagine. To philosophize is to live the life we would consciously choose. To philosophize is to consider: *Why am I doing this? What are my intentions? Who am I in this moment? Why am I here?*

And with that thought, I rest my case.

REFERENCES

Aaronson, D., Barrow, L., & Sander, W. (2007). Teachers and student achievement in Chicago Public High Schools. *Journal of Labor Economics*, 24(1), 95–135.

Aelterman, N., Vansteenkiste, M., Haerens, L., Soenens, B., Fontaine, J. R. J., & Reeve, J. (2019). Toward an integrative and fine-grained insight in motivating and demotivating teaching styles: The merits of a circumplex approach. *Journal of Educational Psychology*, 111(3), 497–521.

Alberini, C. M. (2009). Transcription factors in long-term memory and synaptic plasticity. *Physiological Reviews*, 89(1), 121–145.

Alexander, M. (2010). *The new Jim Crow: Mass incarceration in the age of colorblindness.* New Press.

Anderman, E. M. (2020). Achievement motivation theory: Balancing precision and utility. *Contemporary Educational Psychology*, 101864.

Aptheker, H. (1975). The history of anti-racism in the United States. *The Black Scholar*, 6(5), 16–22.

Arum, R., Beattie, I. R., & Ford, K. (2021). *The structure of schooling: Readings in the sociology of education.* SAGE Publications, Inc.

Au, W. (2010). *Unequal by design: High-stakes testing and the standardization of inequality.* Routledge.

Avenanti, A., Sirigu, A., & Aglioti, S. M. (2010). Racial bias reduces empathic sensorimotor resonance with other-race pain. *Current Biology*, 20(11), 1018–1022.

Baldwin, J. (1962). The creative process. *Creative America*: 17–21.

Ballantine, J. H., Spade, J. Z., & Stuber, J. M. (2018). *Schools and society: A sociological approach to education*. SAGE.

Bandura, A. (1982). Self-efficacy mechanism in human agency. *American Psychologist*, 37(2), 122.

Bandura, A. (1985). Model of causality in social learning theory. *Cognition and Psychotherapy*, 81–99. doi:10.1007/978-1-4684-7562-3_3.

Bandura, A. (1988). Self-regulation of motivation and action through goal systems. In: *Cognitive perspectives on emotion and motivation* (pp. 37–61). Springer, Dordrecht.

Bandura, A. (1991). Self-regulation of motivation through anticipatory and self-reactive mechanisms. In: R. A. Dienstbier (Ed.), *Perspectives on motivation: Nebraska symposium on motivation* (Vol. 38, pp. 69–164). Lincoln: University of Nebraska Press.

Bandura, A. (1997). *Self-efficacy: The exercise of control*. Macmillan.

Bandura, A. (2001). Social cognitive theory: An agentic perspective. *Annual Review of Psychology*, 52(1), 1–26.

Bandura, A., & Walters, R. H. (1977). *Social learning theory* (Vol. 1). Prentice Hall: Englewood cliffs.

Barber, N. (2005). Educational and ecological correlates of IQ: A cross-national investigation. *Intelligence*, 33(3), 273–284.

Barrett, L. F. (2020). *Seven and a half lessons about the brain*. Picador.

Barrett, L. F., & Simmons, W. K. (2015). Interoceptive predictions in the brain. *Nature Reviews Neuroscience*, 16(7), 419–429.

Barsalou, L. W., Simmons, W. K., Barbey, A. K., & Wilson, C. D. (2003). Grounding conceptual knowledge in modality-specific systems. *Trends in Cognitive Sciences*, 7(2), 84–91.

Bayles, D., & Orland, T. (1993). *Art & Fear: Observations on the perils (and rewards) of Artmaking*. Continuum Press.

Berreby, D. (2008). *Us and them: The science of identity.* University of Chicago Press.

Bertolotti, T., & Magnani, L. (2016). Theoretical considerations on cognitive niche construction. *Synthese,* 194(12), 4757–4779.

Borman, G. D., & Dowling, M. (2010). Schools and inequality: A multilevel analysis of Coleman's equality of educational opportunity data. *Teachers College Record,* 112(5), 1201–1246.

Bowles, S. (1968). Towards equality of educational opportunity? *Harvard Educational Review,* 38(1), 89–99.

Boyd, R., & Richerson, P. J. (1983). Why is culture adaptive? *The Quarterly Review of Biology,* 58(2): 209–214.

Boyd, R., & Richerson, P. J. (1985). *Culture and the evolutionary process.* University of Chicago Press.

Brown v. Board of Education, 347 U.S. 483 (1954). The Library of Congress. (n.d.). Retrieved October 24, 2021.

Brown, D. E. (2004). Human universals, human nature & human culture. *Daedalus,* 47–54.

Bruner, J. (2004). A short history of psychological theories of learning. *Daedalus,* 133(1), 13–20.

Bruner, J. S. (2003). *The culture of education.* Harvard University Press.

Burtless, G., & Jencks, C. (2003). American inequality and its consequences. No. 339. LIS Working Paper Series.

Chetty, R., Friedman, J. N., & Rockoff, J. E. (2014). Measuring the impacts of teachers II: Teacher value-added and student outcomes in adulthood. *American Economic Review,* 104(9), 2633–2679.

Cole, M. (1998a). Can cultural psychology help us think about diversity? *Mind, Culture, and Activity,* 5(4), 291–304.

Cole, M. (1998b). *Cultural psychology: A once and future discipline.* Harvard University Press.

Cole, M., & Bruner, J. S. (1971). Cultural differences and inferences about psychological processes. *American Psychologist,* 26(10), 867.

Coleman, J. (1968). The concept of equality of educational opportunity. *Harvard Educational Review*, 38(1), 7–22.

Cushing, I. (2022). Raciolinguistic policy assemblages and white supremacy in teacher education. *The Curriculum Journal*, 34(1), 43–61.

Davis, K., & Moore, W. E. (1945). Some principles of stratification. *American Sociological Review*, 10(2), 242–249.

Davis, T. (2010). *Jean-Michel Basquiat: The radiant child*. SND (Société Nouvelle de Distribution) International.

Deci, E. L., & Ryan, R. M. (2012). Motivation, personality, and development within embedded social contexts: An overview of self-determination theory. In: Ryan, R. M. (Ed.), *The Oxford handbook of human motivation*. OUP USA.

Delgado, M. R., Schotter, A., Ozbay, E. Y., & Phelps, E. A. (2008). Understanding overbidding: Using the neural circuitry of reward to design economic auctions. *Science*, 321(5897), 1849–1852.

Dewey, J., Montessori, M., Strzemiński, W., Piaget, J., Vygotsky, L., von Foerster, H., . . . & Morin, E. (1997). Constructivism (learning theory). *Journal of Social Sciences, Literature and Languages*, 9–16.

Dodel, S., Tognoli, E., & Kelso, J. S. (2020). Degeneracy and complexity in neuro-behavioral correlates of team coordination. *Frontiers in Human Neuroscience*, 14, 328.

Dweck, C. S. (2017). The journey to children's mindsets—and beyond. *Child Development Perspectives*, 11(2), 139–144.

Eisman, A. B., Zimmerman, M. A., Kruger, D., Reischl, T. M., Miller, A. L., Franzen, S. P., & Morrel-Samuels, S. (2016). Psychological empowerment among urban youth: Measurement model and associations with youth outcomes. *American Journal of Community Psychology*, 58(3–4), 410–421.

Ennis, F. R. (1976). Equality of educational opportunity. *Educational Theory*, 26(1), 3–18.

Feinberg, W., & Soltis, J. F. (1998). *Schools and society* (3rd ed.). Teachers College Press.

Fink, L. (2014). *Larry Fink on composition and improvisation*. Aperture.

Franklin, B., & Masur, L. P. (2016). *The autobiography of Benjamin Franklin: With related documents*. Bedford/St. Martin's, Macmillan Learning.

Freedle, R. (2006). How and why standardized tests systematically underestimate African-Americans' true verbal ability and what to do about it: Towards the promotion of two new theories with practical applications. *St. John's Law Review*, 80, 183.

Freedman, K. (2003). *Teaching visual culture: Curriculum, aesthetics, and the social life of art*. New York: Teachers College, Columbia University.

Frith, C., & Frith, U. (2005). Theory of mind. *Current Biology*, 15(17), R644–R645.

Frith, C. D., & Frith, U. (2006). The neural basis of mentalizing. *Neuron*, 50(4), 531–534.

Galef, B. G. (2009). Strategies for social learning: Testing predictions from formal theory. *Advances in the Study of Behavior*, 39, 117–151.

Gendron, M., Mesquita, B., & Barrett, L. F. (2020). The brain as a cultural artifact. *Culture, Mind, and Brain*, 188–222.

Giangrande, E. J., & Turkheimer, E. (2022). Race, ethnicity, and the Scarr-Rowe hypothesis: A cautionary example of fringe science entering the mainstream. *Perspectives on Psychological Science*, 17(3), 696–710.

Golash-Boza, T. M. (2022). *Race and racisms: A critical approach*. Oxford University Press.

Goldman, S. K., & Hopkins, D. J. (2020). Past place, present prejudice: The impact of adolescent racial context on white racial attitudes. *The Journal of Politics*, 82(2), 529–542.

Green, F. T. (1971). Equal educational opportunity: The durable injustice. *Philosophy of Education*, 7977, 121–143

Greenspan, N. S. (2022). Genes, heritability, "race," and intelligence: Misapprehensions and implications. *Genes*, 13(2), 346.

Gutmann, A. (1999). *Democratic education: With a new preface and epilogue*. Princeton University Press.

Harris, L. T., & Fiske, S. T. (2006). Dehumanizing the lowest of the low: Neuroimaging responses to extreme out-groups. *Psychological Science*, 17(10), 847–853.

Harris, L. T., & Fiske, S. T. (2007). Social groups that elicit disgust are differentially processed in mPFC. *Social Cognitive and Affective Neuroscience*, 2(1), 45–51.

Hattie Effect Size List—256 influences related to achievement. *Visible Learning*. Accessed October 22, 2022.

Havighurst, R. J. (1973). Opportunity, equity, or equality. *The School Review*, 81(4), 618–633.

Haykir, M., & Çalışkan, O. (2021). Is there a relationship between empowering chefs and the culinary creativity process? *Journal of Culinary Science & Technology*, 1–26. https://doi.org/10.1080/15428052.2021.1955793

Heider, F., & Weiner, B. (2002). Attribution theory. *The Motivation Handbook*, 31.

Henrich, J. (2020). *The WEIRDest people in the world: How the West became psychologically peculiar and particularly prosperous*. Penguin UK.

Henrich, J., Boyd, R., Bowles, S., Camerer, C., Fehr, E., & Gintis, H. (Eds.). (2004). *Foundations of human sociality: Economic experiments and ethnographic evidence from fifteen small-scale societies*. OUP Oxford.

Henrich, J., Heine, S. J., & Norenzayan, A. (2010). Most people are not weird. *Nature*, 466(7302), 29–29.

Henrich, J. P. (2016). *The secret of our success: How culture is driving human evolution, domesticating our species, and making us smarter*. Princeton University Press.

Hess, K. K., Carlock, D., Jones, B., & Walkup, J. R. (2009). What exactly do "fewer, clearer, and higher standards" really look like in the classroom? Using a cognitive rigor matrix to analyze curriculum, plan lessons, and implement assessments. Presentation at CCSSO, Detroit MI. http://www.nciea.org/cgi-bin/pubspage.cgi?sortby=pub_date.

Hess, K. K., Jones, B. S., Carlock, D., & Walkup, J. R. (2009). Cognitive rigor: Blending the strengths of Bloom's taxonomy and Webb's depth of knowledge to enhance classroom-level processes. Online Submission.

Hmelo-Silver, C. E. (2003). Analyzing collaborative knowledge construction. *Computers & Education*, 41(4), 397–420. doi:10.1016/j.compedu. 2003.07.

Hofstadter, D. R. (2007). *I am a strange loop*. Basic Books.

Hofstadter, D. R., & Sander, E. (2013*). Surfaces and essences: Analogy as the fuel and fire of thinking*. Basic Books.

Hoppitt, W., & Laland, K. N. (2013). Social learning. In: *Social Learning*. Princeton University Press.

Hoppitt, W., & Laland, K. N. (2013). *Social Learning*. Princeton University Press. Kindle Edition.

Houge Mackenzie, S., Son, J. S., & Hollenhorst, S. (2014). Unifying psychology and experiential education: Toward an integrated understanding of why it works. *Journal of Experiential Education*, 37(1), 75–88.

Howe, K. R. (1999). Equality of educational opportunity. *Issues in Educational Research*, 215–221.

Hurwitz, E., & Tesconi, C. A. (Eds.). (1972). *Challenges to education: Readings for analysis of major issues*. Dodd Mead.

Immordino-Yang, M. H. (2016). Ed-talk: Learning with an emotional brain. American Educational Research Association. https://youtu.be/DEeo350WQrs.

Integrated knowledge. SUNY Empire State College. Accessed July 28, 2022.

Jencks, C., & Smith, M. (1973*). Inequality: A reassessment of the effect of family and schooling in America*. Allen Lane.

Johnson, T. J. (2020). Racial bias and its impact on children and adolescents. *Pediatric Clinics of North America*, 67(2), 425–436. https://doi .org/10.1016/j.pcl.2019.12.011.

Jost, J. T., & Hunyady, O. (2005). Antecedents and consequences of system-justifying ideologies. *Current Directions in Psychological Science*, 14(5), 260–265.

Jurado de los Santos, P., Moreno-Guerrero, A.-J., Marín-Marín, J.-A., & Soler Costa, R. (2020). The term *equity* in education: A literature review with scientific mapping in web of science. *International Journal of Environmental Research and Public Health*, 17(10), 3526.

Kahlenberg, R. D. (2001). Learning from James Coleman. *Public Interest*, (144), 54.

Keller, M. M., Goetz, T., Becker, E. S., Morger, V., & Hensley, L. (2014). Feeling and showing: A new conceptualization of dispositional teacher enthusiasm and its relation to students' interest. *Learning and Instruction*, 33, 29–38.

Kepinska, O., de Rover, M., Caspers, J., & Schiller, N. O. (2017). On neural correlates of individual differences in novel grammar learning: An fMRI study. *Neuropsychologia*, 98, 156–168.

Khushal, S. (2021). Suddenly diverse: How school districts manage race and inequality. *Canadian Journal of Education*, 44(1), XII–XV.

Kindermann, T. A. (1993). Natural peer groups as contexts for individual development: The case of children's motivation in school. *Developmental Psychology*, 29, 970–977.

King, R. B., & McInerney, D. M. (2016). Culturalizing motivation research in educational psychology. *British Journal of Educational Psychology*, 86(1), 1–7.

Kolbert, E. (2018, April 4). There's no scientific basis for race—it's a made-up label. *National Geographic* Retrieved October 25, 2021, from https://www.nationalgeographic.co.uk/people-and-culture/2018/04/theres-no-scientific-basis-race-its-made-label

Koster-Hale, J., & Saxe, R. (2013). Theory of mind: A neural prediction problem. *Neuron*, 79(5), 836–848.

Kovacs, K., & Conway, A. R. (2019). A unified cognitive/differential approach to human intelligence: Implications for IQ testing. *Journal of Applied Research in Memory and Cognition*, 8(3), 255–272.

Krishnamurti, J. (1953). *Education and the significance of life*. Harper.

Kubota, J. T., Banaji, M. R., & Phelps, E. A. (2012). The neuroscience of race. *Nature Neuroscience*, 15(7), 940–948.

Labov, W. (1970). The logic of nonstandard English. In: *Language and poverty* (pp. 153–189). Academic Press.

Ladson-Billings, G. (1995). But that's just good teaching! The case for culturally relevant pedagogy. *Theory into Practice*, 34(3), 159–165.

Laidre, M. E., & Kraft, T. S. (2015). In: William Hoppitt & Kevin N. Laland, *Social learning: An introduction to mechanisms, methods, and models*. Princeton University Press.

Lee, S. M. (1993). Racial classifications in the US Census: 1890–1990. Ethnic and Racial Studies, 16(1), 75–94.

Legal Information Institute. (n.d.). *McLaurin v. Oklahoma State Regents for Higher Education et al*. Legal Information Institute. Retrieved October 30, 2021.

Leslie, A. M., Friedman, O., & German, T. P. (2004). Core mechanisms in "'theory of mind." *Trends in Cognitive Sciences*, 8(12), 528–533.

Leyens, J. P., Paladino, P. M., Rodriguez-Torres, R., Vaes, J., Demoulin, S., Rodriguez-Perez, A., & Gaunt, R. (2000). The emotional side of prejudice: The attribution of secondary emotions to ingroups and outgroups. *Personality and Social Psychology Review*, 4(2), 186–197.

Linn, M. C. (2006). *The knowledge integration perspective on learning and instruction*. Cambridge University Press.

Luquet, W. (2015). Everything I know about teaching I learned from jazz. *Journal of Effective Teaching*, 15(2), 60–68.

Maehr, M. L. (1974). Culture and achievement motivation. *American Psychologist*, 29, 887–896.

Mallon, T. (2009). Leibovitz, Annie: Annie Leibovitz at Work. *Biography*, 32(1), 238–239.

Mann, H. (2015). *Lectures on education*. Forgotten Books.

McClelland, J. L., Hill, F., Rudolph, M., Baldridge, J., & Schütze, H. (2020). Placing language in an integrated understanding system: Next steps toward human-level performance in neural language models. *Proceedings of the National Academy of Sciences*, 117(42), 25966–25974.

McGhee, H. (2022). *Sum of us: What racism costs everyone and how we can prosper together*. Profile Books LTD.

Mehlman, M. J., Logan, A., Lantzer, J., Stern, A. M., Dorr, G., McCabe, E., . . . & Carlson, E. A. (2011). *A century of eugenics in America: From the Indiana experiment to the human genome era*. Indiana University Press.

Meier, D., & Knoester, M. (2017). *Beyond testing: Seven assessments of students and schools more effective than standardized tests*. Teachers College Press.

Meltzoff, A. N., Waismeyer, A., & Gopnik, A. (2012). Learning about causes from people: Observational causal learning in 24-month-old infants. *Developmental Psychology*, 48(5), 1215.

Morgan, T. J., Rendell, L. E., Ehn, M., Hoppitt, W., & Laland, K. N. (2012). The evolutionary basis of human social learning. *Proceedings of the Royal Society B: Biological Sciences*, 279(1729), 653–662.

Morrison, S., Decety, J., & Molenberghs, P. (2012). The neuroscience of group membership. *Neuropsychologia*, 50(8), 2114–2120.

Muhammad, K. G. (2019). *The condemnation of Blackness: Race, crime, and the making of modern urban America, with a new preface*. Harvard University Press.

Murray, C. (2021). *Facing reality: Two truths about race in America*. Encounter Books.

Myers, A. F., & Harshman, F. E. (1929). *Training secondary-school teachers: A manual of observation and participation*. American Book Co.

National Commission on Excellence in Education. (1983). A nation at risk: The imperative for educational reform. *The Elementary School Journal*, 84(2), 113–130.

Nieto, S. (2000). Placing equity front and center—Some thoughts on transforming teacher education for a new century. *Journal Teacher Education*, 51, 180–187.

Nisbett, R. E. (2009). *Intelligence and how to get it: Why schools and cultures count*. New York: W. W. Norton.

Nolen, S. B. (2015). Situating motivation. *Educational Psychologist*, 50(3), 234–247.

Nordine, J., Krajcik, J., & Fortus, D. (2011). Transforming energy instruction in middle school to support integrated understanding and future learning. *Science Education*, 95(4), 670–699.

Odling-Smee, J., & Laland, K. N. (2011). Ecological inheritance and cultural inheritance: What are they and how do they differ? *Biological Theory*, 6(3), 220–230.

Osher, D., Cantor, P., Berg, J., Steyer, L., & Rose, T. (2020). Drivers of human development: How relationships and context shape learning and development. *Applied Developmental Science*, 24(1), 6–36.

Page, N., & Czuba, C. E. (1999, January 1). Empowerment: What is it?: Semantic scholar. *The Journal of Extension*. Retrieved May 20, 2021.

Painter, N. I. (2010). *The history of white people*. WW Norton & Company.

Penuel, W. R., & Wertsch, J. V. (1995). Vygotsky and identity formation: A sociocultural approach. *Educational Psychologist*, 30(2), 83–92.

Perkins, D. D., & Zimmerman, M. A. (1995). Empowerment theory, research, and application. *American Journal of Community Psychology*, 23(5), 569–579.

Perry, S., Skinner Dorkenoo, A. L., Abaied, J. L., Osnaya, A., & Waters, S. (2020). Initial evidence that parent-child conversations about race reduce racial biases among white U.S. children. *PsyArXiv*. May 18. doi:10.31234/osf.io/3xdg8.

Pinker, S. (2010). The cognitive niche: Coevolution of intelligence, sociality, and language. *Proceedings of the National Academy of Sciences,* 107(supplement_2), 8993–8999.

Pollock, M. (2008). *Everyday antiracism: Getting real about race in school.* New Press.

Pollock, M., Deckman, S., Mira, M., & Shalaby, C. (2009). "But what can I do?" Three necessary tensions in teaching teachers about race. *Journal of Teacher Education,* 61(3), 211–224.

Portz, J. (2021). "Next-Generation" accountability? Evidence from three school districts. *Urban Education,* 56(8), 1297–1327.

Price, C. J., & Friston, K. J. (2002). Degeneracy and cognitive anatomy. *Trends in Cognitive Sciences,* 6(10), 416–421.

Pulliam, H. R., & Dunford, C. (1980). *Programmed to learn: An essay on the evolution of culture.* New York: Columbia University Press.

Rappaport, J., Seidman, E., & Zimmerman, M. A. (2000). Empowerment theory: Psychological, organizational, and community levels of analysis. In: *Handbook of Community Psychology* (pp. 43–59). Essay, Kluwer Academic.

Reese, W. J. (2011). *America's public schools: From the Common School to "No Child Left Behind."* The Johns Hopkins University Press.

Reis, H. T. (2014). *Responsiveness:* Affective interdependence in close relationships. *Mechanisms of Social Connection: From Brain to Group,* 255–271.

Reis, H. T., & Clark, M. S. (2013). Responsiveness. In: J. A. Simpson & L. Campbell (Eds.), *The Oxford handbook of close relationships* (pp. 400–423). Oxford University Press.

Rendell, L., Fogarty, L., Hoppitt, W. J., Morgan, T. J., Webster, M. M., & Laland, K. N. (2011). Cognitive culture: Theoretical and empirical insights into social learning strategies. *Trends in Cognitive Sciences,* 15(2), 68–76.

Renninger, K. A., & Su, S. (2012). Interest and its development. In: R. M. Ryan (Ed.), *The Oxford handbook of human motivation* (pp. 167–187). Oxford University Press.

Richerson, P. J., & Boyd, R. (2008). *Not by genes alone: How culture transformed human evolution.* University of Chicago Press.

Roeser, R. W., Urdan, T. C., & Stephens, J. M. (2009). School as a context of student motivation and achievement. In: K. Wentzel & A. Wigfield (Eds.), *Handbook of motivation at school* (pp. 381–410). Erlbaum.

Rossell, C. H. (1980). Chapter 5: Social science research in educational equity cases: A critical review. *Review of Research in Education,* 8(1), 237–295.

Rothstein, R. (2017). *The color of law: A forgotten history of how our government segregated America.* Liveright Publishing.

Rowat, A. C., Lammerding, J., Herrmann, H., & Aebi, U. (2008). Towards an integrated understanding of the structure and mechanics of the cell nucleus. *Bioessays,* 30(3), 226–236.

Rowlands, J. (1999). *Empowerment examined. Development with Women,* 141–150.

Ryan, R. M. (Ed.). (2012). *The Oxford handbook of human motivation.* Oxford University Press. https://doi.org/10.1093/oxfordhb/9780195399820.001.000.

Ryan, R. M., & Deci, E. L. (2017). *Self-determination theory: Basic psychological needs in motivation, development, and wellness.* Guilford Publications.

Sage, N. A., & Kindermann, T. A. (1999). Peer networks, behavior contingencies, and children's engagement in the classroom. *Merrill-Palmer Quarterly,* 454, 143–171.

Saltz, J. (2020). *How to be an artist.* Riverhead Books.

Saphier, J., Gower, R. R., & Haley-Speca, M. A. (1997). *The skillful teacher: Building your teaching skills* (p. 544). Research for Better Teaching.

Sapolsky, R. M. (2017). *Behave: The biology of humans at our best and worst.* Penguin.

Schaafsma, S. M., Pfaff, D. W., Spunt, R. P., & Adolphs, R. (2015). Deconstructing and reconstructing theory of mind. *Trends in Cognitive Sciences,* 19(2), 65–72.

Schunk, D. H., & DiBenedetto, M. K. (2020). Motivation and social cognitive theory. *Contemporary Educational Psychology*, 60, 101832.

Seifert, L., Komar, J., Araújo, D., & Davids, K. (2016). Neurobiological degeneracy: A key property for functional adaptations of perception and action to constraints. *Neuroscience & Biobehavioral Reviews*, 69, 159–165.

Skinner, E. A., & Belmont, M. J. (1993). Motivation in the classroom: Reciprocal effects of teacher behavior and student engagement across the school year. *Journal of Educational Psychology*, 85, 571–581.

Skinner, E. A., Kindermann, T. A., & Furrer, C. (2009). A motivational perspective on engagement and disaffection: Conceptualization and assessment of children's behavioral and emotional participation in academic activities in the classroom. *Educational and Psychological Measurement*, 69, 493–525.

Smith, E. (2019). *A critique of anti-racism in rhetoric and composition: The semblance of empowerment*. Lexington Books.

Sprague, E., & Taylor, P. M. (1959). *Knowledge and value: Introductory readings in philosophy*. Harcourt Brace.

Spring, J. (2021). *American education*. Routledge.

Stanley, W. O. (1967). *Social foundations of education*. Holt, Rinehart and Winston.

Starck, J. G., Riddle, T., Sinclair, S., & Warikoo, N. (2020). Teachers are people too: Examining the racial bias of teachers compared to other American adults. *Educational Researcher*, 49(4), 273–284.

Stembridge, A. (2019). *Culturally responsive education in the classroom: An equity framework for pedagogy*. Routledge.

Sternberg, R. J., Grigorenko, E. L., & Kidd, K. K. (2005). Intelligence, race, and genetics. *American Psychological Association*, 60(1).

Stoskopf, A. (1999). The forgotten history of eugenics. *Rethinking Schools*, 13(3), 12–13.

Stoskopf, A. (2002, June). Echoes of a forgotten past: Eugenics, testing, and education reform. In: *The Educational Forum* (Vol. 66, No. 2, pp. 126–133). Taylor & Francis Group.

Strmic-Pawl, H. V., Jackson, B. A., & Garner, S. (2018). Race counts: Racial and ethnic data on the US Census and the implications for tracking inequality. *Sociology of Race and Ethnicity*, 4(1), 1–13.

Tesconi, C. A. (1975). *Schooling in America: A social philosophical perspective*. Houghton Mifflin.

Tesconi, C. A., & Hurwitz, E. (1974). *Education for whom? The question of equal educational opportunity*. Harper & Row.

Thomas, K., Wong, K. C., & Li, Y. C. (2014). The capstone experience: Student and academic perspectives. *Higher Education Research & Development*, 33(3), 580–594.

Thurman, H. (1951). *Deep is the hunger: Meditations for apostles of sensitiveness*. Harper & Brothers.

Turner, J. C., & Patrick, H. (2008). How does motivation develop and why does it change? Reframing Motivation Research. *Educational Psychologist*, 43(3), 119–131.

Turner, S. L. (2019). Measuring what matters: Rethinking middle grades accountability systems in the era of the Every Student Succeeds Act. *International Handbook of Middle Level Education Theory, Research, and* Policy, 357–366.

Tyler, Stephen A. (1970). *Cognitive anthropology*. New York: Holt, Rinehart & Winston.

Urban, W. J., & Wagoner, J. L. (2004). *American education: A history*. McGraw Hill.

Usher, E. L. (2018). Acknowledging the Whiteness of motivation research: Seeking cultural relevance. *Educational Psychologist*, 53(2), 131–144.

Van Schaik, C. P., & Burkart, J. M. (2011). Social learning and evolution: The cultural intelligence hypothesis. *Philosophical Transactions of the Royal Society B: Biological Sciences*, 366(1567), 1008–1016.

Vollet, J. W., Kindermann, T. A., & Skinner, E. A. (2017). In peer matters, teachers matter: Peer group influences on students' engagement depend on teacher involvement. Journal of *Educational Psychology*, 109, 635–652.

Weiner, B. (1972). Attribution theory, achievement motivation, and the educational process. *Review of Educational Research*, 42(2), 203–215.

Weiner, B. (2012). An attribution theory of motivation. *Handbook of Theories of Social Psychology*, 1, 135–155.

Weiner, B. (2014). Searching for the roots of applied attribution theory. In: *Attribution theory* (pp. 1–13). Psychology Press.

Wentzel, K. R. (1998). Social relationships and motivation in middle school: The role of parents, teachers, and peers. *Journal of Educational Psychology*, 90, 202–209.

Wentzel, K. R. (2009). Students' relationships with teachers as motivational contexts. In K. R. Wentzel & A. Wigfield (Eds.), *Handbook of motivation at school* (pp. 301–322). Routledge.

Whitehead, A. N. (1929). *The aims of education: And other essays*. New York: New American Library.

Whiten, A. (2017). A second inheritance system: The extension of biology through culture. *Interface Focus*, 7(5), 20160142.

Wigfield, A., Eccles, J. S., Fredricks, J. A., Simpkins, S., Roeser, R., & Schiefele, U. (2015). Development of achievement motivation and engagement. In: R. M. Lerner (Series Ed.) & M. Lamb (Volume Ed.), *Handbook of child psychology and developmental* science, Vol. 3. Socioemotional processes (7th ed., pp. 657–700). Wiley.

Wiggins, G., & McTighe, J. (1998). *Understanding by design*. Association for Supervision and Curriculum Development.

Wilkerson, I. (2020). *Caste: The origins of our discontents*. Random House.

Wrangham, R., & Conklin-Brittain, N. (2003). Cooking as a biological trait. Comparative Biochemistry and Physiology Part A. *Molecular & Integrative Physiology*, 136(1), 35-46.

Wrangham, R. (2009). *Catching fire: How cooking made us human*. Basic Books.

Yang, P. Q., & Koshy, K. (2016). The "becoming white thesis" revisited. *The Journal of Public and Professional Sociology*, 8(1), 1.

Yee, E. (2019). Abstraction and concepts: When, how, where, what and why? *Language, Cognition and Neuroscience*, 34(10), 1257–1265.

Yosso, T. J. (2005). Whose culture has capital? *Race, Ethnicity and Education*, 8(1), 69–91.

Yudof, M. G. (1972). Equal educational opportunity and the courts. *Texas Law Review*, 51, 411.

Zimmerman, M. A. (1995). Psychological empowerment: Issues and illustrations. *American Journal of Community Psychology*, 23(5), 581–599.

Zimmerman, M. A. (2000). Empowerment theory. In: *Handbook of community psychology* (pp. 43–63). Springer.

Zucker, J. K., & Patterson, M. M. (2018). Racial socialization practices among white American parents: Relations to racial attitudes, racial identity, and school diversity. *Journal of Family Issues*, 39(16), 3903–3930.

INDEX

D

E